Manage[...] Theory

From

Taylorism

to

Japanization

Management Theory

From
Taylorism
to
Japanization

John Sheldrake

INTERNATIONAL THOMSON BUSINESS PRESS

I(T)P   An International Thomson Publishing Company

London • Bonn • Boston • Johannesburg • Madrid • Melbourne • Mexico City • New York • Paris
Singapore • Tokyo • Toronto • Albany, NY • Belmont, CA • Cincinnati, OH • Detroit, MI

Management Theory: from Taylorism to Japanization

Copyright ©1996 John Sheldrake

First published by International Thomson Business Press

 A division of International Thomson Publishing Inc.
I(T)P The ITP logo is a trademark under licence

British Library Cataloguing-in-Publication Data
A catalogue record for this book is available from the British Library

First edition 1996

Typeset in the UK by Hodgson Williams Associates, Tunbridge Wells and Cambridge
Printed in the UK by the Alden Press, Oxford

ISBN 0-412-57240-0

International Thomson Business Press
Berkshire House
168–173 High Holborn
London WC1V 7AA
UK

International Thomson Business Press
20 Park Plaza
14th Floor
Boston MA 02116
USA

http://www.thomson.com/itbp.html

Contents

Preface

This book traces the development of management theory during the twentieth century. It does not seek to provide an encyclopaedic account of the ideas of every thinker who has contributed to the subject, nor does it consider every concept or trend. Instead it provides a clear outline of the subject's main contours through a consideration of the life and writings of twenty thinkers (including, in the case of the Gilbreths, a husband and wife partnership) who have made a significant contribution to the development of management theory since the turn of the present century. Additionally, numerous other thinkers are dealt with in passing. Although the narrative moves forward chronologically and pieces together patterns of interaction and influence between the various thinkers, each chapter nevertheless provides a free-standing essay. Thus the reader is not necessarily constrained to traverse the entire text but, if so disposed, can shift from thinker to thinker as desired or required. Each chapter identifies the particular thinker's main contribution to the subject and also provides a critical summary, discussion questions and a guide to further reading. Of course, many of the theorists strongly disagree with each other – some of the differences being so radical that they can never be reconciled. An important outcome of this is that, although there might be general agreement from time to time on what constitutes best management practice, the theoretical ingredients will tend to vary. Management theories are therefore contestable rather than definitive and, although there is a sense of progressive, evolutionary refinement, there is no master narrative to reassure us that the latest theory is necessarily the best. Management theory did not, of course, arrive fully articulated at the beginning of this century, it already had a considerable history. Chapter 1 traces the development of management theory from the final years of the eighteenth century through to the end of the nineteenth century – broadly speaking from the emergence of the factory system in Britain to the emergence of scientific management in the USA.

Chapters 2, 3 and 4 deal with the development, refinement and subsequent international spread of the techniques and philosophy of scientific management. These chapters deal with such issues as management control, financial and other incentives, and the growing emphasis on industrial efficiency. In Chapter 3 the emerging influence of industrial psychology is noted, together with the study of fatigue in the work situation. Chapters 5 and 6 deal with the classic expositions of organizational structure in the form of bureaucracy and hierarchy. The limitations of bureaucracy as an organizational form are examined through a brief account of the work of Henry Mintzberg. Chapter 7 deals with workers' resistance to management's attempts to control the labour process through an examination of the work of Carter Goodrich. In Chapter 8 an account of the work of Mary Parker Follett serves as a linkage between the technical/classical era of Taylor, Weber and Fayol and the human factor era of Elton Mayo. Chapter 9 provides an account of the work of Henry Ford. As well as dealing with the technical elements involved in the mass production of automobiles, the chapter also covers Ford's social interventions and his managerial failings. Chapter 10 examines the work of Lyndall Urwick, particularly his efforts to spread the 'gospel' of scientific management in a British context. Chapter 11 is devoted to the work of Elton Mayo, specific emphasis being placed on his role in the design and interpretation of the Hawthorne experiments. In Chapter 12 an account of the thinking of the 'manager/philosopher' Chester Barnard is given. Barnard, like Mayo, was associated with the influential Harvard Pareto Circle and an account of this group illustrates the importance of ideology in the development of management theory. Chapter 13 deals with the work of Alfred Sloan at General Motors and his development of the decentralized organization structure with centrally co-ordinated control. Chapters 14, 15 and 16 analyse the impact on the development of management theory of the behavioural scientists Maslow, Herzberg and McGregor. These chapters deal with such issues as personality, human motivation, job design, and managerial beliefs and styles. An examination of the work of Schumacher and Braverman in Chapters 17 and 18 provides a critique of modern industrial society and its associated management structures and techniques. Braverman was a Marxist and a brief account of Marxism is given accordingly. Chapter 19 chronicles the impact of Japanese economic success on the development of management theory, specifically through an examination of the work of William Ouchi. In Chapter 20, the changing nature of work and organizational structures in post-industrial society is examined through consideration of the later writings of Charles Handy. Chapter 21 provides a brief conclusion.

This book is a work of synthesis and the materials used in its creation are listed in the Bibliography. I received the greatest assistance with locating the many books and articles which I used from my colleagues in the Calcutta House Library of London Guildhall University, particularly Richard Delahaye. I would also like to thank the many friends and colleagues who read and commented on various parts of the draft, particularly Sarah Vickerstaff who read the final version in its entirety. Finally, I would like to thank my wife Susan for the infinite pains she has taken in word-processing a difficult manuscript. This book is dedicated to her and our children, Sophie and Lewis.

Chapter 1

Introduction

Management as a self-conscious activity is a creation of the nineteenth century although systematic consideration of the elements that constitute it can certainly be dated to the late eighteenth century. Adam Smith in his *The Wealth of Nations* of 1776, for example, begins with an account of the improvements to productivity that can be gained as a result of the division of labour. In his own words:

> To take an example...the trade of pin-maker; a workman not educated to do this business...could scarce, perhaps, with his utmost industry, make one pin in a day, and certainly could not make twenty. But in the way in which this business is now carried on, not only the whole work is a peculiar trade, but it is divided into a number of branches, of which the greater part are likewise peculiar trades. One man draws out the wire, another straights it, a third cuts it, a fourth points it, a fifth grinds it at the top for receiving the head; to make the head requires three distinct operations; to put it on is a peculiar business, to whiten the pins is another; it is even a trade by itself to put them into the paper; and the important business of making a pin is, in this manner, divided into about eighteen distinct operations...I have seen a small manufactory...where ten men only were employed (who) could, when they exerted themselves, make among them about 12 pounds of pins in a day. There are in a pound upwards of four thousand pins of a middling size. Those ten persons, therefore, could make among them upwards of forty-eight thousand pins in a day...But if they had all wrought separately and independently, and without any of them having been educated to this peculiar business, they could certainly not each of them had made twenty, perhaps not one pin in a day; that is, certainly, not the two hundred and fortieth, perhaps not the four thousand eight hundredth part of what they are at present performing, in consequence of a proper division and combination of their different operations. In every other art and manufacture, the effects of the division of labour are similar to what they are in this very trifling one...The

1

> division of labour...so far as it can be introduced, occasions in every art, a proportionable increase of the productive powers of labour.
>
> *(Smith, 1776/1986, pp.109–110)*

While praising the immense improvements in productivity that could be achieved as a result of the division of labour, Smith was also aware of the tedium that such a system could impose on the workers. Nevertheless he considered that the advantages to society as a whole, measured in terms of the general increase in wealth that accrued as a result of specialization, outweighed the disadvantages experienced by the individual workers. Specialization, increasing mechanization and an expanding market for products all combined to give the factory system the edge in many industries over the traditional domestic system of production which preceded it. This was particularly the case in cotton textiles which became the most prominent factory-based industry during the early nineteenth century. The factory system brought new problems in terms of disciplining a workforce to the rigours of production directed by the entrepreneurs' desire to maximize the level of production in order to justify their capital investment. During the early years of the nineteenth century some of the skilled workers who were being marginalized by new technology and factory production sought to resist change by a campaign of intimidation and machine breaking. One response to the problems of industrial dislocation and the demands of the new factory system was made by Robert Owen, the self-made cotton manufacturer and social thinker.

In his middle and later life Owen became increasingly involved with radical programmes for social reconstruction; rejecting industrialization, urbanization and the market and placing immense faith in programmes for rationally constructed communes and co-operatives. However, in his early years he was a thrusting manager and entrepreneur. In the words of his biographer :

> At the age of seventeen Owen (arrived) in Manchester which was just then becoming the leading centre of cotton-manufacturing in Britain. Most spinning and weaving still took place at home. But forms of production were quickly being altered by technical developments, notably the invention of Samuel Crompton's 'mule' for producing fine yarn and the introduction of the steam engine in place of water power at the end of the eighteenth century. Owen soon saw the implications of these changes, and not only in terms of the rapid expansion of production, but equally the increase in urban overcrowding, the rising rate of disease and premature death, the intensification of work and discipline for the new factories. Arriving in 1788, Owen remained twelve years in Manchester. The progress of his career was meteoric (and) when the position of manager of the first large cotton-spinning mill fell open...Owen offered his services. Soon superintending 500 men and women, he was enormously

successful, vastly increasing the quality of the cotton spun, and quickly becoming the owner's partner.

(Claeys in Owen, 1991, p.viii)

In 1800 Owen acquired the cotton mills at New Lanark on the banks of the Clyde south of Glasgow where a labour force of some 2000 people were employed, including 500 pauper children as young as five years of age apprenticed from local workhouses. As a 'foreigner' Owen's arrival was resented by the indisciplined and generally low-quality workforce. However, with considerable charm and patience he began an experiment in enlightened, paternalistic management inspired by his belief that human beings were moulded by their surroundings and were therefore improvable. Among the benefits he provided for his workforce were housing, free education for the children and a village store operated on a non-profit making basis. He also raised the age at which children could begin work in the mill from five to ten years of age and reduced the working day for the workforce from fourteen hours to twelve. Of course the novelty of Owen's approach meant that it was easy for him to demonstrate to his workforce the advantages of working at New Lanark rather than elsewhere. Further, his approach was underpinned by various disciplinary elements such as the 'silent monitor', a device suspended above each workplace which indicated the level of the individual worker's performance. Also cleanliness in New Lanark village was enforced, drunkenness in public punished by fines and a curfew operated during winter. Having said this, however, Owen did succeed in demonstrating that workers could be motivated and improved by taking an enlightened approach to their welfare. He also showed that such an approach could be good for business too, for he succeeded in consistently improving the quality of the cotton thread produced at New Lanark while achieving a high level of profit for himself and his partners. Indeed the profits were such that Owen's approach to management could easily be funded.

During the 1830s the extent and value of the new industrial arrangements were surveyed by two outstanding individuals – Charles Babbage and Andrew Ure. Babbage's contribution to the development of management theory is contained in his book *On the Economy of Machinery and Manufactures* (1832) which sold over 10 000 copies and has been claimed as 'the first management best seller' (Clutterbuck and Crainer, 1990, p.13). Among other things he examined the comparative advantage of machine production over handwork. Returning to Adam Smith's example of the division of labour in the manufacture of pins he analysed the operation of a newly devised American pin-making machine observing that 'it is highly ingenious in point of contrivance, and, in respect to its economical principles, will furnish a strong and interesting contrast with the manufacture of pins by the human hand' (Babbage, 1832/1971, pp.187–190). On balance he found handwork to be more productive but conceded that the advantage of the machine emerged where labour was in short supply 'for all processes are executed by the machine, and a single labourer can easily work it'. Of course this was the situation that prevailed in the United States and, as will be.

seen, partly accounts for the extensive application of labour-saving equipment in that country while Britain held to more labour-intensive methods. Babbage's analysis of work had a close resemblance to that later carried out by some of the scientific managers, particularly Frank Gilbreth (see Chapter 3).

Again in a similar fashion to the scientific managers Babbage was concerned with issues of human motivation, the application of incentives and the avoidance of industrial conflict. At the time Babbage was writing the era of machine breaking, known as Luddism after a mythological workers' leader known as Ned Ludd, was still fairly recent. The hostility of some craftworkers to the introduction of new machinery resulted in bitter resentment, attacks on factories and even murder. For example at the York Assizes of January 1813, 64 people were tried on charges associated with Luddism, 17 of whom were hanged; 3 for the murder of a mill owner, 5 for an attack on a factory and 9 for stealing arms and money to support Luddite violence (Stevenson, 1992, p.196). During the early 1830s the so called Swing Riots occurred in areas of the rural south of England, which included demonstrations, arson, robbery and assault as well as the breaking of threshing machines. The response of Babbage to the hostility between employers and workers (specifically in the manufacturing sector of the economy) was close to F. W. Taylor's advocacy of the 'mental revolution' some 70 years later (see Chapter 2). Babbage asserted the mutuality of interest between masters and workers and claimed that, given proper recognition, this could transcend any differences between the parties. As he put it:

A most erroneous and unfortunate opinion prevails amongst workmen…that their own interest and that of their employers are at variance. The consequences are that valuable machinery is sometimes neglected, and even privately injured, that new improvements, introduced by the masters, do not receive a fair trial, and that the talents and observations of the workmen are not directed to the improvement of the processes in which they are employed…Convinced as I am from my own observation, that the prosperity and success of the master manufacturer is essential to the welfare of the workmen, I am yet compelled to admit that this connection is, in many cases, too remote to be always understood by the latter: and whilst it is perfectly true that workmen, as a class, derive advantage from the prosperity of their employers, I do not think that each individual partakes of that advantage exactly in proportion to the extent to which he contributes towards it; nor do I perceive that the resulting advantage is as immediate as it might become under a different system.

(Babbage, 1832/1971, pp.257–258)

Babbage's panacea for healing the antagonism between masters and men was the extension of the profit-sharing schemes that were already operating in the Cornish tin mines, the lead mines of Flintshire and Yorkshire, and some of the copper mines of Cumberland. He claimed that the introduction of profit-sharing into a factory would, among other things, generate circumstances in which 'every person engaged in it would have a direct interest in its prosperity; since the effect of any success, or falling off, would almost immediately produce a corresponding change in his own weekly receipts'. Further, Babbage claimed, profit-sharing would obviate the need for 'combinations' (i.e. trade unions) 'because the only combination which could exist would be a most powerful union between both parties to overcome their common difficulties' (Babbage, 1832/1971, pp.257–258).

Andrew Ure was professor of chemistry and natural philosophy at Anderson's College, Glasgow during a 25 year period from 1804 to 1839. The central purpose of the college was to provide technical education for working men, many of whom subsequently became managers in the local factories. Ure's thinking on management is contained in *The Philosophy of Manufactures* (1835) which was calculated to serve as both a survey of the developing factory system and a handbook of best operational practice. The specific industrial focus of the book was concerned with the technical aspects of the machine production of such textiles as cotton, wool, flax and silk. Ure was an unashamed apologist for the factory system, celebrating its productive superiority over the domestic system and also claiming that it provided a better working environment than either the small workshop or the home. He specifically defended the employment of children in textile mills, for many years a matter of concern in philanthropic circles and the subject of protective legislation in 1833. Reflecting on the plight of the factory children Briggs has observed that 'conditions were often deplorable, one model mill in Manchester working its children 74 hours a week' (Briggs, 1979, p.61). As has been seen even as enlightened a mill owner as Robert Owen employed 10 year olds for 12 hours a day. Nevertheless Ure felt able to defend the practice both on grounds of industrial necessity and also of the children's own welfare, observing that:

> I have not met with a single instance…of deformity that is referable to factory labour. It must be admitted that factory children do not present the same blooming robust appearance as is witnessed among children who labour in the open air but I question if they are not more exempt from acute diseases and do not, on average, suffer less sickness than those who are regarded as having more healthy employments.
>
> *(Ure, 1835/1967, p.379)*

In a similar vein Ure blamed the general poor health suffered by many of the factory operatives of Manchester as springing from their consumption of too much rank bacon, the smoking of too much tobacco, and the drinking of too much gin coupled with their morbid hypochondria and tendency to indulge 'too much in the desires of the flesh'.

Laying aside Ure's rather primitive approach to questions of human resources, he did provide many sensible observations in his book relating to factory layout, the organization of work and the productive advantages to be gained from the replacement of water, wind and animal power by the steam engine. As he put it :

Steam-engines furnish the means not only of their support but of their multiplication. They create a vast demand for fuel; and, while they lend their powerful arms to drain the pits and to raise the coals, they call into employment multitudes of miners, engineers, shipbuilders, and sailors, and...while they enable these rich fields of industry to be cultivated to the utmost, they leave thousands of fine arable fields free for the production of food to man, which must have been otherwise alloted to the food of horses. Steam-engines moreover, by the cheapness and steadiness of their action, fabricate cheap goods, and procure in their exchange a liberal supply of the necessaries and comforts of life, produced in foreign lands.

(Ure, 1835/1967, p.29)

Like Adam Smith, whose ideas he enthusiastically embraced, Ure argued that any disadvantages accruing to the individual as a result of the division of labour were far outweighed by the benefits accruing to society as a whole. Indeed the individual would gain a double dividend for their labours receiving not just better wages than they would obtain, for example, in agriculture but also enjoying the generalized benefits of economic growth. Ure adapted Smith's insights of the 1770s to fit the changed circumstances of the 1830s, noting the ability of machinery to replace the skill of the artisan while also reducing the tedium inherent in specialization. As he put it, 'the grand object...of the modern manufacturer is, through the union of capital and science, to reduce the task of his workpeople to the exercise of vigilance and dexterity' (Ure, 1835/1967, pp.20–21). There is much in this statement that brings Ure close to the American system of manufacturing and scientific management examined later in this chapter and that which follows.

Both Babbage and Ure were well aware of the vulnerability of the new production processes to industrial unrest. Although Luddite violence was reactionary in its nature and perpetrated by those outside the new factory system, opposition to the discipline of the factory also came from those employed within. As Belchem has observed:

Reduced to wage-earning proletarians without rights to the materials and product of their labour...workers fought hard to retain residual control over the 'labour process', over the speed, intensity and rhythm of work. Through a variety of strategies – cultural and linguistic as well as organizational and economic – they managed...to defend their workplace autonomy against the new time and labour discipline favoured by political economists, preachers and employers.

(Belchem, 1991, p.43)

One of the strategies adopted by the factory operatives was the organization of various elements of the new division of labour in such a way as to reconstruct skilled worker status. The outcome of this was that the factory labour force itself became organized on a hierarchical basis with 'skilled' men at the top and supposedly 'unskilled' women at the bottom. Whereas men were able to defend their newly reconstructed 'skills' through the establishment and grudging acceptance of trade unions, women were left more or less defenceless. Many employers were content to collude in this process which gradually formed the accepted culture of factory life (Joyce, 1982). Again in the words of Belchem:

> lacking the ideological and technological apparatus to assert managerial authority, employers welcomed these reformulations of skill and gender, hierarchical constructions which solved the problem of labour discipline. Compulsion, the inefficient and much–resented management of the early factory system, was abandoned in favour of benevolent paternalism, a strategy designed to elicit deferential consent at the workplace.
>
> *(Belchem, 1991, p.43)*

The tacit collaboration between industrial elites and employers was, however, fragile and at times severely strained by adverse economic circumstances and pressures for technological change, not only in Britain (see Chapter 7) but in industrializing countries generally including the United States.

In terms of technological developments, the growing reliability of the stationary steam engine was followed by the application of steam to locomotion thereby inaugurating the transport revolution which began in Britain and was soon replicated throughout the world. Between 1822 and the turn of the century 22 000 miles of railway were engineered in Britain alone and engaged literally millions of labourers (i.e. navvies) organized on the basis of contract and sub-contract. In the words of Coleman:

> the making of a railway was organized in this way: first the company, the London and Birmingham or the Great Western, appointed an engineer – say Robert Stephenson or Brunel – to devise the route, specify the works to be done, superintend their construction, and to be responsible to the company for the whole venture. The company then invited tenders for part or whole of the work, and appointed a principal contractor, or contractors, to carry out these works. This main contractor...was the grand entrepreneur. The contractor then appointed agents for each section of the line, and these agents were empowered to let parcels of the work, a cutting here, an embankment there, to sub-contractors. These sub-contractors in turn appointed the gangers, the corporals of the enterprise, and the gangers took on the navvies.
>
> *(Coleman, 1965, p.51)*

This system was fraught with a whole range of problems not least the control of the vast numbers of navvies. These men, given to hard drinking and subject to extortion and primitive living conditions, moved across the countryside levelling, tunnelling and taking out cuttings as they went. Treatment of these workers was at the very opposite end of the spectrum from those employed by Robert Owen at New Lanark.

Notwithstanding the excessive level of injuries and deaths among the railway navvies, the railways were nevertheless built. Further, a primitive notion of work measurement did exist as a guide to anticipated daily output. Thomas Brassey, the major contractor, estimated a day's work for a navvy as fourteen 'sets' – a set being a train of wagons drawn by horses on a temporary line of rails. As work progressed along a cutting or embankment the line of rails would be extended and each wagon filled by two men working together using shovels:

> if the train was filled and carted away fourteen times in a day then each pair of men would have filled fourteen wagons, and each individual navvy seven. A wagon was reckoned to hold $2\frac{1}{4}$ cubic yards of muck, which was the navvy name for all kinds of earth and rock, so each man would lift nearly twenty tons of earth a day on a shovel over his own head into a wagon. This was the fourteen–set day. Some men did sixteen.
>
> *(Coleman, 1965, p.39)*

Such work, supported in the British case by only minimal labour-saving equipment, perforce engendered its own discipline and not surprisingly stimulated respect in those non-labourers who witnessed it in action. One of Brassey's timekeepers, for example, was moved to observe, in terms reminiscent of those F. W. Taylor would later use with regard to the elite yard labourers at Bethlehem Steel, 'I think it as fine a spectacle as any man could witness, who is accustomed to look at work, is to see a cutting in full operation, with about twenty wagons being filled, every man at his post, the gangers looking about, and everything going like clockwork' (quoted in Coleman, 1965, p.44).

Although the engineering of the railways in Britain was achieved using primitive methods, the outcome (i.e. a substantial network of lines throughout the country) generated the need for substantial management expertise. The operation of reliable timetables, the requirement to ensure safe operation and the almost regimented organization of large numbers of staff, totalling 250 000 in the 1870s and rising to 600 000 by 1914, across wide geographic areas provided a challenge not encountered in the confines of the factory (Mingay, 1976, p.11). A similar situation developed in the United States where the rapid development of the railways, together with Samuel Morse's invention of the telegraph, radically improved transportation and communications. In the case of the telegraph some 50 000 miles of lines were constructed across the eastern half of the country between 1844 and 1860 (Wren, 1994, p.75). Taken together the railways and the telegraph facilitated the extensive expansion of trade within the United States, enabling the exploitation of new markets and taking inexpensive, factory-produced goods to areas of the country where the domestic system had previously prevailed. In the years following the ending of the Civil War in 1865 the United States began seriously to challenge Britain for industrial leadership of the world.[1] In mounting this challenge the Americans adopted different ideas on manufacturing and management from those of their British counterparts. Partly these ideas arose from different circumstances relating to labour costs, natural resources and so on prevailing in the two countries. Partly also they derived from the fact that the United States' first industrial revolution occurred later than Britain's (Habakkuk, 1962). Above all, however, they sprang from something less tangible; a national genius for enterprise which chose to celebrate economic success and welcome innovation to an extent hardly encountered in Britain or for that matter most of Europe (Levine, 1967). The origins and development of industrialization in the United States are traced in the section which follows.

The rise of American industry

In a study of the rise of the modern industrial enterprise, Chandler has observed that:

> the coming of the railroad and the telegraph and the simultaneous availability of large quantities of coal quickly brought the modern enterprise to the United States – first in transportation and communications, then in distribution, and finally in production. The new technologies made possible much greater speed and volume in the production and movement of goods and necessitated the creation of managerial hierarchies to supervise, monitor, and co-ordinate the new processes of production and distribution. In transportation and communications, the managers of the railroad, telegraph and steamship companies began to co-ordinate the movement of goods from one commercial centre to another. In distribution, new mass-marketing enterprises, which relied on new means of transportation and communication, administered the flow of goods from processors or producers to retailers or ultimate consumers. In manufacturing, the new mass producers came to co-ordinate the flow from the extraction of raw material through production to distribution to retailers or final consumers. In sectors dominated by the new, large enterprises, the top–level managers of a few modern multi-unit companies made the decisions that had previously been made by the owners of thousands of small firms.
>
> *(Chandler, 1980, p.15)*

In 1880 there were roughly 2 700 000 workers employed in manufacturing in the United States. By 1900 the number had increased to 4 500 000 and by 1920 it had

---

1 Together with Germany following the defeat of France in the Franco–Prussian War of 1870 and unification of the country in 1871.

reached 8 400 000 (Nelson, 1975, p.4). Although some of these workers were employed in small workshops, and even sweatshops, the vast bulk worked in modern factories. By 1900 there were over 1000 factories in the USA which employed between 500 and 1000 workers per plant and almost 450 employing in excess of 1000 per plant. The largest factories were concentrated in a relatively narrow band of industries, most prominently cotton textiles, metals (particularly steel) and machinery. In 1900 the largest manufacturing plants (i.e. those employing between 8000 and 10 000 workers) were Cambria Steel, Carnegie Steel and Jones and Loughlin Steel. The only non-steel plant employing workers on a comparable scale was that of Baldwin Locomotive. All of these plants were situated in Pennsylvania. Midvale Steel, where F. W. Taylor worked out the basic framework of his system, employed between 2 and 3000 workers in 1900 while Bethlehem Steel, where he put many of his controversial ideas into practice, employed between 3 and 4000 (Nelson, 1975, pp.7 and 8). Steel plants were unrivalled in scale of operation until the emergence of the automobile industry in the early years of the century. Henry Ford's Highland Park plant, for example, employed almost 13 000 workers in 1914, 19 000 in 1915 and 33 000 in 1916. By 1924 the Highland Park plant was employing over 42 000 workers while Ford's new River Rouge plant had almost 70 000. The Rouge subsequently 'became the largest manufacturing plant in the United States and probably in the world (and) the automobile factory...the universal symbol and stereotype of the large manufacturing plant' (Nelson, 1975, p.9).

The sheer scale of operations in the factories prompted managements to explore new methods of controlling and deploying labour. The new techniques were calculated to replace a system based on the judgement of workers and supervisors with the certainty of what became known as scientific management. One outcome of these changes was an increasing professionalization of management, particularly in the sphere of mechanical engineering. The American Society of Mechanical Engineers (ASME) was formed in 1880 and held its inaugural meeting at the Stevens Institute of Technology in Hoboken, New Jersey. The purpose of the ASME 'was to address those issues of factory operation and management neglected by the other engineering groups' such as the American Society of Civil Engineers and the American Institute of Mining Engineers (Wren, 1994, pp.88–89). At a meeting of the ASME held in Chicago in 1886, Henry Towne (co-founder and president of the Yale and Towne Lock Company) presented his paper *The Engineer as an Economist*. He advocated the organized exchange of management experience among the works managers of different companies and urged the ASME to create an economic section to act as a focus of best practice in shop management and shop accounting. As he put it:

A vast amount of accumulated experience in the art of workshop management already exists, but there is no record of it available to the world in general, and each old enterprise is managed more or less in its own way, receiving little benefit from the parallel experience of other similar enterprises and imparting as little of its own to them, while each new enterprise, starting *de novo* and with much labor, and usually at much cost for experience, gradually develops a more or less perfect system of its own, according to the ability of its managers, receiving little benefit or aid from all that may have been done previously by others in precisely the same field of work. Surely this condition of things is wrong and should be remedied. But the remedy must not be looked for from those who are 'business men' or clerks and accountants only; it should come from those whose training and experience has given them the experience of both sides (*viz.* the mechanical and the clerical) of the important questions involved. It should originate, therefore, from those who are also engineers, and...particularly from mechanical engineers. Granting this, why should it not originate from, and be prompted by the American Society of Mechanical Engineers?

(Towne in Merrill, 1960, pp.60–61)

Although Towne's idea was not immediately accepted by the ASME it nevertheless pointed in the direction subsequently taken by Taylor and his associates. At the same Chicago meeting of the ASME Captain Henry Metcalfe (who managed army arsenals) described a shop-order system of accounting which he had devised using cards. The cards accompanied each batch of work as it made its way through the workshops and facilitated better co-ordination and control of work. Metcalfe suggested that a 'science of administration' might be developed based on more or less universal principles applicable in the bulk of situations. His paper, *The Shop Order System of Accounts*, was to a large extent a summary of a pioneering book on cost accounting which he had published in 1885. This work, *The Cost of Manufactures and the Administration of Workshops, Public and Private*, detailed methods of cost and materials control, issues subsequently investigated by Taylor, Gantt and, in a different national context, Fayol (see Chapters 2, 4 and 5).

The growing scale of industrial operation in the United States was linked to the system of manufacturing itself. As early as 1812 Eli Whitney described the objective of the American system of manufacturing as being 'to substitute correct and effective operations of machinery for that skill of the artist which is acquired only by long practice and experience'. Thus the skill of the apprenticed craftsman was, wherever possible, to be replaced by the machine. Although this process was inherent in the ideas on the division of labour explored by Adam Smith, Whitney was directly inspired by the example of Oliver Evans who had experimented with such techniques at his cotton mills in Philadelphia. Together with his partner, Simeon North, a Connecticut clockmaker, Whitney applied these techniques to the manufacture of rifles and developed the idea of using interchangeable parts which enabled his workers to assemble the weapons more quickly than ever before (Clutterbuck and Crainer, 1990, pp.4–5). As Heskett has observed 'throughout most of the nineteenth century the progress of the American system...emphasized the analysis of objects and mechanisms, breaking them down into inter-changeable constitutent parts and designing them for mechanized production' (Heskett, 1987, p.65). Improvements in factory construction, increased demand and the application of electricity all facilitated the transition from the American system of manufacturing to the sophisticated processes of mass production pioneered by Henry Ford (see Chapter 9). These changes provided the context for the development of systematic management thought in the early years of the twentieth century to which we now turn.

Discussion questions

1. What did Adam Smith see as the advantages and disadvantages of the division of labour?
2. In what ways did Robert Owen seek to improve the motivation of his workers?
3. How plausible were Babbage's ideas for profit-sharing as a means to reduce industrial conflict?
4. What were the advantages and disadvantages of the factory system?
5. In what ways did the development of the railways stimulate improved management techniques?
6. What specific elements characterized the American system of manufacturing?

Suggested reading

Belchem, J. (1991) *Industrialization and the Working Class: The English Experience, 1750–1900*, Scholar Press, Aldershot.

Dintenfass, M. (1992) *The Decline of Industrial Britain 1870–1980*, Routledge, London.

Drucker, P. F. (1942/1945) *The Future of Industrial Man*, Transaction Publishers, New Brunswick.

Harris, J. (1994) *Private Lives, Public Spirit: Britain 1870–1914*, Penguin Books, Harmondsworth, ch. 5.

Landes, D. (1969) *The Unbound Prometheus: Technological Change and Industrial Development in Western Europe from 1750 to the Present*, Cambridge University Press, Cambridge.

Pollard, S. (1965) *The Genesis of Modern Management: A Study of the Industrial Revolution in Great Britain*, Edward Arnold, London.

Wiener, M. (1981/1985) *English Culture and the Decline of the Industrial Spirit 1850-1980*, Penguin Books, Harmondsworth.

Wren, D. (1994) *The Evolution of Management Thought*, Wiley & Sons, Chichester, chs. 3–5.

Chapter 2

F. W. Taylor and scientific management

Frederick Winslow Taylor was born in 1856 in Germantown, Pennsylvania into a prosperous Quaker–Puritan family. His parents intended him to become a lawyer like his father and, after completing his preparatory studies at Phillips Exeter Academy, and travelling in Europe he passed the entrance examinations for Harvard Law School. His studies impaired his eyesight, however, and he withdrew for the time being from further study and never practiced as a lawyer.[1] Instead he took the unusual step of becoming a manual worker and learning a trade. Between 1874 and 1878 he worked for Enterprise Hydraulic, a pump manufacturing company in Philadelphia, where he learned the skills of pattern maker and machinist. He also observed what he considered to be poor management, 'soldiering' (i.e. skiving) and generally poor relations between workers and managers. In 1878 he went to work for the Midvale Steel Company in Philadelphia as a labourer and spent twelve years there, rising to become chief engineer. While working for Midvale he resumed his studies, this time in engineering, and in 1883 gained a Masters degree in the subject through night study at the Stevens Institute. He also began patenting the first of his many inventions, which were mainly concerned with improvements to machinery and included the design and construction of the largest successful steam hammer ever constructed in the USA. At Stevens Institute Taylor came into contact with Dr Robert Henry Thurston, the founder of the American Society of Mechanical Engineers (ASME), who pioneered the application of scientific knowledge to machine shop practice and influenced Taylor's

---

1 It has been claimed that Taylor's change of tack was due not to deficient eyesight but to a rejection of his parents' plans for his career. Certainly his eyesight seems to have been satisfactory in 1881 for in that year he was one of the successful pair who won the US amateur doubles tennis championship.

subsequent theorizing. In 1885 Taylor himself became a member of the ASME and began attending its meetings and discussions. At the ASME he heard Henry Towne's influential paper *The Engineer as an Economist* and presented his own papers on *A Piece Rate System* (1895) and *Shop Management* (1903). It was in the course of his day to day work at Midvale that he began to develop the management technique outlined in these papers which he described as 'the task system' and that later became known as the Taylor system, Taylorism or scientific management (see Chapter 3). Between 1890 and 1893 Taylor was general manager of the Manufacturing Investment Company which, although it was based in Philadelphia, operated large paper mills in Maine and Wisconsin. When Taylor left this company he set up as a consultant and, using his experience of management and the shop floor, he claimed (as his business card put it) to be able to 'systematize shop floor management'.

In 1893 Taylor's services were retained exclusively by the Bethlehem Steel Company where, as will be seen, his ideas concerning scientific management became fully developed. While working for Bethlehem Steel Taylor collaborated with J. Maunsel White in the discovery of what became known as the Taylor–White process of heat treatment for tool steel. This produced 200–300 per cent improvements in cutting capacity and, by the 1930s, tools treated by the process were in use in machine shops throughout the industrialized world. Following his resignation from Bethlehem Steel in 1901, he returned to Philadelphia where he devoted the remaining years of his life to expounding his system with an almost evangelical zeal. He became president of the ASME in 1906, giving as his presidential address a paper entitled *On the Art of Cutting Metals*, consisting of 248 pages plus tables and illustrations and described by Henry Towne as a masterpiece and the most important contribution to the knowledge of the subject that had ever been made. In 1910 the Society for the Promotion of Scientific Management (renamed after his death in 1915 the Taylor Society) was established and brought together engineers and industrialists throughout the world with the intention of carrying on Taylor's work.

Taylor's system of task management

As has been noted Taylor's system of task management was substantially developed during his years as an employee at Midvale Steel and also as a consultant primarily at Bethlehem Steel. He took a somewhat low opinion of workers (based it has to be said on his long experience as a worker, first line supervisor and manager) although he was not anti-worker. In *Shop Management* he made what became his characteristic distinction between what he termed the first class man and the average man. In Taylor's view a first class man is highly motivated and pushes forward with his work rather than wasting time or restricting output. Ideally such men should be selected for the appropriate task and supported by management through financial incentives. In Taylor's experience restriction of output was the norm in the many workshops he had encountered and he described this phenomenon as 'soldiering'. He further classified soldiering as either natural or systematic and commented on the issue in the following terms:

> There is no question that the tendency of the average man (in all walks of life) is towards working at a slow, easy gait, and that it is only after a good deal of thought and observation on his part or as a result of example, conscience, or external pressure that he takes a more rapid pace...This tendency to take it easy is greatly increased by bringing a number of men together on similar work and at a uniform rate of pay by the day. Under this plan the better men gradually but surely slow down to that of the poorest and least efficient.
>
> *(Taylor, 1903/1972, pp.30–31)*

Thus even if a first class man should exist in such circumstances he will tend to slow down to the average partly through lack of incentive and partly, as we now know, through peer group pressure.

The tendency of workers to take it easy (i.e. natural soldiering) was considered by Taylor to be unfortunate. Worse than this, however, was systematic soldiering which led workers to reduce their output according to what Taylor saw as a narrow calculation of their own self interest (i.e. 'with the deliberate object of keeping their employers ignorant of how fast work can be done') (Taylor, 1903/1972, p.33). Taylor depicted such activity as pathetic in that it blunted the competitive edge of the enterprise and was also generally demoralizing, leading workers to restrict their output even when they could produce more without extra effort. Such activity Taylor viewed as stemming partly from what he considered to be the erroneous notion that greater production would result in fewer workers being required and partly from management's willingness to settle for far less than optimum levels of production. In Taylor's words:

> the great defect ...common to all the ordinary systems of management is that their starting point, their very foundation, rests upon ignorance and deceit, and that throughout their whole course in the one element which is most vital both to employer and workmen, namely, the speed at which work is done, they are allowed to drift instead of being intelligently directed and controlled.
>
> *(Taylor, 1903/1972, p.45)*

Taylor's response to these problems was the application of what he termed 'systematic and scientific time study', breaking each job down into simple, basic elements and, with the co-operation of the workers, timing and recording them. Timings of the basic elements were then placed on file and, with appropriate weightings built in, used as the means to construct standard times for various jobs. The extent to which all of this was scientific rather than, given the various weightings relating to fatigue etc., intuitive is questionable. Certainly, however, in the context of Taylor's immediate industrial milieu his approach provided more accurate information on how long a job should take than the old rule of thumb methods could ever do. Task management also stimulated management's ability to take greater control of all the aspects of production including tooling, machines, materials, methods and job design, thereby enhancing the continued replacement of skill with the standardized approach favoured by American production techniques.

Taylor's system or Taylorism

In terms of incentives Taylor believed in paying each individual worker by results. This ran counter to the norms of trade unionism which promoted collective solidarity and therefore tended to displace what Taylor believed was the natural desire of first–class men for material gain and personal advancement based on their own talents and application. Taylor deprecated any notion of endemic conflict between capital and labour, seeing their relationship instead as one of mutual interest. Collaboration of managers and workers would ensure the success of the enterprise and provide economic growth with benefits for all. When he produced his authoritative statement on scientific management in 1911 Taylor represented his system as offering the key to future national prosperity in the following terms:

> The principal object of management should be to secure the maximum prosperity for the employer, coupled with the maximum prosperity for each employee. The words 'maximum prosperity' are used, in their broad sense, to mean not only large dividends for the company or owner, but the development of every branch of the business to its highest state of excellence, so that the prosperity may be permanent. In the same way maximum prosperity for each employee means not only higher wages than are usually received by men of his class, but, of more importance still, it also means the development of each man to his state of maximum efficiency, so that he may be able to do, generally speaking, the highest grade of work for which his natural abilities fit him, and it further means giving him when possible, this class of work to do.
>
> It would seem so self-evident that maximum prosperity for the employer, coupled with maximum prosperity for the employee, ought to be the two leading objects of management, that even to state this fact should be unnecessary. And yet there is no question that, throughout the industrial world, a large part of the organization of employers, as well as employees, is for war rather than for peace, and that perhaps the majority on either side do not believe that it is possible so to arrange that their interest become identical. The majority of these men believe that the fundamental interests of employees and employers are necessarily antagonistic. Scientific management on the contrary, has for its very foundation that the true interests of the two are one and the same; that prosperity for the

employer cannot exist through a long term of years unless it is accompanied by prosperity for the employee, and *vice versa*.

(Taylor, 1911/1972, pp.9–10)

This is a statement which refutes the vulgar view of Taylor as seeing workers as akin to robots and merely being interested in greater levels of production at whatever human cost. Instead there is the advocacy of enabling workers to progress in accordance with their abilities and an awareness that the prosperity of employees should never be sacrificed in the interests of profits.

It has been noted that Taylor joined Bethlehem Steel as a consultant in 1893 and also that it was there that his ideas on scientific management became fully developed. He was retained by Joseph Wharton, founder of the USA's first business school and a major stockholder in Bethlehem Steel. Operation of the company was weak and Taylor's ideas were resisted by the management who were suspicious of his methods. By the time he reached Bethlehem Steel Taylor had already carried out successful consultancies including one at Simonds Rolling Machine Company, a manufacturer of ball bearings for bicycles. At Simonds he conducted a study of the inspection department where some 120 women were engaged in scrutinizing ball bearings for defects. These women worked for 10½ hours a day, 5½ days a week; work that, in Taylor's words, 'required the closest attention and concentration, so that the nervous tension of the inspectors was considerable, in spite of the fact that they were comfortably seated' (Taylor, 1903/1972, p.87). He decided that much of the women's time was wasted as a result of the tedium caused by the excessively long hours. Instead of pushing on with their work the women were engaged in developing strategies to alleviate boredom. Taylor was a believer in adequate relaxation periods so that, as he put it, 'workers can really "work while they work and play while they play", and not mix the two'. By changing the method of work, substantially reducing working hours, introducing careful staff selection, providing rest periods and applying incentive payments, he eventually succeeded in reducing the number of women employed on inspection from 120 to 35 and improving accuracy by two-thirds. Regarding the women, their wages increased by an average of 80 to 100 per cent; their working day was reduced by two hours and each 'was made to feel that she was the object of especial care and interest on the part of the management, and that if anything went wrong with her she could always have a helper and teacher in the management to lean upon' (Taylor 1903/1972, pp.95–96). Such substantial loss of jobs (if accompanied by redundancy rather than redeployment) would no doubt disturb workers and their trade unions alike. Nevertheless, there are facets of Taylor's work at Simonds that are reminiscent of the Hawthorne experiments (see Chapter 11), although, of course, Taylor's work pre-dated these by over thirty years.

Taylor was assisted at Bethlehem Steel by Henry Gantt (see Chapter 4) who had worked with him at Midvale Steel and supervised some of the work at Simonds. He was also joined by Dwight V. Merrick, an expert in time study, and Carl Barth a mathematician who developed a slide rule to solve the many complex equations involved in Taylor's experiments on metal cutting. Taylor thus pushed forward at Bethlehem Steel with his empirical work in two spheres, developing his studies in metallurgy and machine tools while perfecting, as he saw it, his system of task management. Indeed Taylor's work often directly linked his findings in metallurgy (and particularly the processes involved in cutting metals) with improvements in productivity as a result of rationalizing and standardizing production techniques. He was able to demonstrate that the application of a scientific knowledge of machine tools, together with the application of his management techniques, could revolutionize the nature of the production process. For Taylor, long experience of a particular trade provided little advantage in terms of maximizing efficiency. Instead it was more likely to mean that things went on in much the same way, thereby ensuring the uncritical perpetuation of techniques and processes. He therefore advocated a complete separation between the role of the operatives and that of management. As he remarked:

> It is true that whenever intelligent and educated men find that the responsibility for making progress in any of the mechanical arts rests with them, instead of upon workmen who are actually labouring at the trade, that they almost invariably start on the road which leads to the development of a science where, in the past, has existed mere traditional or rule of thumb knowledge.
>
> *(Taylor, 1903/1972, p.103)*

This sharp division of functions between management and workers assumed that the former would take all the major decisions concerning the methods of production, while the latter would more or less passively accept their role in the overall production process. Of course, Taylor's 'managers' were not to be the old guard entrepreneurs and traditional foremen but a new technical elite trained in the methods of Taylorism. To objections that the sharp division of labour between those who managed and those who were to be managed would degrade the work of the operatives, Taylor responded that careful staff selection would ensure that only individuals suited to undertake (or, one might say, endure) the requirements of each specific aspect of the production process should be recruited. He summed all of this up in three central principles as follows:

> (1) the substitution of a science for the individual judgement of the workmen; (2) the scientific selection and development of the workmen, after each man has been studied, taught, and trained…instead of allowing the workmen to select themselves and develop in a haphazard way; and (3) the intimate co-operation of the management with the workmen, so that they together do the work in accordance with the scientific laws which have been developed, instead of leaving the solution of each problem in the hands of the individual workman.
>
> *(Taylor, 1911/1972, pp.114–115)*

Whether Taylor was indeed justified in claiming that his analysis of work had generated 'scientific laws' is doubtful. However, notwithstanding the resistance that his methods sometimes met from managers and operatives alike, he was certainly able to demonstrate that expert knowledge of the technical means of production, coupled with time study and financial incentives, could substantially improve efficiency levels. He was of course aware that the greater the level of technical complexity, the greater the need for managerial control. Self-evidently the autonomy of the individual worker in such a situation would be severely constrained and a visit to any present day automobile plant provides ample evidence of Taylor's legacy in terms of production techniques. Ironically, however, the greatest publicity has been given not to Taylor's management of the interface between complex technology and the worker but to a situation where the level of technical complexity was negligible and the attributes of the worker limited to brute strength and stamina. In 1899 Taylor set himself the task of undertaking a systematic study of the labourer's working in what was called 'the yard' at Bethlehem Steel. There were between 400 and 600 of these men and they were employed in gangs under foremen who had previously been yard labourers themselves. The men's work consisted mainly of unloading goods from railway trucks and shovelling materials into piles. From the piles they would then transport the various raw materials, such as ore, coke, limestone, sand, coal and so on, to the blast furnaces and open-hearth furnaces for smelting. The men would also transport and load the finished products such as pig iron from the furnaces and billets from the rolling mills, onto railway trucks for outward dispatch. The labourers earned $1.15 a day for their efforts and Taylor was informed that they were 'steady workers, but slow and phlegmatic, and that nothing would induce them to work fast'.

Using a trained assistant, Taylor set out to establish how much work a first class man could do in a day without undue strain. He utilized his system of task management, breaking the work into elements and using a stopwatch to record the time taken for each of these. When the times had been reconstituted, and rest pauses added, he calculated that a first class man should be able to load between 45 and 48 tons of pig iron each day. In fact the average quantity loaded by men working in gangs of 5 to 20 was between 12 and 13 tons a day. Taylor offered an incentive piece rate of 60 per cent more pay (i.e. $1.85) to men able to meet his standard requirement of $47\frac{1}{2}$ tons of pig iron loaded each day. He selected a likely individual, a Dutch immigrant called Henry Knolle, and, after instructing him in the correct method of loading, set him to achieve the new production target.[2] Knolle succeeded in the task and, notwithstanding opposition from many of the men working in the yard, Taylor managed to transfer

2 In *The Principles of Scientific Management* pp.44–46 Taylor calls Knolle 'Schmidt' and provides an account of their conversation. However, although many of Taylor's critics have quoted the dialogue as an example of Taylor's callousness the conversation probably never took place.

practically all of the yard labour from day to piecework over a two year period. He summed up the improvements as he saw them in the following terms:

> When the writer left the steelworks, the Bethlehem pieceworkers were the finest body of picked labourers that he has ever seen together. They were practically all first class men, because in each case the task which they were called upon to perform was such that only a first class man could do it. The tasks were all purposely made so severe that not more than one out of five labourers (perhaps even a smaller percentage than this) could keep up. It was clearly understood by each newcomer as he went to work that unless he was able to average at least $1.85 per day he would have to make way for another man who could do so . . . Perhaps the most notable different between these men and ordinary pieceworkers lay in their changed mental attitude toward their employers and their work, and in the total absence of soldiering on their part.
>
> *(Taylor, 1911/1972, pp.55–56)*

Not surprisingly perhaps, the tone of this statement was used by Taylor's many detractors as evidence that he pursued efficiency whatever the costs in human terms and has haunted his reputation ever since. Although, as has been shown above, this was certainly not the case, early antagonism to 'the speed up' gave Taylorism a bad reputation which has endured to the present day. In the context of his own times, Taylor's methods, together with those of his associates and followers, attracted increasing opposition from American trade unions and eventually resulted in his appearance before a committee of Congress established to investigate his, and other associated, systems of shop management.

Taylor's testimony

In August 1911 the first strike against scientific management as it was now termed (see Chapter 3) occurred at the army munitions arsenal at Watertown, Massachusetts. General William Crozier, head of the Army Ordnance Department, had studied Taylor's work and considered that the techniques of scientific management might be appropriate for use in the army arsenals. Crozier chose Watertown, together with Rock Island, Illinois, as pilot plants to test scientific management and hired Dwight V. Merrick (who it will be recalled had worked under Taylor at Bethlehem Steel) to undertake the task. Although the initial work at Watertown went well, opposition developed at Rock Island where the International Association of Machinists began agitation among the workers against time study. It soon became clear that organized labour, and particularly the craft trade unions, was beginning a concerted campaign to resist the spread of scientific management. Taylor personally counselled Crozier to tread carefully at Watertown and to implement scientific management on a piecemeal basis and only after careful consultation with the workers. Indeed, he subsequently blamed the problems at Watertown on bad communications rather than trade union resistance to his methods. However, whatever the underlying reasons for the strike at Watertown, the immediate cause was the dismissal of a moulder who refused to be time studied by Merrick. Although it was short lived the industrial unrest at Watertown was represented to Congress by labour interests as stemming from the poor treatment of workers as a result of the attempt to introduce Taylorism.

The Special House Committee appointed by Congress to investigate the issue consisted of William B. Wilson, a former United Mine Workers Official, chairman of the House Labour Committee and subsequently secretary of labour under President Wilson; William C. Redfield, a manufacturer who became secretary of commerce under Wilson; and John Q. Tilson, the only Republican among the three, to act as umpire. The hearings began in October 1911 and ended in February 1912 and Taylor spent twelve hours, spread over four days, giving evidence. The atmosphere was both adversarial and hostile and, in the words of Wren, 'baited, insulted and made to appear a beast, Taylor staggered from the stand at the close of his testimony. Taylor's pride was sorely wounded, his life work reviled before a congressional committee' (Wren, 1994, p.125). However, when the final report of the committee emerged it was inconclusive. No evidence was found to show abuse of workers under the techniques of scientific management and no demand for protective legislation emerged. Nevertheless, interests sympathetic to organized labour ensured that riders were added to appropriation bills banning the use of scientific management, and specifically the use of the stopwatch. Although such riders were calculated to keep Taylorism out of government installations, they did not succeed. As Judith Merkle, a strong critic of Taylorism, has conceded 'congressional intervention did not eliminate the implementation of Taylor's ideas, even in the Watertown Arsenal itself. Rather, it forced them underground. The banning of the stopwatch failed to bannish Taylorism' (Merkle, 1980, p.29). This statement could almost stand as an epitaph to Taylorism which often in the face of opposition from organized labour wherever it appeared, and more or less wholly lacking in the support of academic commentators, nevertheless made a huge impact on the modern world.

In its printed form Taylor's testimony before the Special House Committee runs to over 280 pages, the bulk of which are taken up with questions posed by William B. Wilson and Taylor's responses. Broadly speaking Wilson took the position that the combination of scientific management, improved methods and new technology would lead to the erosion of workers' residual control over the labour process and create unemployment. This of course was often to be the attitude of craft trade unions when confronted by scientific management. It resurfaced, in Marxist guise, in the work of Harry Braverman during the 1970s (see Chapter 18). Taylor's view, in contrast, was that all of these things were justified by the demands for improvement and would tend to stimulate economic activity and growth thereby ensuring an aggregate expansion of employment rather than a loss. Workers displaced by innovation would therefore readily find alternative jobs if they were prepared to re-train and/or relocate. Further, while Wilson advocated the benefits of collective bargaining, Taylor confirmed his strong belief in individual incentive payments. As Aitken has commented:

> Taylor's insight into the general logic of industrial work…was combined with particular assumptions about human psychology and a particular approach to the problem of incentives. Taylor, like almost all his contemporaries, accepted with little question the view of human nature implied by Benthamite utilitarianism. This acceptance determined Taylor's approach to the problem of incentives in the workshop…The goals of the worker had to be brought into co-incidence with the goals of the enterprise. The problem was to be solved by gearing the worker's wage to his production through a system of incentive wages.
>
> *(Aitken, 1960, pp.34–35)*

However, ensuring that the goals of the worker and the enterprise coincided required much more than merely time study and incentive wages. As Taylor expressed it in his testimony it meant a total reconstruction of attitudes and a decisive shift in the relationship between management and workers. Far from generating conflict Taylor considered that scientific management, if properly applied and fully accepted by the parties, would create an atmosphere of trust, harmony and mutual prosperity. He considered this to be the true essence of scientific management. In his own words:

> Scientific management is not any efficiency device, not a device of any kind for securing efficiency…in its essence (it) involves a complete mental revolution on the part of the working man engaged in any particular establishment or industry – a complete mental revolution on the part of these men as to their duties towards their work, toward their fellow men, and toward their employers. And it involves the equally complete mental revolution on the part of those on the management's side – the foreman, the superintendent, the owner of the business, the Board of Directors – a complete mental revolution on their part as to their duties toward their fellow workers in the management, toward their workmen, and toward all of their daily problems. And without this complete mental revolution on both sides scientific management does not exist.
>
> *(Taylor, 1911/1972, pp.26–27)*

Taylor's statement encapsulates the division in his work between the narrow techniques of time study and the far more ambitious project of scientific management with its aim of obviating industrial conflict. As Lyndall Urwick observed 'it was not high speed steel, the care of belting, planning (or) mnemonic classification…which were his great gifts to the world, but that "mental revolution" which he so often emphasized as necessary to the application of his methods' (Urwick, 1929, p.57).

Critical summary

F. W. Taylor, in the words of Aitken, 'was the first to synthesize and systematize the best that was known about the management of men and to point out the techniques by which this art might be advanced in the future' (Aitken, 1960, p.35). Engineering was at the heart of Taylor's theorizing, providing the context for its development, the world view by which it was sustained and, finally, the justification for its widespread application. Scientific management aimed to analyse and control the activities of people in the same way that engineers analysed and controlled machines. Thus the success of engineers in bringing together the productive capacities of physical materials was to be extended not just in engineering but in all spheres of work. Central to Taylor's system was the desire to rationalize and standardize production techniques in the interests of economy, efficiency and mutual prosperity. His primary point of interest was the individual worker pursuing individual goals and motivated by incentive payments. Undoubtedly Taylor's view of human motivation was somewhat simplistic and his apprehension of the significance of groups limited and generally negative. Nevertheless, his grasp of the mutual responsibilities of managers and workers in the aggregate, together with his advocacy of the 'mental revolution', provide some evidence that his belief in individualism was far from being total. Taylor's influence on subsequent mangement theory was immense. In Britain the initial reaction to scientific management was a combination of indifference on the part of management – who thought they didn't need it – and hostility on the part of trade unions – who felt they didn't want it. Among British managers interest in Taylor's work was narrowly focused on his technical expertise in the area of high speed steel rather than management theory. The trade unions seized on the much publicized opposition of the American unions to scientific management and took the view that it was synonymous with the harsh treatment of workers (Urwick and Brech, 1945, p. 89).

The hostility of the American unions to scientific management received its exposition in the pages of the Hoxie Report published in 1915 which contained all of the conventional complaints about Taylor's work. Robert Franklin Hoxie, an associate professor of political economy at the University of Chicago, undertook (on behalf of the US Commission on Industrial Relations) an investigation into 35 workshops where scientific management had been implemented. His report, published under the title *Scientific Management and Labor* scrutinized the claims of management in support of scientific management and those of the trade unions against. He made no distinction in his investigation between scientific management in its theoretical form and scientific management as he saw it operating in practice. Briefly, he was antagonistic to its aims generally and sceptical concerning its claims, particularly those relating to industrial democracy. He depicted scientific management as leading inevitably to de–skilling and as inimical to the establishment and maintenance of trade unionism generally but in particular the craft unions. The following passage gives the flavour:

Scientific management, fully and properly applied, inevitably tends to the constant breakdown of the established crafts and craftsmanship and the constant elimination of skill in the sense of narrowing craft knowledge and workmanship, except for the lower orders of workmen...Were the scientific management ideal as at present formulated fully realized, any man who walks the street would be a practical competitor for almost any workman's job. Such a situation would inevitably break down the basis of present day unionism in its dominant form and render collective bargaining as now practiced impossible in any effective sense in regard to the matters considered by the unions most essential...Add to all this the advantage gained by the employers in the progressive gathering up and systematization for their own uses, and the destruction of apprenticeship which cuts the workers off from the perpetuation among them of craftsmanship, and the destructive tendencies of scientific management, as far as present day unionism and collective bargaining are concerned, seem inevitable.

(Hoxie, 1915, pp.129–131)

Interestingly, Hoxie's opposition to scientific management, and his strong advocacy of craft prerogatives and the industrial *status quo*, tended to reinforce rather than erode the support for scientific management and greater efficiency among employers. Thus as Claude S. George observed 'Hoxie should be remembered because he caused men to re-examine their faith in the new science of management and to stand foursquare in their beliefs in its efficiency and value to society. His scorching derision of the movement did more to anchor it more firmly than his approbation would have' (George 1968, p.118). Thus, notwithstanding criticism and opposition, the influence of Taylor's ideas steadily grew. They entered the French–speaking world through the efforts of Henri Le Chatelier (see Chapter 5). In Britain his work was popularized by the efforts of Lyndall Urwick (see Chapter 10). In the Soviet Union, *Pravda*, in 1918, quoted Lenin as saying 'we should try out every scientific and progressive suggestion of the Taylor system' (Wrege and Greenwood, 1991, p.254). Similarly the insights and techniques of Taylor's work were introduced into Japan at an early stage, translations of his work appearing there in 1912 (see Chapter 19). Thus, as Christel Lane has aptly observed, 'Taylorism...spread from the USA all over the industrialized and industrializing world' (Lane 1989, pp.144–5).

Discussion questions

1. What did Taylor mean by the terms natural and systematic soldiering?
2. How convincing were Taylor's claims that 'systematic and scientific time study' would improve productivity?
3. If Taylorism was pro-management then why was it resisted by many managers?

4. What were the three core principles of Taylor's system?
5. Why were trade unions generally hostile to Taylor's ideas?
6. How convincing were Taylor's arguments for individual incentive payments?
7. Why did Taylor call for a mental revolution on the part of managers and workers?

Suggested reading

Copley, F. (1923) *Frederick W. Taylor: Father of Scientific Management,* Harper & Row, New York.

Daunten, P. (ed) (1962) *Current Issues and Emerging Concepts in Management,* Houghton, Boston, chs. 1 and 2.

Pugh, D. and Hickson, D. (eds) (1989) *Writers on Organizations,* Penguin Books, Harmondsworth, ch.3.

Rose, M. (1988) *Industrial Behaviour: Research and Control,* Penguin Books, Harmondsworth, chs. 3 and 4.

Taylor, F. W. (1903) *Shop Management,* Harper & Row, New York.

Taylor, F. W. (1911) *The Principles of Scientific Management,* Harper & Row, New York.

Taylor, F. W. (1972 edition) *Scientific Management,* Greenwood Press, Westport, Connect.

Wren, D. (1994) *The Evolution of Management Thought,* Wiley & Sons, Chichester, ch.7.

Wrege, C. and Greenwood, R. (1991) *Frederick W. Taylor, Father of Scientific Management: Myth and Reality,* Business One Irwin, Homewood, Illinois.

Chapter 3

The Gilbreths and motion study

Frank Bunker Gilbreth was born in Fairfield, Maine in 1868.[1] The son of a hardware merchant, he inherited the habits of hard work and thrift which characterized New England puritanism. When Gilbreth was three years old his father died and his widowed mother moved her young family to Andover, Massachusetts where he attended the local academy. In 1878 the family moved once again, this time to Boston, where Gilbreth at first attended Rice Grammar School and later the English High School, where he prepared for entry to the Massachusetts Institute of Technology. Although he passed the entrance examinations for MIT he made the surprising decision to abandon his studies and start working at once as an apprentice bricklayer. During a ten-year period between 1885 and 1895 Gilbreth worked for the Whidden Construction Company, rising from apprentice to become a foreman and eventually the chief superintendent at the age of 27. During this period he initiated his early observations of motion study and also began to devise improved construction equipment such as scaffolding which could be readily raised to facilitate bricklaying.

In April 1895 Gilbreth, by now a member of the American Society of Mechanical Engineers, left Whidden and established his own company specialising in concrete construction which was then in its infancy. Like Taylor (and, as will be seen, Gantt) Gilbreth had considerable innovative talents and during the 1890s he began patenting the first of his many inventions including concrete mixers, conveyors and reinforcing bars. His business prospered and he soon widened its geographical base to include much of north America from Montreal to Louisiana and from Maine to California. He

1 The bulk of the biographical information contained in this chapter is based on Lillian Moller Gilbreth's *The Quest for the One Best Way: A Sketch of the Life of Frank Bunker Gilbreth*, Hive, Easton 1973.

also began undertaking contracts in Europe, eventually opening an office in Victoria Street, London. Similarly the types of work undertaken gradually expanded from small jobs such as waterproofing cellars to building houses, factories and mills and major civil engineering undertakings such as dams and canals. In Woodland, Maine, Gilbreth presided over the building of an entire town. The scope of these activities, together with the necessity of delegating their management to others, prompted him to devise the set of standardized accounting and working procedures which formed the subject of his first two books, *Field System* and *Concrete System* which were published in 1908. These were followed by *Bricklaying System* (1909) in which Gilbreth began the process of systematically setting down his research into motion study. He introduced the subject in the following terms:

> The motion study in this book is but the beginning of an era of motion study, that will eventually affect all our methods of teaching trades. It will cut down production costs and increase the efficiency and wages of the workman...To be pre-eminently successful: (a) a mechanic must know his trade; (b) he must be quick motioned; and (c) he must use the fewest possible motions to accomplish the desired result.

> *(Gilbreth in Spriegel and Myers, 1953, p.55)*

Scrutinizing his own trade of bricklaying Gilbreth was able to demonstrate that the number of motions involved could be reduced from as many as 18 to as few as $4\frac{1}{2}$ thereby substantially increasing productivity and earnings. He set out his method of bricklaying in charts illustrating what he considered to be 'the wrong way' and 'the one best way' of undertaking the job. His intention was that new recruits to the trade would in future be systematically trained according to the set of techniques embodied in 'the one best way', thereby enabling them to attain skilled status at a far earlier date than could be achieved using rule of thumb methods.

Although Gilbreth was working quite independently of Taylor his work obviously paralleled the latter's own endeavours. While Gilbreth was, of course, engaged in construction work rather than engineering, and interested primarily in motion rather than time study, they nevertheless shared many concerns and assumptions not least the desire for standardization, systematic work study and high levels of productive efficiency. Gilbreth must have been aware of Taylor's work through their mutual association with the ASME and he had already read the latter's *Shop Management* when the two men first met in 1907. Gilbreth immediately became an apostle of the Taylor system. In July 1910 Gilbreth, together with Gantt, accompanied Taylor on the latter's only professional visit to Britain to attend a joint meeting of the Iron and Steel Institute and the ASME in Birmingham. In 1911 Gilbreth became the driving force in establishing the Society for the Promotion of Scientific Management which subsequently became the Taylor Society. By this time Taylor had developed his thinking into a general ideology of efficiency and, when the Eastern Railways requested permission from the Interstate Commerce Commission for an increase in freight rates, Taylor's ideas were taken up by 'the people's lawyer' – Louis D. Brandeis. Brandeis supported the cause of the shippers against the railways and argued against increasing rates, claiming that they would be unecessary if the railways were operated efficiently using Taylor's ideas. Brandeis wished to publicize the 'Taylor system' and convened a meeting at Henry Gantt's New York apartment to discuss the issue. Among those present at the meeting were James Mapes Dodge (President of the Link Belt Company and a President of the ASME) and Frank Gilbreth. In the event Brandeis coined the term 'Scientific Management' as the slogan to publicize Taylor's work, and this was readily accepted by the other engineers although only reluctantly adopted by Taylor himself.

Taylor's influence is to be seen in Gilbreth's first substantial book *Motion Study* (1911) in which he extended his sphere of concern beyond bricklaying and construction to embrace work as a whole. Gilbreth began by alluding to the waste of natural resources, particularly the land through the process of erosion, and went on to observe that this dreadful loss was as nothing compared to the loss of human productivity as a result of wasted motion. As he expressed the situation:

> tremendous savings are possible in the work of everybody, – they are not for one class, they are not for the trades only, they are for the offices, the schools, the colleges, the stores, the households, and the farms. But the possibilities of benefits from motion study in the trades are particularly striking, because all trades, even at their present best are bungled…We start at present in the first stage of motion study, i.e. the stage of discovering and classifying the best practice. This is the stage of analysis. The following are the steps to be taken in the analysis:
>
> 1. Reduce present practice to writing.
> 2. Enumerate motions used.
> 3. Enumerate variables which affect each motion.
> 4. Reduce best practice to writing.
> 5. Enumerate motions used.
> 6. Enumerate variables which affect each motion.
>
> *(Gilbreth in Spriegel and Myers, 1953)*

Gilbreth identified 15 'variables of the worker' including anatomy, creed, experience, mode of living, skill, temperament and training. He also identified 14 'variables of the surroundings, equipment and tools' such as lighting, heating, cooling, ventilation, supervision, colour of the surrounding walls etc. Finally, he identified 13 'variables of the motion' including acceleration, automaticity, inertia and momentum overcome, direction and effectiveness. Gilbreth paid particular attention to fatigue and here he received the help of his wife, Lillian Moller Gilbreth, an important management thinker in her own right. Together they developed a list of 17 basic motions such as 'select', 'hold', 'search' and so on, each of which they called a 'therblig' (i.e. Gilbreth spelled backwards with the 'th' transposed). Using a 'therblig chart' the Gilbreths were able to analyse the exact motions involved in any particular operation.

The Gilbreth's partnership

Lillian Moller was born in Oakland, California in 1878 where her German born father was a prosperous sugar refiner. She was exceptionally gifted academically and overcame the contemporary prejudice against women in order to obtain Bachelors and Masters degrees in English from the University of California. Following her success in her Masters work she began a Doctoral thesis. However, during a trip East she met Frank Gilbreth, became engaged to him and they were married in 1904. Following her marriage Lillian decided to change the focus of her studies to psychology, reasoning that this subject would best complement the work of her husband. From the early 1900s until Frank Gilbreth's premature death in 1924, the Gilbreths embarked on a partnership which embraced both the domestic (they had 12 children) and professional spheres. Lillian Moller Gilbreth completed her doctorate in 1912 and submitted it for scrutiny to the University of California. Unfortunately, although her thesis was accepted, the University insisted that she return to California and spend a year on campus before her degree could be awarded. This she steadfastly refused to do, choosing instead to publish the thesis as *The Psychology of Management* (1914) a book which, in the words of Wren, 'stands in the literature as one of the earliest contributions to understanding the human factor in industry' (Wren, 1994, p.143). In the event the University of California decided that Lillian Gilbreth's year of residency could be spent at any college which awarded an advanced degree in management or industrial psychology. Brown University in Providence, Rhode Island was then in the process of launching a PhD programme in applied management and, for reasons of convenience that will be examined in a moment, Lillian Gilbreth spent the necessary year there, finally receiving her doctorate in 1915.

In 1912 Frank Gilbreth set up as a management consultant and obtained his first major job at the New England Butt Company in Providence, as has been seen the home of Brown University. Such was the magnitude of the task that the whole Gilbreth family relocated, enabling Lillian to attend university lectures and assist Frank in extending the techniques of motion study. Also in 1912 they published a *Primer of Scientific Management* in which, somewhat to the chagrin of Taylor and his immediate circle, they expounded the philosophy of scientific management for a mass audience.[2] However, in describing scientific management the Gilbreths also undertook to rede-

2 For an account of the tensions between Taylor and Gilbreth see Nadworny, M. (1957) Frederick Taylor and Frank Gilbreth: Competition in Scientific Management. *Business History Review* **31**(1) 23–34.

fine it, downplaying the emphasis on time study and, not surprisingly, emphasizing the importance of motion study. At New England Butt, a company which braided materials for electrical wiring, the Gilbreths began to use the technique they described as 'micromotion study'. In the words of Nadworny, they:

> employed a motion picture camera to record the performance of a worker on a job, with a clock calibrated in hundredths of a minute placed in viewing range. With this technique (they) could record the motions, the time, and the conditions surrounding the job. (The) major objective was the recording, and ultimate simplification in improvement, of the motions of the worker. (This) method permitted the timing of both the methods of the worker and the total job, and also provided an opportunity to reproduce the performance of the worker a relatively unlimited number of times.
>
> *(Nadworny, 1957, p.27)*

Taylor was not much impressed with 'micromotion study' and, as occurred in the case of Gantt (see Chapter 4), became critical of Frank Gilbreth and his work. In fact Frank Gilbreth's ideas, complemented by the insights derived from industrial psychology provided by Lillian, were moving beyond the original confines of scientific management and pointing in the direction subsequently pursued by Elton Mayo and his associates (see Chapter 11).

In 1920 the Gilbreths made a veiled attack on Taylor in their paper *An Indictment of Stop-Watch Time Study*, delivered to the Taylor Society in New York. They 'characterized time study as unethical, wasteful and inaccurate...(it) employed questionable statistical methodology in arriving at standard times, and was costly because of the inaccurate and useless data it developed' (Nadworny, 1957, p.31). The Gilbreths were careful not to reject Taylor's work out of hand, even though he had of course been the leading advocate of time study. Instead they sustained Taylor in the role of visionary and prophet, claiming merely to be refining his pioneering work in the light of their own researches and the availability of new techniques. Among the new techniques used by the Gilbreths 'micromotion study' has already been mentioned. A further technique was the 'chronocylegraph' which involved attaching a tiny, flashing lightbulb to the hand, finger or arm of a worker and causing a film to be made showing acceleration or deceleration of movements as a series of dots. This technique facilitated the identification of the most effective patterns of motions thus enabling the Gilbreths to improve methods and utilize them in training new workers.

It has been mentioned that the Gilbreths became interested in industrial fatigue as an adjunct to Frank Gilbreth's work on motion study. In 1916 they published *Fatigue Study* which provided a synthesis of classic scientific management and insights derived from industrial psychology. As they put it:

> There has come, in the past twenty-five years, a strong general realization that the important factor in doing work is the human factor, or the human element.

Improvement in working apparatus of any type is important in its effect upon the human being who is to use the apparatus. The moment one begins to make man; the worker, the centre of activity, he appreciates that he has two elements to measure. One is the activity itself. This includes the motions, seen or unseen, made by the worker, what is done and how it is done. The other is fatigue. This includes the length and nature of the interval or rest period required for the worker to recover his original condition of working power. Anyone who makes a real motion study, or analyses motion study data, cannot fail to realize constantly the relationship of motion study to fatigue study.

(Gilbreth and Gilbreth in Spriegel and Myers, 1953, p.305–6)

The Gilbreth's divided fatigue into what they characterized as 'unnecessary' (i.e. resulting from effort or work which does not need to be done at all) and 'necessary' (i.e. resulting from work that must be done in order to achieve the task). The key to minimizing fatigue was, they claimed, to be located through scientific motion study and the implementation of improved methods. Thus 'unnecessary' fatigue (such as lifting and carrying) could be largely eliminated through better design of the workplace and 'necessary' fatigue could be minimized through the introduction of improved techniques and the provision of rest periods. Other ways of reducing fatigue advocated by the Gilbreths were the reduction of the working day and the introduction or increase of holidays with pay.

As was seen in Chapter 2, Taylor had certainly been aware of the problems caused by fatigue and was an advocate of appropriate rest periods. Nevertheless, he had in the main chosen to ignore the issue, opting instead to rely on the physical capacity of the individual worker to overcome fatigue and put forth greater effort through the stimulus of cash incentives. The Gilbreths took a different approach, down playing the idea of the 'first class man' and emphasizing the significance of the total working environment in the maintenance of high levels of productivity. The following quotation, touchingly whimsical as it may seem, indicates the difference that had developed between the approach of Taylor and that of the Gilbreths.

The final test of fatigue elimination, as of a very other change made in doing things, is its influence upon the total output of 'Happiness Minutes'. The aim of life is happiness, no matter how we differ as to what true happiness means. Fatigue elimination, starting as it does from a desire to conserve human life and to eliminate waste, must increase 'Happiness Minutes', no matter what else it does, or it has failed in its fundamental aim. Have you reason to believe that your workers are really happier because of the work that you have done on fatigue study? Do they look happier, and say they are happier? Then your fatigue eliminating work has been worthwhile in the highest sense of the term, no matter what the financial outcome.

(Gilbreth and Gilbreth in Spriegel and Myers, 1953, p.55)

This is a far cry from the starker realities of 'the yard' at Bethlehem Steel and points in the direction of the considerations concerning human motivation at work which formed the core of the Hawthorne experiments (see Chapter 11).

Critical summary

Frank Bunker Gilbreth's work paralleled and complemented that of F. W. Taylor. Although the emphasis in the latter's approach was on time study, where Gilbreth's early work concentrated entirely on motion study, they were basically interested in the same things, namely standardization, systematic work study and high levels of productive efficiency. In any case 'time study' and 'motion study' soon became conflated to form 'time and motion' study. Like Taylor, Gilbreth was keenly interested in improving methods and adapting work techniques to meet the demands of changing technology. However, whereas Taylor tended to lay the greatest stress on the quality of the operative combined with financial incentives to achieve 'the speed up', Gilbreth downplayed the idea that the best results could be obtained merely by prompting the operative to work harder. Instead he sought to improve operator performance through reducing unnecessary motions and limiting fatigue by placing far greater emphasis on the total working environment. In his mature work Gilbreth was strongly influenced by Lillian Moller Gilbreth and her research in the sphere of industrial psychology. Between them the Gilbreths advanced the agenda of work study beyond the search for the 'first class man' and, through their significant appreciation of the human factor in industry, towards the modern science of ergonomics.

Discussion questions

1. Why did the Gilbreths favour motion study over time study?
2. How accurate is it to call the Gilbreths followers of F. W. Taylor?
3. What were the circumstances which led to the coining of the term scientific management?
4. In what ways did the Gilbreths develop their work beyond the confines of scientific management?
5. What did the Gilbreths mean by the terms necessary and unnecessary fatigue?

Suggested reading

Gilbreth, F. (1911) *Motion Study*, Van Nostrand Rheinhold, New York.
Gilbreth, F. (1912) *Primer of Scientific Management*, Van Nostrand Rheinhold, New York.

Gilbreth, L. (1914) *The Psychology of Management*, Sturgis & Walton, New York.

Gilbreth, F. and L. (1917) *Applied Motion Study*, Sturgis & Walton, New York.

Merrill, H. (ed) (1960) *Classics in Management*, American Management Association, New York, ch.11.

Nadworny, M. (1953) The Society for the Promotion of the Science of Management. *Explorations in Entrepreneurial History* **5** 244–247.

Spriegel, W. and Myers, C. (eds) (1953) *The Writings of the Gilbreths*, Richard Irwin, Holmwood, Illinois.

Wren, D. (1994) *The Evolution of Management Thought*, Wiley & Sons, Chichester, ch.8.

Chapter 4

Henry Gantt and humanized scientific management

Henry Laurence Gantt was born into a prosperous Maryland family in 1861, during the American Civil War.[1] Although Maryland was held to the cause of the North, many of its people nevertheless sympathized with the Confederacy, including Gantt's parents, Virgil and Mary. Gantt's father ran a successful plantation but when President Lincoln issued the Emancipation Proclamation in September 1862, his 69 slaves, not surprisingly, deserted. Ultimately Virgil Gantt was financially ruined and his family compelled to abandon the plantation and move to Baltimore in search of a new life. From a position of comfort, security and prosperity the Gantts were reduced to a situation of near poverty. Owing to his deafness, Virgil Gantt was unable to make much contribution to the family's upkeep and it was Mary Gantt who became the breadwinner by operating a boarding house until her eldest daughter, Margaret, was able to help support the family by working as a schoolteacher. One result of this dramatic change in family fortunes was that Henry Gantt left home when he was 12 years old to enter McDonagh School which had recently been established near Baltimore as a free farm school for poor boys. The school was run on the basis of strict military discipline and Gantt's biographer provides the flavour of life at McDonagh in the following extract:

1 The biographical information in this chapter is based on L. Alford's 'Henry Laurence Gantt: Leader in Industry' the condensed version of which is contained in Rathe A. (ed) (1960) *Gantt on Management: Guidelines for Today's Executive*, American Management Association and The American Society of Mechanical Engineers, New York.

It was located about twelve miles north east of Baltimore. Five or six labourers cared for the animals and did the hardest part of the work. The students did the rest. In summer, the rising hour was 4.30am; and in winter, 5.30am. The boys planted, hoed, cut, stacked, and husked corn; stacked the wheat after it was cut and bundled; and later on assisted in tending the threshing machine when it was threshed. After the hay had been cut, they did all the work of curing it, loading it on the wagons, and towing it away to the barns. They did the gardening, which included raising all the vegetables for the school and small fruits such as strawberries and raspberries.

(Alford in Rathe, 1960, p.241)

The discipline and training for hard unremitting work which Gantt imbibed at McDonagh was to stay with him for the rest of his life. Gantt was an outstanding success at McDonagh and won a scholarship to Johns Hopkins University, although he continued to live at the school and commute to the university daily. On graduating from Johns Hopkins in 1880 he spent three years teaching natural sciences and physics at McDonagh before resuming his studies, this time at the Stevens Institute of Technology. Gantt went to the Stevens Institute in 1883 (the year that F. W. Taylor gained his Masters Degree from Stevens) concentrating his studies in the areas of physics and electricity and graduating as a mechanical engineer in 1884. When Gantt left Stevens he returned to Baltimore and spent two years as a draughtsman at Poole & Hunt, a firm of ironfounders and machinists. In 1886 he returned once again to McDonagh, this time as an instructor in manual training, before joining Midvale Steel in 1887.

By the time Gantt arrived at Midvale Steel as an assistant in the engineering department, F. W. Taylor was already chief engineer at the plant. In 1888 Gantt was elected to membership of the American Society of Mechanical Engineers and also became Taylor's assistant. In the words of Urwick and Brech, Gantt was now 'engaged less in technical work than in determining the most economical methods of working the machine tools in the machine shop' (Urwick and Brech, 1945, p.73). Although temperamentally very different, Gantt and Taylor embarked on a close working relationship which lasted for several years and included experimental work in metallurgy as well as the development of scientific management. Initially, as Wren has observed:

Gantt's ideas were largely influenced by Taylor, and the same elements appear in his early writings. The stress on the mutuality of interests between labour and management, the scientific selection of workmen, the incentive rate to stimulate performance, detailed instructions on work and all the other familiar concepts are reflected in Gantt's work.

(Wren, 1994, pp. 135–36)

However, Gantt tempered Taylor's work with greater insight into human psychology and greater emphasis on method as opposed to measurement. Like Taylor, Gantt was a practical inventor and between 1901 and 1904 the two men took out six joint patents, all of which were concerned with controlling temperatures for heating metal–cutting tools. Gantt also collaborated with Taylor and Carl Barth on the development of a slide rule which was patented in 1904. His most significant patent, however, concerned a mould for steel ingots which reduced the tendency of the ingots to crack, thereby reducing the amount of waste. As Alford commented, by '1934 certainly 25 per cent, and possibly as much as 50 per cent, of all steel ingot tonnage in the United States was cast in moulds on the Gantt principle' (Alford in Rathe, 1960, p.161).

Although Taylor left Midvale Steel in 1890 to become general manager of the Manufacturing Investment Company, Gantt remained and was promoted to superintendent of the castings department, a post he held until 1893. Gantt did subsequently resign, however, and during 1894–95 set himself up as a consulting engineer based in Philadelphia, before taking a post as superintendent of the Thurlow, Pennsylvania works of the American Steel Castings Company. Gantt was not particularly successful as a manager, suffering from severe headaches that rendered his temper uncertain, and in 1897 he once again teamed up with Taylor, this time at Simonds Rolling Machine Company. When Taylor went to Bethlehem Steel Gantt joined him there in March 1899 becoming closely involved with Taylor's metal cutting experiments and developing his own task-and-bonus incentive plan. He considered Taylor's approach to incentives to be too punitive and lacking in sensitivity to the human needs of operatives. In turn Taylor characterized Gantt's approach as mere pussy-footing and the relationship between the two men became somewhat cooler. As Alford described the situation:

> The underlying cause was something far more than a difference in temperament. Rather, it was a difference in fundamental thinking, in industrial philosophy. Taylor's attitude was an unwillingness to consider matters except in their technologic aspects. In contrast, Gantt sensed and felt the problems of the general management as well as those of the technological management, and proceeded to take them into account in his practice. Taylor disapproved of many of these methods; to him they were compromises rather than true scientific determinations.

> *(Alford in Rathe, 1960, p.259)*

In any case both Taylor and Gantt left Bethlehem Steel in 1901. As was observed in Chapter 2 Taylor spent the remaining years of his life campaigning in the cause of scientific management while Gantt, in the words of his biographer, 'began his real life's work as a consultant in modern industrial management'. In 1901 Gantt read a paper to the ASME (*viz. A Bonus System of Rewarding Labour*) which formed the basis of his book *Work, Wages and Profits* published in 1913. He read a further paper in 1903, this time dealing with the pictorial charting of production flows and entitled

A Graphical Daily Balance in Manufacturing which was subsequently developed into the 'Gantt Chart'. Meanwhile he undertook projects at the American Locomotive Company, Brighton Mills, Williams Brothers, the Portland Company, and Tabor Manufacturing, installing the Taylor system of management as he had learned it at Midvale, Simonds and Bethlehem but with the addition of his methods of task–and–bonus, and a procedure to give a graphical daily balance. In 1904 he became the first 'efficiency expert' to work in a textile plant when, on the recommendation of Taylor, he undertook an assignment at Sayles Bleacheries, Saylesville, Rhode Island.

Gantt at Sayles Bleacheries and Remington Typewriter

Taylor's system was as often resisted by managers and supervisors, who resented the ways in which the new scientific management diluted their prerogatives, as it was by the operatives who were apparently most obviously affected. This was certainly Gantt's experience at Sayles Bleacheries where:

> the internal situation of the mills was typical of the times. It might be described as a group of small kingdoms. Each was ruled by a foreman who possessed certain trade secrets, and endeavoured to hold his position by keeping his information to himself. Many of these foremen were English. They were ultraconservative, obstinate, and difficult to deal with. The internal affairs of the plant were actually in their hands and not those of management.
>
> *(Alford in Rathe, 1960, p.257)*

Gantt spent four turbulent years at Sayles encountering opposition and criticism at every turn. His work covered every aspect of shop management including the installation of his task–and–bonus system, the establishment of time study, the creation of a planning office, the setting up of cost and stock control systems and the introduction of substantial technical improvements some of which he patented. Gantt also reorganized the plant so as to shatter the informal control exercised by the foremen. Resistance to the changes he introduced eventually led to a strike in one of the bleacheries which spread and brought the entire plant to a standstill. Gantt responded by importing a new workforce including foremen which was trained and deployed in the plant so that production could be resumed. This exercise in strike breaking could hardly be described as 'pussy-footing' and cost Gantt dearly in terms of personal energy. Nevertheless the urgent need to train a replacement workforce served to crystalize his thinking on the subject of industrial training at large and prompted him to write his paper *Training Workmen in Habits of Industry* which he read to the ASME in December 1908. Gantt subsequently submitted the manuscript to Taylor for his opinion on whether or not it should be published. Although Taylor's view of the paper was a negative one, Gantt decided to ignore the advice and pushed forward with publication thereby precipitating the final break between the two men.

Gantt later amplified his views on industrial training in his paper *Modern Methods of Training* which he produced in 1915.

Gantt's association with Remington Typewriter began in 1910 and continued until 1917. His work was initially concerned with the flow of materials from purchase and receipt, through the various manufacturing processes to the final product. This was a complex problem in that each individual typewriter consisted of some 2500 components and Remington were currently producing over 480 different models with 1113 authorized and listed keyboards. Further, the disparity in the size of components, the number required and differences in the manufacturing procedures made the production process highly complex. Gantt spent two years on the necessary preliminary work required to fully monitor and control the production process. The success of his efforts at the end of seven years at Remington may be judged by Alford's observation that they:

> included an increase in factory production in the proportion of 100 to 164 at the same time that the ratio of capital invested to production volume was reduced. The work week was cut from 59 to 50 hours and wage rates increased, but the total wage bill was reduced. In addition there were such subtler benefits as improved quality and better morale.
>
> *(Alford in Rathe, 1960, pp.261–262)*

Gantt provided a formal consideration of the question of the ratio between output and costs in a paper entitled *The Relation Between Production and Costs* which he presented to the ASME in June 1915.

Wartime initiatives

The United States entered the First World War in April 1917 and Gantt rapidly became closely involved in the task of co-ordinating war production. Working initially for the Ordnance Bureau he subsequently joined the War Industries Board and later the Emergency Fleet Corporation and Shipping Board. His role was mainly concerned with co-ordinating production both in the privately owned munitions plants and the government arsenals. This was, of course, a huge task which tested his capacities as an organizer to the limit. For example, in the sphere of shipping, German submarines sank 6 618 623 tons of shipping during 1917 alone. World production of new shipping during that year amounted to only 2 703 245 tons of which 2 100 000 was constructed by the USA and the UK combined. Thus, during the first year of the USA's participation in the war, the amount of shipping destroyed was two and a half times the quantity of new building. Under the auspices of the Emergency Fleet Corporation a massive shipbuilding programme was initiated which produced 533 ships of a total of 3 030 406 tons during 1918 alone. Alford has described this vast programme of shipbuilding as 'one of the greatest outpourings of creative energy the world has ever known' and it certainly represented a demonstration of the enormous productive capacities of the United States (*Alford in Rathe*, 1960, p.266). By the end of the war the USA had 341 ship yards, employing 350 000 workers and had constructed almost 1300 ships during a period of 18 months. Among the techniques applied to stimulate the productivity of ship yard workers, Gantt developed a simple means of measuring effort using the yardstick of 'rivets driven'. Rival ship yards vied with each other to set and break records on the basis of 'rivets driven' and the results of what became an intense rivalry were reported daily in the press. It was also during the war that Gantt fully developed the 'Gantt Chart'. The task of co-ordinating the work of the various plants and departments involved in the war effort prompted him to develop a bar chart for the purposes of accurate scheduling. Gantt used the charts to provide a graphical depiction of time rather than quantity, thereby enabling a manager to monitor the progress of a project and take appropriate action should it fall behind schedule. As he claimed at the time, the:

> principles upon which the charting method is founded are easily comprehended:
>
> First: The fact that all activities can be measured by the amount of time needed to perform them.
>
> Second: The space representing the time unit on the chart can be made to represent the amount of activity which should have taken place in that time.
>
> Bearing in mind these two principles the whole system is readily intelligible; it affords a means of charting all kinds of activities, the common measure being time.
>
> *(quoted in Rathe, 1960, pp.223–224)*

The chart was never patented and, following Gantt's death in 1919, Wallace Clark (a member of Gantt's consulting firm) popularized the idea in *The Gantt Chart: A Working Tool of Management* which was published in 1922. This book did much to spread international appreciation of the practical aspects of Gantt's work. In the words of Wren it:

> was translated into eight languages, formed the basis for the Russian central planners to control their 'five year plans' and provided the whole world with a graphic means of planning and controlling work. All subsequent production control boards and charts drew their inspiration from Gantt's original work.
>
> *(Wren, 1994, p.139)*

The experience of wartime conditions moved Gantt's interests far beyond the limited sphere of improving industrial efficiency, towards an attempt to understand and influence the dynamics of industrial society at large. In 1916 he formed an organization called the New Machine with a membership made up of engineers and other individuals sympathetic to the cause of limited industrial democracy. Rose has situated the concerns and aspirations of the New Machine firmly in the context of the war as follows:

> On American entry to the First World War: an Ordnance Department General Order decreed that war supplies should be purchased only from manufacturers who maintained working conditions that included opportunities for joint consultation. These and other acts heightened the public status of unionists, and prominent leaders were drawn into the war machine as propagandists. The federal authorities also made wide use of Taylorians as management consultants during the war. This taste of power, and the explosive growth of union membership to 5 million by 1920, encouraged some Taylorians to anticipate an imminent new social order in which they would play a leading part. A short lived propaganda movement, the New Machine, foretold the approaching collapse of capitalism unless it could substitute service (a favourite term of Henry Ford) for profit. Only the scientific manager could handle the problems of this transformation.
>
> *(Rose, 1988, pp.54–55)*

Many of the ideas of the New Machine were outlined by Gantt in a paper to the ASME, titled *Efficiency and Democracy*, in 1918 and also in his book *Organizing for Work* of 1919. Briefly he advocated an 'aristocracy of the capable' which would provide industrial leadership on the basis of fact rather than opinion and on merit rather than privilege. The relationship between managers and workers would be one of mutualism rather than conflict and the final purpose of economic activity service rather than profit. In Gantt's own words:

> The doctrine of service is more than good economics; it is eminently practical. Because of the increased production of goods obtained by it, this doctrine promises to lead us safely through the maze of confusion into which we seem to be headed. It can give us that industrial democracy which alone can afford a basis for industrial peace…It should be perfectly evident that, with the increasing complexity of the modern business system, successful operation can be attained only be following the lead of those who understand the controlling forces practically and are willing to recognize their social responsibility in operating them. Any attempt to operate the business system by people who do not understand the driving forces is sure to reduce its effectiveness; any attempt to operate it in the interests of a class is not much longer possible. For instance, under present conditions the attempt to drive the workman to do that which he does not understand results in failure, even if he is willing to be driven, which he no longer is. He has learned that real democracy is something more than the privilege of expressing an opinion. Whether we like it or not, we will have to realise that only those who know what to do and how to do it will have a

sufficient following to make their efforts worthwhile. In other words, the conditions under which the great industrial and business system must operate to keep our complicated system of modern civilization going successfully can be directed only by real leaders – men who understand the operation of the moving forces and whose prime objective is to render such service as the community needs.

(quoted in Rathe, 1960, pp.223–24)

Thus successful management would in future depend on the establishment and maintenance of self-conscious consent on the part of those being managed. Such consent could not be forthcoming merely as a result of ownership or coercion. Instead it would be based on the workers' recognition that management possessed legitimacy based on a combination of knowledge and merit. The ability to manage would therefore be earned by management rather than assumed as of right. Many of these themes, particularly that of 'service', were subsequently to be examined by Mary Parker Follett (see Chapter 8).

Critical summary

Much of Gantt's work can be seen as an extension of the scientific management approach pioneered by F. W. Taylor. Gantt was a close associate of Taylor's and the development of his original ideas only occurred during the final ten years or so of Gantt's life. Above all he moderated the emphasis on the efficiency of the individual operative with a broader approach that included greater concern with systematic training and method. His experience of wartime conditions infused his work with a spirit of idealism calculated to replace old fashioned 'bossism' and militant labourism with industrial harmony. Gantt's ideas, and their tangible expression the New Machine, stopped short of advocating socialism but called for a greater mutualism as a means of achieving economic prosperity. Wren's verdict on Gantt (i.e. that he was 'the most unorthodox of Taylor's followers (and) had come to the ultimate conclusion that the mental revolution must be in the hands of the engineer and that the mutuality of interests was to be found in cartels and public service corporations') comes closest to an accurate categorization (Wren, 1979, p.169).

Discussion questions

1. Why did Gantt favour method study over time and motion study?
2. How would you account for Gantt's interest in industrial training?
3. What was the Gantt Chart and what was its impact on production planning?
4. What was the New Machine and how did it seek to nurture industrial harmony?

5. How convincing was Gantt's claim that in future successful management would be based on consent?

Suggested reading

Clark, W. (1922) *The Gantt Chart: A Working Tool of Management*, Ronald Press, New York.

Gantt, H. (1910) *Work, Wages and Profit*, Engineering Magazine Co., New York.

Gantt, H. (1916) *Industrial Leadership*, Yale University Press, New Haven, Conn.

Gantt, H. (1919) *Organizing for Work*, Harcourt Brace Jovanovich, New York.

Merrill, H. (ed) (1960) *Classics in Management*, American Management Association, New York, ch.6.

Rose, M. (1988) *Industrial Behaviour: Research and Control*, Penguin Books, Harmondsworth, ch.4.

Urwick, L. and Brech E. (1945) *The Making of Scientific Management Volume 1: Thirteen Pioneers*, Management Publications Trust, London.

Wren, D. (1994) *The Evolution of Management Thought*, Wiley & Sons, Chichester, ch.8.

Chapter 5

Henri Fayol and administration

Henri Fayol spent the bulk of his very long life managing mining and metallurgical undertakings and much of his extensive bibliography deals with the technical and geological aspects of those related industries. He was born in 1841 and educated at the Lycée in Lyon and the National School of Mines at St Etienne. In 1860 he was appointed as engineer to the Commentry group of pits which were owned by a mining and metallurgical combine popularly known as Comambault. Fayol spent his entire working life with the combine, retiring as managing director in 1918 and remaining a director until his death in 1925 at the age of 84. As Urwick observed, Fayol's career can be usefully divided into four periods. From 1860 to 1872 he was a subordinate executive and his research and writings were mainly concerned with problems of mining engineering, particularly the fire hazards of coal mining. In 1872 he was appointed director of a group of pits and his intellectual inquiries turned to geological questions, including the factors which would determine the life span of the coal mines for which he was responsible. In 1888 he became managing director of the Comambault combine, taking control at a time when it was facing financial disaster. No dividend had been paid to stockholders since 1885, its metallurgical operations at Fourchambault and Montluçon were making heavy losses and its coal mines at Commentry and Montvicq were approaching exhaustion. Urwick has claimed that Fayol's success in turning the combine round was 'one of the romances of French industrial history' describing it in the following glowing terms:

> From the day he took charge the tide turned. The only works which had to be closed were Fourchambault. Montluçon was kept in action, the only surviving blast furnace in central France. Imphy rapidly attained a leading position as a producer of special steels. The approaching exhaustion of Commentry was forestalled by the purchase of the Bressac pits in 1891 and the pits at Decazeville

45

> in 1892. Decazeville was a difficult field, and the company had an unfortunate history. It needed all the skill of the engineers Fayol had trained at Commentry and all his own scientific genius and practical sense to wring success from such an unpromising situation...Comambault went on growing (and) in 1900 it extended its activities into the eastern coal field with the purchase of Joudreville...When Fayol retired at the age of 77 its financial position was unassailable
>
> *(Urwick in Fayol, 1916/1949, p.vii)*

During the final period of his life Fayol, rather like Taylor before him, spent much of his time popularizing his managerial theories. He founded the Centre d'Etudes Administratives and chaired weekly meetings of prominent industrialists, writers, officials, philosophers and members of the military. One result of this was the circulation by Marshal Lyautey of 2000 copies of a pamphlet (through the French army in Morocco) applying Fayol's principles to military administration. Fayol himself gave a series of lectures at the Ecole Supérieure de la Guerre and his ideas were also taught at the French navy's supply school. In the last year of his life Fayol commented on the relationship between Taylorism and what was already being referred to in France as Fayolisme, denouncing any attempt to place the two theories in competition. As Urwick observed:

> The work of Taylor and Fayol was, of course, essentially complementary. They both realized that the problem of personnel and its management at all levels is the key to industrial success. Both applied scientific method to this problem. That Taylor worked primarily on the operative level, from the bottom of the industrial hierarchy upwards, while Fayol concentrated on the managing director and worked downwards, was merely a reflection of their very different careers.
>
> *(Urwick in Fayol, 1916/1949, pp.9–10)*

Nevertheless there was competition between Fayolisme and Taylorism. Henri Le Chatelier translated Taylor's *The Principles of Scientific Management*, became a friend of Taylor's and introduced his work to French-speaking Europe. Together with Charles de Freminville he founded the Conférence de l'Organization Française to publicize Taylor's work, one effect of which was to overshadow the work of Fayol.[1] However, in 1926 the Conférence de l'Organization Française merged with the Centre

---

1 Henri Le Chatelier (1850–1936) was a chemist and metallurgist who at one time held the Chair of Chemistry at the Sorbonne. Charles de Freminville (1856–1936) was a leading railway and motor engineer.

d'Etudes Administratives to form the Comité Nationale de l'Organization Française which became the leading management organization in France.

Fayol's major work, *Administration, industrielle et générale* (*General and Administrative Management*), was not published until he was 75 years old. He originally planned to produce a four part work including sections on the teaching of management; the principles and elements of management; reflections on his own experience of management; and the lessons gained from the First World War. In the event, however, only the first two sections appeared in a single volume amounting to little more than 100 pages. Fayol's influence in the English–speaking world was inhibited by the lack of a readily available translation of his book. In 1927 the American retailer and philanthropist, Edward Albert Filene initiated the establishment of the International Management Institute (IMI) in Geneva which was part funded by the International Labour Organization and acted as an international clearing house for the exchange of information on better methods of management.[2] Lyndall Urwick became director of the IMI in 1928 (see Chapter 10) and, in 1930, published a translation of Fayol's book by J. A. Coubrough. However, its availability was limited and it was not until 1949 that a popular English edition appeared. This edition was translated by Constance Storr under the title *General and Industrial Management* and published by Pitman with an introduction by Urwick who had written a preliminary account of Fayol's ideas during the 1930s. Notwithstanding some controversy concerning the interchangeability, or otherwise, of the words 'management' and 'administration', it has become the standard version used both in Britain and the USA.

General and industrial management

According to Fayol the activities of industrial undertakings could be divided into six groups as follows:

1. Technical activities (production, manufacture, adaptation).
2. Commercial activities (buying, selling, exchange).
3. Financial activities (search for and optimum use of capital).
4. Security activities (protection of property and persons).
5. Accounting activities (stock taking, balance sheet, costs, statistics).
6. Managerial activities (planning, organization, command, co-ordination, control).

(Fayol, 1916/1949, p.3)

2 Edward Albert Filene (1860-1937) was a pioneer of retail management who endowed a research
institution – the Twentieth Century Fund. His department store in Boston was among the organizations
studied by Mary Parker Follett (see Chapter 8).

He claimed that 'be the undertaking simple or complex, big or small, these six groups of activities or essential functions are always present'. Obviously, in non-industrial, non-profit making organizations the importance or relevance of groups 1 to 5 would vary. However the five elements which made up the list of managerial activities would retain their significance irrespective of the type of organization involved. Fayol discriminated between management and what he described as ' government'. Thus:

> management…is an activity spread, like all other activities between head and members of the body corporate. The managerial function is quite distinct from the other five essential functions. It should not be confused with government. To govern is to conduct the undertaking towards its objective by seeking to derive optimum advantage from all available resources and to assure the smooth working of the six essential functions. Management is merely one of the six functions whose smooth working government has to ensure.
>
> *(Fayol, 1916/1949, p.6)*

Fayol appears to be drawing a distinction between what would now be termed 'day to day' management and ' strategic' management – government equating to the latter.

Having outlined the five elements of management Fayol postponed detailed examination of them until later in his book, turning instead to what he considered to be the general principles of management. He did not claim that the principles were immutable or amenable to being applied in a rigid manner or even that his list was exhaustive. On the contrary, he argued that 'there is no limit to the number of principles of management…a change in the state of affairs can be responsible for change of rules which had been engendered by that state' (Fayol, 1916/1949, p.19). He then went on to examine those fourteen principles of management which, in his own career, he most often had cause to apply, *viz*.

1. Division of work;
2. Authority;
3. Discipline;
4. Unity of command;
5. Unity of direction;
6. Subordination of individual interest to the general interest;
7. Remuneration;
8. Centralization;
9. Scalar chain (line of authority);
10. Order;
11. Equity;
12. Stability of tenure of personnel;
13. Initiative;
14. Esprit de corps.

1. Division of work – the object of this was 'to produce more and better work with the same effort'. Specialization, claimed Fayol, was part of the natural order, observable in the animal world and in human societies. He did not, however, consider that division of work should be limited only to technical activities but extended across all aspects of an organization. Interestingly he did not go as far as the scientific managers in advocating the breaking down of tasks into basic elements. Instead he claimed that 'division of work has its limits which experience and a sense of proportion teach us may not be exceeded'.

2. Authority – was 'the right to give orders and the power to exact obedience'. Fayol drew a distinction between 'official' authority (which derived from a manager's appointed position in an organization) and 'personal' authority (which stemmed from such attributes as intelligence, experience, integrity and leadership ability). Further, he claimed that in a first class manager personal authority is the 'indispensible complement' of official authority. Authority, Fayol argued, is always allied to responsibility and the proper exercise of both required the ability to make judgements and, if necessary, impose sanctions. In all of this a high level of personal integrity was required. As Fayol put it:

> judgement demands high moral character, impartiality and firmness...Responsibility valiantly undertaken and borne merits some consideration; it is a kind of courage everywhere much appreciated...A good leader should possess and infuse into those around him courage to accept responsibility...The best safeguard against abuse of authority and against weakness on the part of a higher manager is personal integrity and particularly high moral character of such a manager, and this integrity, it is well known, is conferred neither by election nor ownership.
>
> *(Fayol, 1916/1949, pp.21–22)*

3. Discipline – was 'in essence obedience, application, energy, behaviour and outward marks of respect observed in accordance with standing agreements between the firm and its employees'. Fayol conceded that discipline would take different forms in various organizations but maintained that it is nevertheless, in all circumstances, an essential ingredient. He noted that a shift away from agreements between individual owners and their workers was currently developing. Instead, agreements were increasingly being made between employers' associations and trade unions with, in the immediate context of the First World War, a growing element of state intervention. In Fayol's view the move away from individual bargaining towards collective bargaining merely adjusted the rules governing discipline. It did not release management from the task of enforcing discipline using, where necessary, such sanctions as warnings, fines, suspensions, demotions and dismissals as appropriate.

4. Unity of command – was the notion that 'an employee should receive orders from one superior only'. According to Fayol dual command was bound to generate tension, confusion and conflict. He noted the tendency to divide command between individuals and also to blur the lines of demarcation between departments. The outcome, he claimed, was a dilution of responsibility and the erosion of clear lines of communication. Further, a higher manager might sometimes give orders directly to workers further down the hierarchy and thereby bypass middle management. As Fayol put it 'if this mistake is repeated there is dual command with its consequences, *viz.* hesitation on the part of the subordinate, irritation and dissatisfaction on the part of the superior set aside, and disorder in the work' (Fayol, 1916/1949, p.24).

5. Unity of direction – was expressed as 'one head and one plan for a group of activities having the same objective' . Whereas unity of command required that each employee should receive orders from one superior only, unity of direction could be summed up in the phrase 'one head, one plan' . In Fayol's own words 'it is the condition essential to unity of action, co-ordination of strength and focusing of effort. A body with two heads is in the social as in the animal sphere a monster, and has difficulty in surviving'. (Fayol, 1916/1949, p.25).

6. Subordination of individual interest to general interest – 'calls to mind the fact that in a business the interest of one employee or group of employees should not prevail over that of the concern'. Fayol drew attention to the fact that one of the greatest problems of management was to reconcile the general interest with that of individual and group interests. As he put it 'ignorance, ambition, selfishness, laziness, weakness and all human passions tend to cause the general interest to be lost sight of in favour of individual interest and a perpetual struggle has to be waged against them'. (Fayol, 1916/1949, p.26).

7. Remuneration of Personnel – was 'the price of services rendered'. Fayol considered the factors which determined levels of pay but are independent of the employer's will such as the cost of living, availability of labour, the business environment and the economic situation. He also examined the various modes of compensation available such as time rates, job rates, piece rates, bonuses, profit-sharing, payment in kind and various non-financial incentives. He concluded that 'whether wages are made up of money only or whether they include various additions such as heating, light, housing, food, is of little consequence provided that the employee be satisfied' (Fayol, 1916/1949, p.32). However, Fayol did not limit his consideration of non-financial incentives to compensation issues alone. Instead he went beyond this advocating a modestly paternalistic view of the employment relationship in the following terms:

> there is no doubt that a business will be better served in proportion as its employees are more energetic, better educated, more conscientious and more permanent. The employer should have regard…for the health, strength, education, morale, and stability of his personnel…Therefore, the employer comes to be concerned with his employees outside the works…the employer's activity may be used to good purpose outside the factory confines provided that there be discretion and prudence, that it be sought after rather than imposed, be

in keeping with the general level of education and taste of those concerned and
that it have absolute respect for their liberty.

(Fayol, 1916/1949, p.32)

8. Centralization – 'like division of work…belongs to the natural order'. In considering the extent to which any organization should have a centralized or decentralized
structure, Fayol used the example of a living organism. Thus 'in every organism,
animal or social, sensations converge towards the brain or directive part, and from the
brain or directive part orders are sent out which set all parts of the organism in
movement' (Fayol, 1916/1949, p.33). The notion that organizations are akin to living
organisms rather than machines was a central theme in Fayol's work. Consistent with
this was his view that his principles should not be forced but applied pragmatically
depending on circumstances. As he put it in the case of centralization, 'the question
of centralization or decentralization, is a simple question of proportion, it is a matter
of finding the optimum degree for the particular concern… Everything which goes to
increase the importance of the subordinate's role is decentralization, everything which
goes to reduce it is centralization' (Fayol, 1916/1949, p.33).

9. Scalar chain – was 'the chain of superiors ranging from the ultimate authority to
the lowest ranks'. More familiar terms for the scalar chain would be 'hierarchy' and
'channels or lines of communication'. Fayol combined these two concepts in his
examination of the scalar chain, establishing the need for an ultimate authority but
conceding that reference of every issue up the organization to the highest point 'is not
always the swiftest. It is even at times disastrously lengthy in large concerns, notably
in governmental ones' (Fayol, 1916/1949, p.34). In order to maintain control but avoid
unnecessary delay he proposed a system of delegated authority which he termed a
'gang plank' approach. This facilitated lateral communication between similarly
ranked individuals in an organization without the requirement to refer every issue
upwards.

10. Order – was 'a place for everything and everything in its place' and, by extension,
'a place for everyone and everyone in his place'. Fayol advocated the maintenance of
tidy material order with appropriate and well kept storage facilities, general cleanliness and the preparation of a diagram or plan of the premises showing the various
sections and facilities. Similarly he insisted that 'for social order to prevail there
must…be an appointed place…for every employee and every employee be in his
appointed place…in the English idiom, 'the right man in the right place' (Fayol,
1916/1949, p.37). This drew Fayol into a consideration of the importance of adequate
job design and staff selection techniques. He noted that maintaining the correct balance
of human resources is by no means an easy task. As he put it:

this balance is most difficult to establish and maintain and all the more difficult
the bigger the business, and when it has been upset and individual interests

resulted in neglect or sacrifice of the general interest, when ambition, nepotism, favouritism or merely ignorance, has multiplied positions without good reason or filled them with incompetent employees, much talent and strength of will…are required in order to sweep away abuses and restore order.

(Fayol, 1916/1949, pp.37–38)

As in the case of material control Fayol advocated the creation of detailed organization charts which 'represent the personnel in entirety, and all sections of the concern together with the people occupying them'.

11. Equity – whereas, claimed Fayol, justice was merely the putting into practice of conventions already established, equity is the combination of justice and kindliness. Although equity was calculated, on the part of management, to ensure devotion and loyalty on the part of employees it did not reduce the individual manager's duty to maintain discipline. Striking the correct balance between equity and discipline demanded, in Fayol's words, 'much good sense, experience and good nature' (Fayol, 1916/1949, p.38).

12. Stability of tenure of personnel – dealt with issues relating to personnel planning, management development and labour turnover. Fayol called for a suitable induction period to enable employees, and particularly managers, to acclimatize themselves to new work and situations. As he observed 'insecurity of tenure (is) especially to be feared in large concerns…much time is needed indeed to get to know things in a large concern in order to be in a position to decide on a plan of action, to gain confidence in oneself, and inspire it in others…Instability of tenure is at one and the same time cause and effect of bad running' (Fayol, 1916/1949, p.39).

13. Initiative – was the power to conceive a plan and ensure its success. It was central to ensuring high motivation and job satisfaction, being 'one of the most powerful stimulants to human endeavour'. Broadly speaking, claimed Fayol, the maximum opportunity to exercise initiative should be extended to all employees through delegated authority. As he put it, 'the manager must be able to sacrifice some personal vanity in order to grant this sort of satisfaction to subordinates…a manager able to permit the exercise of initiative on the part of subordinates is infinitely superior to one who cannot do so' (Fayol, 1916/1949, p.40).

14. Esprit de corps – was the building and maintaining of harmony among the workforce. Fayol strongly attacked the use of the management style based on a belief in divide and rule. As he expressed it:

dividing enemy forces to weaken them is clever, but dividing one's own team is a grave sin against business. Whether this ever results from inadequate managerial capacity or imperfect grasp of things, or from egoism which sacrifices general interest to personal interest, it is always reprehensible because harmful to the business. There is no merit in sowing dissention among subordinates; any beginner can do it. On the contrary, real talent is needed to co-ordinate effort, encourage keenness, use each man's abilities, and reward each one's merit without arousing possible jealouses and disturbing harmonious relations.

(Fayol, 1916/1949, p.40)

The elements of management

It will be recalled that Fayol identified the five elements of management as planning, organization, command, co-ordination and control. According to Fayol **planning** (that is attempting to assess the future and making provision for it) was an essential part of management. Central to the process was the development of a formal plan of action which he described as:

a kind of future picture wherein proximate events are outlined with some distinctness, whilst remote events appear progressively less distinct, and it entails the running of the business as forseen and provided against over a definite period.

(Fayol, 1916/1949, p.43)

Such a plan should be based on the organization's resources, the type and significance of the work in progress and likely future trends. Fayol viewed the preparation of the plan of action as being one of the most difficult and important tasks facing management and, moreover, one that required the active participation of the entire organization. An ideal plan of action would combine unity (i.e. an overall masterplan supported by specific plans for each activity), continuity (i.e. the guiding action must be consistent as plans develop over time), flexibility (i.e. possess the ability to adjust to unforeseen events), and, finally, precision (i.e. be as accurate as possible). Consistent with Fayol's advocacy of proper planning was his system of forecasting which required daily, weekly, monthly, annual, five–year and ten–year forecasts to be prepared and modified as necessary according to circumstances. Fayol's emphasis on planning and forecasting were unique in his own day and remain relevant at the present time.

The second element of management identified by Fayol was **organizing** by which he meant providing a business 'with everything useful to its functioning: raw materials, tools, capital, personnel' (Fayol, 1916/1949, p.53). He paid particular attention to what he termed the 'composition of the body corporate' (i.e. the organizational structure) claiming that the form taken by an organization would depend almost entirely on the number of people employed. Thus he claimed that as organizations grew and became more complex the number of functions would expand horizontally. Similarly increases in the number of employees would generate the need for more layers of supervision. The outcome of all of this was the familiar (although now partially discredited) organizational pyramid or, to use Fayol's term, scalar chain. As he put it:

> Each fresh group of ten, twenty, thirty workers brings in a fresh foreman; two, three or four foremen make necessary a superintendent, two or three superintendents give rise to a departmental manager, and the number of links of the scalar chain continues to increase in this way up to the ultimate superior, each new superior having usually no more than four or five immediate subordinates…The personnel of enterprises of all kinds is constituted in similar fashion to that of industrial concerns, so much so that all organizations at the same stage of expansion are alike.
>
> *(Fayol, 1916/1949, p.22)*

Fayol's third element was **command** and its object was 'to get the optimum return from all employees…in the interest of the whole concern' (Fayol, 1916/1949, p.97). Successful command depended on a combination of personal qualities and a knowledge of the general principles of management. In Fayol's view a manager who has command should be mindful of the following precepts:

1. Have a thorough knowledge of his personnel.
2. Eliminate the incompetent.
3. Be well versed in the agreements binding the business and its employees.
4. Set a good example.
5. Conduct periodic audits of the organization and use summarized charts to further this.
6. Bring together his chief assistants by means of conferences, at which unity of direction and focusing of effort are provided for.
7. Not become engrossed in detail.
8. Aim at making unity, energy, initiative and loyalty prevail among personnel.

> *(Fayol, 1916/1949, pp.98–99)*

Self-evidently these precepts contained a reiteration of some of Fayol's principles, including the need for personal integrity and the centrality of unity of command secured by maintaining good communications with subordinates. Further, there was an emphasis on what subsequent thinkers would term motivation and the advocacy of, albeit carefully monitored, delegation. The manager, as Fayol put it:

> can develop initiative among his subordinates by allowing them the maximum share of activity consistent with their position and capability, even at the cost of some mistakes, whose magnitude, however, may be circumscribed by means of watchful attention. By showing them discreetly without acting for them, by encouraging them with appropriate praise, by sometimes sacrificing his own

personal vanity for their benefit, he can quickly transform men with latent abilities into employees of the first water.

(Fayol, 1916/1949, pp.102–3)

Co-ordination was Fayol's fourth element and was aimed at securing the optimum harmonization of all the activities of an organization in such a way as to 'facilitate its working, and its success'. He was concerned here with maintaining balance between the various activities of the organization thereby ensuring, for example, that expenditure was proportionate to income; sales to production; equipment procurement to production needs; and stocks to consumption. Central, in Fayol's view, to this process was the weekly conference of departmental heads which, as he put it:

> has for its aim to inform management about the running of the concern, to make clear co-operation to be expected as between various departments, to utilize the presence of departmental managers for solving various problems of common interest. In such conferences, it is not a case of drawing up the plan of action of the business, but of facilitating the carrying out of this plan in the light of current events. The scope of each conference extends over a short period only, normally a week, during which the harmonizing of activity and focussing of effort are to be ensured.

(Fayol, 1916/1949, pp.104–5)

Fayol's final element was **control** which was concerned with ensuring that everything which occured in the organization conformed to the plan adopted, established principles and issued instructions. The object of control in this context was to point up weaknesses and errors so that they could be rectified and prevented from reoccuring. As Fayol put it control 'operates on everything, things, people, actions'. Control stimulated the process of feedback whereby the organization adapted to changing circumstances and constantly renewed itself. In Fayol's view control could not reside entirely in the hands of management and he advocated the appointment of impartial inspectors who were not linked with, or under obligation to, the person whose work was to be inspected. Control, in this form, was 'a precious auxiliary to management and can afford it certain necessary data which official supervision might at times fail to furnish' (Fayol, 1916/1949, p.109).

Critical summary

The view that higher grade employees (and others for that matter) should receive management training is now part of the received wisdom. However, this was not the case in Fayol's day when systematic thinking about the nature and content of the management function was in its infancy. As he put it :

whilst the greatest effort is being made, and profitably so, to spread and perfect technical knowledge...management does not even figure in the syllabuses of our colleges...– why? Is it that the importance of managerial ability is mis-understood? No ...the real reason for the absence of management teaching in our vocational schools is absence of theory; without theory no teaching is possible.

(Fayol, 1916/1949, p.14)

General and Industrial Management was Fayol's attempt to overcome the absence of theory and facilitate the teaching of management by setting down a set of generaliza-tions based on his own long experience. In structure the book is like a rather old fashioned treatise on statecraft, with Fayol putting forward a series of precepts which he considers likely to be applicable in most situations. Unlike Taylor he did not view organizational arrangements as something that could be constructed or bolted together on a more or less mechanical basis. Instead he viewed organizations as akin to living organisms, possessing a life of their own and requiring the maintenance of harmony in order to function satisfactorily. Nevertheless, Fayol considered that all organiza-tions were pretty much the same, the main factor of differentiation being size. To the modern eye this view seems somewhat simplistic given the insights provided by, for example, studies of such variables as technology and organizational culture. Having said this, however, Fayol did succeed in providing, if not a fully worked theory, at least a 'conceptual schema' capable of being taught on management courses and hugely influential in terms of analysing and refining management practice. Of course, Fayol considered that becoming a successful manager demanded more than attending a course of lectures and, in today's terms, gaining an MBA. It also required latent capacities of judgement and leadership ability that could only be perfected through experience. Thus Fayol advocated a combination of classroom teaching, learning through doing, and natural gifts or inherent traits. Finally, Fayol insisted that the successful manager must possess a high level of personal integrity and moral rectitude which, in the modern world of moral relativism, seems at first sight slightly pretentious and old fashioned. On reflection, however, it is clear that Fayol is stating the need for a moral underpinning to business activity that is becoming increasingly prominent in contemporary debates on business ethics. Perhaps the best brief verdict on Fayol's contribution to management theory has been offered by Lyndall Urwick who stated that:

the unique character of Fayol's work cannot be over emphasized. For the first time a successful business leader of long experience submitted, not the work of others, but his own duties and responsibilities to close scientific analysis. He viewed what he had to do as an administrator with a detachment as rare as it is valuable. In the first quarter century of the scientific study of business management, his is the only European figure worthy of a place beside that of F. W. Taylor. To Taylor belongs the glory of the pioneer. He it was who initiated the idea that management and administration might be studied scientifically. But Fayol showed beyond question, what Taylor himself appreciated, but what many of his imitators have failed to emphasize, that better management is not merely a question of improving the output of labor and the planning of subordinate units of organization, it is above all a matter of closer study and more administrative training for men at the top.

(Urwick in Gulick and Urwick, 1937, p.129)

Discussion questions

1.   How convincing is Fayol's claim that the activities of industrial undertakings can be divided into six groups?
2.   What were Fayol's fourteen principles of management?
3.   According to Fayol, there are five elements of management. What are they?
4.   In what ways did Fayol's work pre-figure modern debates on business ethics?
5.   To what extent does Fayol consider that managers are born rather than made?

Suggested reading

Fayol, H. (1937) The Administrative Theory in the State in Gulick, L. and Urwick, L. (eds) *Papers on the Science of Administration*, Institute of Public Administration, Columbia University, New York.

Fayol, H. (1916/1949) *General and Administrative Management*, Pitman, London.

Pugh, D. and Hickson, D. (eds) (1989) *Writers on Organizations*, Penguin Books, Harmondsworth, ch.3.

Pugh, D. (ed) (1990) *Organization Theory: Selected Readings*, Penguin Books, Harmondsworth, ch.10.

Urwick, L. (1937) The Function of Administration with Special Reference to the Work of Henry Fayol in Gulick, L. and Urwick, L. (eds) *Papers on the Science of Administration,* Institute of Public Administration, Columbia University, New York.

Chapter 6

Max Weber and bureaucracy

Weber was born in 1864 in Erfurt, Thuringia, now part of the reunified Germany but then part of the Prussian dominion. Weber's family were wealthy Protestants and his father was a member of the Prussian Diet and the imperial parliament or Reichstag. In order to pursue his political career his father moved the family to the Charlottenburg district of Berlin in 1869, and it was here that Weber began his education. In 1882 he went to university in Heidelberg to study law, breaking his studies in 1884 to spend a year in Strasbourg as a conscripted junior officer in the army. Weber's student life was characterized by duelling and heavy drinking. As MacRae has noted, when Weber's puritanical mother first saw his scarred and coarsened features on his return from university, she slapped his face in disgust (MacRae, 1974, p.27). Weber completed his university studies at Göttingen in 1886 and spent the next 3 years in Berlin, working in a minor legal position while preparing his doctoral thesis *On the History of Medieval Trading Companies*. He received his doctorate in 1889 and, in 1891, qualified as a university teacher with a further thesis, this time on *The Significance of Roman Agrarian History for Public and Private Law*. In 1894 Weber became a professor when the University of Freiburg-im-Breisgau awarded him a chair in political economy and, in 1897, he moved to Heidelberg as professor of economics. In the same year Weber's father died, an event which precipitated a serious crisis in his life and severely damaged his mental and physical health. He resigned from his professorship and, gripped by a compulsion to travel, journeyed throughout Europe and the United States, avoiding teaching for a period of 20 years during which his academic interests gradually shifted from law and economics to sociology. His relative financial security enabled him to live as a private scholar during the many years spent as a semi-invalid following his breakdown. During the First World War Weber worked in hospital administration, regained his health and displayed a strong sense of opposition to the regime of Wilhelm II in articles on current events which he wrote for the *Frankfurter Zeitung*. His opposition to the Kaiser and, in the context of Germany, liberal credentials gained him a place on the Commission which drafted the memorandum on German war guilt for the Peace Conference and also the Commission which prepared the Weimar Constitution. In 1918 Weber returned to university teaching, initially in Vienna and subsequently in Munich. In 1920 he fell victim to the influenza pandemic which was then sweeping Europe killing, it has been claimed, more people than the 1914–18 War itself. His influenza turned to pneumonia and Weber died, probably at the height of his intellectual powers and with the vast bulk of his writings uncompleted.

Weber's academic interests were wide ranging and spanned economics, history, religion, politics and sociology. At the time of his death his papers were in a state of chaos and none of his work was available in English. Weber never produced a wholly systematic work and even *Economy and Society*, the text generally agreed to be his most important, was put together from fragmentary manuscripts without a plan. In the English–speaking world his best known work is certainly the empirical, historical essay *The Protestant Ethic and the Spirit of Capitalism* which was translated by the American sociologist Talcott Parsons and published, with a foreword by R. H. Tawney, in 1930. It was Parsons who introduced Weber's writings to an international audience bringing about an interest in the German sociologist's work through his own writings and translations (Kasler, 1988, p.209). One result of this was that the reception of Weber's work in the English–speaking world became intimately associated with Parsons' own controversial output, requiring a subsequent 'de-Parsonization' of Weber to correct the situation. Weber's writings on bureaucracy were set out in two different sections of the uncompleted draft of *Economy and Society*. The first part was translated by Parsons and A. M. Henderson in 1947, accounting for some 12 pages in section 3 of *The Theory of Social and Economic Organization*. The second part appeared in Hans Gerth's and C. Wright Mills' *From Max Weber, Essays in Sociology* in 1946.

Authority and legitimacy

One of the oldest questions in political theory is 'Why do I accept the authority of the ruler?' There are, of course, many immediate responses, including habit, fear, loyalty and so on. In mature democracies the response will also include some element of overt, or at least tacit, belief in the process of election and the legitimacy of the outcome. Authority generates the expectation of obedience and is underwritten by legitimacy. This debate can readily be shifted from the macro-level issues of the polity to the micro-level considerations of the organization. With this transition the actors involved are no longer monarchs and subjects, presidents and citizens but capital and labour; managers and workers. It is in this context that Weber's reflections on authority and legitimacy can be situated and his notion of 'imperative co-ordination' be best understood. Weber defined 'imperative co-ordination' as 'the probability that certain specific commands (or all commands) from a given source will be obeyed by a given group of persons' (Weber, 1947, p.324). He argued that, in any organization:

> members of the administrative staff may be bound to their superior…by custom, by affectual ties, by a purely material complex of interests, or by ideal motives…But these factors…do not, even taken together, form a sufficiently reliable basis for a system of imperative control. In addition there is normally a further element, the belief in legitimacy.
>
> *(Weber, 1947, p.325)*

At this point Weber introduced what he termed the 'three pure types of legitimate authority' as follows:

1. Rational grounds – resting on an established belief in the 'legality' of patterns or normative rules and the right of those elevated to authority under such rules to issue commands (legal authority);
2. Traditional grounds – resting on an established belief in the sanctity of immemorial traditions and the legitimacy of the status of those exercising authority under them (traditional authority); or finally,
3. Charismatic grounds – resting on devotion to the specific and exceptional sanctity, heroism or exemplary character of an individual person, and of the normative patterns or order revealed or ordained by him (charismatic authority).

(Weber, 1947, p.325)

In the case of legal authority, Weber argued that obedience was owed to the impersonal order established by law. Thus the authority which any individual possessed came not from essential personal attributes but from the appointment or office held. In the case of traditional authority by contrast, obedience was owed to the actual person of the leader who, as Weber put it, 'occupies the traditionally sanctioned position of authority and who is (within its sphere) bound by tradition'. Finally, in the case of charismatic authority, Weber claimed that obedience sprang from the leader's personal qualities which, at their highest, would amount to 'the gift of grace'. In Weber's view it was 'legal authority' that characterized the modern organization and was associated with the establishment of bureaucracy.

Legal authority and the concept of bureaucracy

Weber held that a belief in legitimacy was central to almost all systems of authority. In his analysis of 'legal authority with a bureaucratic administrative staff' he began by setting out five concepts on which the legitimacy of legal authority depended. These have been conveniently abbreviated by Albrow as follows:

1. That a legal code can be established which can claim obedience from members of the organization.
2. That the law is a system of abstract rules which are applied in particular cases, and that administration looks after the interests of the organization within the limits of that law.
3. That the man exercising authority also obeys this impersonal order.
4. That only *qua* member does the member obey the law.
5. That obedience is due not to the person who holds authority but to the impersonal order which has granted him his position.

(Albrow, 1970, p.43)

Based on these concepts Weber went on to formulate a set of eight principles concerning the structuring of legal authority systems (again Albrow's abbreviated form is given):

1. Official tasks are organized on a continuous, regulated basis.
2. These tasks are divided into functionally distinct spheres, each furnished with the requisite authority and sanctions.
3. Offices are arranged hierarchically, the rights of control and complaint between them specified.
4. The rules according to which work is conducted may be either technical or legal. In both cases trained men are necessary.
5. The resources of the organization are quite distinct from those of the members as private individuals.
6. The office holder cannot appropriate his office.
7. Administration is based on written documents and this tends to make the office (Bureau) the hub of the modern organization.
8. Legal authority systems can take many forms, but are seen at their purest in a bureaucratic administrative staff.

(Albrow, 1970, pp.44–45)

According to Weber a bureaucratic administrative staff (i.e. bureaucracy in its most rational form) would exist in conformity with the five concepts of legitimacy and the eight principles of authority outlined above. Additionally, however, such a bureaucracy, and the officials which serve it, would also have to conform to the following criteria:

1. They are personally free and subject to authority only with respect to their impersonal official obligations.
2. They are organized in a clearly defined hierarchy of offices.
3. Each office has a clearly defined sphere of competence in the legal sense.
4. The office is filled by a free contractual relationship. Thus, in principle, there is free selection.

5. Candidates are selected on the basis of technical qualifications. In the most rational case, this is tested by examination or guaranteed by diplomas certifying technical training, or both. They are appointed, not elected.

6. They are remunerated by fixed salaries in money, for the most part with a right to pensions. Only under certain circumstances does the employing authority, especially in private organizations, have a right to terminate the appointment, but the official is always free to resign. The salary scale is primarily graded according to rank in the hierarchy; but in addition to this criterion, the responsibility of the position and the requirements of the incumbent's social status may be taken into account.

7. The office is treated as the sole, or at least primary, occupation of the incumbent.

8. It constitutes a career. There is a system of 'promotion' according to seniority or to achievement, or both. Promotion is dependent on the judgement of superiors.

9. The official works entirely separated from ownership of the means of administration and without appropriation of his position.

10.He is subject to strict and systematic discipline and control in the conduct of the office.

(Weber, 1947, pp.333–334)

Critical summary

Weber identified the growing centrality of expert, technical knowledge in modern, industrial societies and recognized the significance of rational, administrative systems in complex organizations. Certainly his notion of rational (or pure) bureaucracy is 'without doubt the single most important statement on the subject in the social sciences' (Albrow, 1970, p.45). However, given the lack of an accessible translation, Weber's work did not make an impact on management theory in the English–speaking world until the 1940s and 1950s. As Wren has commented, 'he had to wait until cultural conditions created the need to think in terms of theory. As organizations grew in size and complexity, the search for a theory of organizations led to Max Weber and his bureaucratic model' (Wren, 1994, p.198). By this time, however, the United States already had a home grown version of organization theory in the form of Chester Barnard's *The Functions of the Executive* published in 1938 (see Chapter 12). Whereas Weber tended to emphasize the significance of the formal organization together with the impact of rules, roles and hierarchies, Barnard highlighted the spontaneous elements of co-operation which characterized the informal organization. In a sense the work of Barnard and Weber was complementary – the one describing the pervasive nature of modern bureaucracy, the other indicating its practical limitations. Contemporary critics, whilst conceding the importance of Weber's pioneering work, have tended to emphasize the negative rather than positive aspects of bureaucracy. Henry Mintzberg, for example, in *Structure in Fives: Designing Effective Organizations*, identifies the defining characteristic of bureaucratic organizational structure as standardization. On this basis the standardization of production techniques advocated by the scientific managers becomes the counterpart of Weber's bureaucracy. Large operating units, extensive division of labour, and above all the need to maintain management control, all lead to what Mintzberg describes as Machine Bureaucracy. These are characterized by:

> highly specialized, routine operating tasks; very formalized procedures...a proliferation of rules, regulations, and formalized communication throughout the organization; large-sized units at the operating level; reliance on the functional basis for grouping tasks; relatively centralized power for decision-making; and an elaborate administrative structure with a sharp distinction between line and staff.
>
> *(Mintzberg, 1983, p.164)*

Mintzberg does not take Machine Bureaucracy to be the universal organizational configuration for industrial society. Instead he depicts it as being of limited utility, appropriate only to those organizations where 'their operating work is routine, the greatest part of it rather simple and repetitive (and), as a result, work processes are highly standardized' (Mintzberg, 1983, p.163). Machine Bureaucracy is the organizational configuration which most closely resembles Weber's ideal type but it is merely one possible configuration among many and by no means the most suitable in all situations. Nevertheless, Mintzberg argues, 'when an integrated set of simple, repetitive tasks must be performed precisely and consistently by human beings, the Machine Bureaucracy is the most efficient structure – indeed, the only conceivable one' (Mintzberg, 1983, p.176). Thus, although bureaucratic organizational structures may be the best configuration in a limited range of situations (Mintzberg gives a national post office, a security agency, a steel company, a custodial prison, an airline and a giant automobile company as examples) it will be wholly inappropriate for others. To the contemporary eye this is an unsurprising conclusion but it does draw attention to the fact that bureaucratic structure misapplied is counterproductive – not least for those who work within it.

Discussion questions

1. What, according to Weber, are the three pure types of legitimate authority?
2. Weber sets out five concepts upon which the legitimacy of legal authority depends. What are they?
3. What are the eight principles of a legal authority system?

4. What are the advantages and disadvantages of bureaucracy?
5. What is the Machine Bureaucracy?

Suggested reading

Albrow, M. (1970) *Bureaucracy*, Pall Mall Press, London.

Aron, R. (1967/1990) Max Weber. *Main Currents in Sociological Thought, Volume 2*, Penguin Books, Harmondsworth.

Mintzberg, H. (1983) *Structure in Fives: Designing Effective Organizations*, Prentice–Hall, Englewood–Cliffs, N. J.

Perrow, C. (1986) *Complex Organizations: A Critical Essay*, Random House, New York, chs. 1 and 2.

Pugh, D. and Hickson, D. (eds) (1989) *Writers on Organizations*, Penguin Books, Harmondsworth, ch.1.

Pugh, D. (ed) (1990) *Organization Theory: Selected Writings*, Penguin Books, Harmondsworth, ch.1.

Weber, M. (1947) *The Theory of Social and Economic Organization*, The Free Press, Illinois.

Chapter 7

Carter Goodrich and the frontier of control

Carter Lyman Goodrich was born in Plainfield, New Jersey in 1897 and educated at Amherst College, Massachusetts where he majored in economics.[1] When he graduated in 1918, Amherst awarded him a fellowship which enabled him to come to Britain to study labour problems. During his time here Goodrich's research was supervised by the economist Henry Clay, a Fellow of New College, Oxford who had played a prominent role in the Ministry of Labour during the latter years of the war. He was also advised by R. H. Tawney who was at that time closely involved with the Guild Socialists and the trade unions. Clay and Tawney were well connected in radical circles and through them Goodrich was enabled to make a number of important contacts including G. D. H. Cole. Clay prompted Goodrich in the direction of studying the phenomenon of workers' control of industry. When Goodrich subsequently returned to the USA he wrote up his research as a University of Chicago PhD dissertation. This work was published in 1920 by Harcourt Brace with a foreword by R. H. Tawney and the full title *The Frontier of Control: A Study of British Workshop Politics*. Following the book's publication Goodrich maintained his interest in labour issues generally, and the issue of control in particular. In 1925 he produced *The Miner's Freedom: A Study of the Working Life in a Changing Industry* in which he examined the impact of changing technology and working methods on the working life of coalminers. In 1931 Goodrich became Professor of Economics at Columbia University, remaining there until 1963 when he became Mellon Professor of History and of Economics at the University of Pittsburgh. Although he maintained his interest

---

1 The biographical information in this chapter is largely based on R. Hyman's foreword to the 1975 edition of Goodrich's *The Frontier of Control*.

in labour matters (becoming closely involved in the work of the International Labour Organization – see Chapter 10) his academic work was increasingly concerned with economic history and particularly the impact of government on transportation. In this context he produced *Government Promotion of American Canals and Railroads* (1960) and *Canals and American Development* (1961). Carter Goodrich died in 1971.

British labour relations in the era of industrialization

The claims and aspirations of scientific management, (such as the assertion of a mutual interest between capital and labour, workers and managers) offended those elements of organized labour which saw their legitimate role as the defence of craft privilege and the protection of workers against what they perceived to be hostile, exploitative attempts by employers to gain control of the labour process. In Britain, for example, the recruitment of craft workers into stable trade unions, with paid officials and national structures, had already emerged by the 1850s. Unions such as the Amalgamated Society of Engineers sought to limit entry into the craft (and thus the workshop) by insisting that new recruits serve a lengthy period of apprenticeship before gaining acceptance into the union. These skilled workers, organized by the so-called 'New Model' unions, represented an artisan elite within the working class, jealous of their privileges and basically hostile to technological change. For these craftsmen their skill was a form of capital, to be protected and nurtured rather than diluted by either the unskilled worker or modernizing employer. By the 1890s trade unionism in Britain was also substantially established among unskilled workers such as dockers, gas stokers and transport workers. This 'New Unionism' tended to be more militant in nature and linked with socialist organizations through many of its prominent activists such as Tom Mann, John Burns, Ben Tillett and Will Thorne. Although the unskilled workers lacked the financial and technical advantages of their skilled counterparts in the older craft unions, they were nevertheless capable of offering a formidable challenge to the employers. Indeed some employers actively mobilized against the new trade unions, seeking to break their power through the deployment of 'free' (i.e. non–union) labour and legal obstruction.

The employer counter attack against the new unions was extended to the craft unions during the 1890s. As Fox has observed:

> Competition was quickening both at home and abroad and American and German rivals had already overtaken the British lead…new methods of production in some firms were destroying craft customs and privileges and forcing other firms to follow suit. New specialist machines lent themselves to the employment of unapprenticed labour and as improvisation gave way increasingly to planning the craftsmen found themselves hedged

about…Shop-floor resistance to these trends led eventually to the formation in 1896 of the Employers Federation of Engineering Associations.

(Fox, 1985, p.187)

The Federation took as its particular object employer resistance to trade union restrictive practices, whether through strike action or other means. When, in 1897, the engineering unions demanded the eight-hour day the Federation responded by locking-out 35 000 workers, precipitating a bitter struggle and engendering lasting bitterness. Although the unions managed to retain the right to collective bargaining they were forced to renounce their craft claims to encroach on managerial prerogatives in the areas of work organization, piecework, overtime, apprenticeship, employment of non-unionists and the introduction of new machinery. Of course this did not mean that craft privileges were immediately or completely stripped away (see Chapter 1). Instead such privileges were eroded as the pace of technological change increased and union strength ebbed or flowed according to the vagaries of the business cycle.

Tensions between British employers and unions continued in the years between the turn of the century and the outbreak of the First World War. Trade union membership grew steadily from under 1 million in 1888 to over 2 million in 1906, doubling again to reach over 4 million in 1913. Although the formal process of conciliation between employers and unions was strengthened during the period, and government increased its expertise through the activities of the Labour Department of the Board of Trade, industrial unrest nevertheless grew sharply and became increasingly politicized. In particular the unrest which occurred in the years between 1910 and 1914 was fuelled by the imported ideas of syndicalism and industrial unionism. Syndicalism originated in the industrial areas of France and Belgium during the 1890s and drew its theoretical content from the writings of Proudhon and Marx. In practical terms it meant workers' control of industry. The existing centralized political system would be replaced by a federalized structure based on local organizations of workers. This replacement would occur either gradually or as a result of a revolutionary crisis culminating in a general strike. Following the overthrow of the existing order industry in each locality would be run by the unions and, over larger areas, by a general labour federation. Industrial unionism, the American counterpart of European syndicalism, was advocated by the Industrial Workers of the World and encouraged by Daniel de Leon's Socialist Labour Party. A British branch of this movement was founded in 1903 by the Irish Labour leader, James Connolly and, from 1910 onwards, Tom Mann introduced French and American ideas on workers' control into Britain through his journal *Industrial Syndicalist*. After 1912 a diluted form of syndicalism was advocated by the Guild Socialists who claimed that the government of industry should involve all those concerned with production, including managerial and professional elements, rather than only manual workers. A further refinement was provided by G. D. H. Cole in his book *The World of Labour* which drew on insights from such anti-industrial thinkers as John Ruskin and William Morris.

Industrial unrest continued right up to the outbreak of war on 4 August 1914. However, the opening of hostilities had a sobering effect on employers and unions alike. In an effort to limit the damage to industry and avoid widespread unemployment the trade unions called an industrial truce and the level of strike activity was dramatically reduced. In the event, however, the rapid recruitment of men to the forces, coupled with the expanding demand for war material, led to dire labour shortages in many areas of industry which were only partially met by the recruitment of women. Labour shortages gave unprecedented bargaining power to workers and, as manufacturers' profits soared, wage demands increased and were backed by unofficial strikes. Whereas in January 1915 only 10 disputes were known to the Labour Department of the Board of Trade, by February the figure had increased to 47 and by March it was 74. During 1915 nearly 3 million working days were lost through strike action and almost 2.5 million were lost in 1916. As the war progressed a heightened mood of militancy developed in the trade unions and the emergence of unofficial leaders brought a shop stewards movement into prominence, particularly in engineering. During 1917 a wave of strikes resulted in the loss of 6 million working days and led the government of David Lloyd George to establish the Commission of Inquiry into Industrial Unrest. Interpretations of the unrest varied from mere war weariness and frustration caused by food and housing shortages to a belief in revolution on the model recently experienced in Russia. In any event there was widespread belief in the strength of organized labour, particularly as by 1918 membership had risen to over 6.5 million and continued to rise to reach 8.3 million during the brief boom which followed the war and ended in 1920. Not surprisingly perhaps in such a situation, the demands of workers and their representatives for a greater say in the operation of industry were louder and more persistent than ever before. This was the backdrop to Carter Goodrich's study of workshop politics *The Frontier of Control*.

Workers' control of industry

The Frontier of Control provided a consideration of the extent to which workers could justifiably expect to control their industries and the various forms such control might take. Goodrich did not provide an answer to the question – who should control industry? preferring instead to let the facts speak for themselves. At the time he carried out his research the issue of workers' control was higher on the political agenda than ever before and, arguably, ever would be again although the subject did enjoy something of a revival during the 1970s, partly inspired by the work of Harry Braverman (see Chapter 18). The experience of bitter industrial conflict in the pre-war years, together with the desire to promote industrial harmony during the war itself, prompted the British government after 1915 into ever greater intervention in industrial matters, including labour relations. Although lasting industrial peace was not achieved, the level of strike action during the war did not reach pre-war levels and the government had some reason to be optimistic concerning post-war developments. During the final years of the war the government embraced Whitleyism, initially as a means of promoting industrial harmony and subsequently as a way of managing the end of the war and the return to the civilian order. Whitleyism, based on the recommendations of the Whitley Committee, advocated a system of labour relations based on voluntary, joint committees of trade unions and employers in each industry meeting on a regular basis to deal with major employment issues such as pay and conditions (Sheldrake, 1988, chapters 2, 3 and 4). To the radical and militant activists committed to the various schemes for workers' control of industry, Whitleyism was a mere sop calculated to buy time for capitalism without delivering much to the workers. Goodrich, however, considered that the claims of the syndicalists, Guild Socialists, nationalizers, proto-communists, advocates of industrial parliaments, 'enlightened' employers and moderate supporters of Whitleyism could be plausibly placed on a continuum. Indeed he considered that the strength of the more radical approaches had prompted the more moderate responses. As he put it 'there is no one break in the long series from syndicalism to Whitleyism, and the widespread acceptance of the latter in middle class thinking is a hint of the driving force of the more drastic doctrines' (Goodrich, 1920/1975, p.7). Of course the onset of trade depression after 1920 severely reduced the potency of the trade union movement, throwing workers on the defensive and often out of a job. Such advances as workers had made in extending the frontier of control in the workplace were soon negated as employers fought for survival in a hostile economic environment. Nevertheless the question of workers' control of industry had been raised and, certainly in radical and labour circles, remained viable at least as an objection to management's assertion of the right to manage. The value of Goodrich's work was in gathering together the various strands of the debate on workers' control at a crucial moment in its development and, through his book, preserving them in a lasting form. As R. H. Tawney put it at the time:

> We must know how much control is wanted, and control over what, and through whom it is to be exercised. We must decide whether the demand is the passing result of abnormal economic conditions produced by the war and seized upon by theorists as a basis for premature generalizations, or whether it represents a movement which is so fundamental and permanent that any future scheme of industrial relationships unless it is to be built upon sand, must take account of it. The first condition of answering these questions is an impartial survey of the actual facts as they exist today. Mr. Carter Goodrich's book supplies it.
>
> *(Tawney in Goodrich, 1920/75)*

With the advantage of hindsight we now know that the radical demands for workers' control of industry in Britain – or anywhere else for that matter – were never realised in spite (or possibly because) of the election of governments sympathetic to the claims of organized labour and a large scale extension of public ownership of industry which has only recently receded. Nevertheless Goodrich's impartial, if sympathetic, survey remains of historic interest as an account of a movement contemporary with, but radically different from, scientific management.

Critical summary

Carter Goodrich provided an account of the various demands for workers' control of industry at a time when the strength of organized labour in Britain was at an unprecedented high. Although sympathetic to the claims of the workers, *The Frontier of Control* took a descriptive, analytical approach rather than a polemical or normative one. Written at a time when scientific management was beginning to have a major impact on industry, the book provides a useful reminder that workers have not always accepted managerial prerogatives or existing patterns of ownership.

Discussion questions

1. How plausible is the notion of workers' control of industry?
2. In what ways did the First World War strengthen the British trade unions?
3. To what extent did Whitleyism offer a means of reconciling the interests of managers and workers?

Suggested reading

Cole, G. D. H. (1917/1972) *Self-Government in Industry*, Hutchinson, London.

Cole, G. D. H. (1923/1973) *Workshop Organization*, Hutchinson, London.

Fox, A. (1985) *History and Heritage: The Social Origins of the British Industrial Relations System*, Allen & Unwin, London.

Goodrich, C. (1920/1975) *The Frontier of Control: A Study in British Workshop Politics*, Pluto Press, London.

Sheldrake, J. (1991) *Industrial Relations and Politics in Britain 1880–1989*, Pinter, London.

Chapter 8

Mary Parker Follett and dynamic management

Mary Parker Follett was born in Quincy, Boston in 1868 and attended the Thayer Academy before going to the Annexe at Harvard (later renamed Radcliffe College). In total she spent six years at Radcliffe, broken during 1890–91 by a period at Newnham College, Cambridge where she studied politics, history and law. Her year at Cambridge stimulated her interest in England and she regularly returned to the country, developing a wide circle of friends including Lyndall F. Urwick (see Chapter 10) and Seebohm Rowntree[1] and spending the final years of her life living in Chelsea. Follett was not a 'business woman' or a conventional academic. Instead she was a political, social and management thinker who derived her early inspiration from involvement in social work in her native city of Boston. As Urwick and Brech observed:

> she had very early become impressed with many of the social evils that followed in the wake of the growing industrialization of the city. She had felt the urge to play her part both in countering the worst effects of these developments and also in seeking a radical cure for the evils themselves. It was the former aim that kept

1 Benjamin Seebohm Rowntree (1871–1954), the social investigator and industrialist, was director of the Industrial Welfare Department of the Ministry of Munitions between 1916 and 1918. In 1923 he succeeded his father as chairman of the Rowntree's confectionery business and set about reorganizing the Rowntree Works in York according to the principles of scientific management. He engaged Lyndall F. Urwick, Britain's pioneer management thinker, and presided over a programme of paternalistic company welfare benefits. When Mary Parker Follett was seeking case study material for her research on the social philosophy of business she chose the Rowntree Works, together with Filene's department store in Boston, as an example.

her actively engaged on her various social pursuits, and it was the latter that lent point to her later studies of industrial organization and management.

(Urwick and Brech, 1945, p.49)

In 1900 Follett established a debating club in the Roxbury Neighbourhood House in Boston. Situated in a poor locality, the purpose of Neighbourhood House was to provide social, recreational and educational facilities for young people – particularly those who had left school early to work in the factories and shops of the city. This experience prompted Follett to begin a campaign for the opening of school premises after hours for the purposes of social and educational activity. As a result of this work the Committee on the Extended Use of School Buildings was established in Boston and pioneered the development of school centres not only in that city but nationally. During 1902 Follett visited Edinburgh and was impressed by a scheme of vocational guidance that was in operation there. On her return to the USA she began to work for the establishment of a similar scheme to operate in connection with the evening schools. When, in 1912, the directors of the Boston School System decided to set up a placement bureau, Follett was invited to join the inaugural Placement Bureau Committee and she sustained an interest in this work for the remainder of her life. Her experience of vocational guidance, in the words of Metcalf and Urwick,

afforded her...valuable contact with industry. Under her guidance, files of information about working conditions in different industries were gradually built up. It was at this time, in fact, that her main interest shifted from political and social issues to problems of industrial relations.

(Metcalf and Urwick, 1941, p.13)

Follett's first publication appeared in 1909 and took the form of a pamphlet entitled *The Speaker of the House of Representatives* based on a paper which she had given when a student at Newnham. However it was not until 1918 that her main work *The New State* appeared being followed, in 1924, by *Creative Experience*. In these latter two works she expounded her belief in the primacy of the group over the individual, thereby challenging the received wisdom of the liberal tradition. She took the view that the 'true self is the group-self' and 'man can have no rights apart from society or independent of society or against society' (Follett, 1918, p.7). By the 1920s such a challenge had become almost commonplace in the sphere of political theory in Europe with the rise of collectivism most clearly manifested in the various forms of socialism. Nevertheless, Follett's theorizing dealt with phenomena which had been somewhat neglected in management literature and Urwick was moved to comment that:

before Mary Follett, industrial groups had seldom been the subject of study of political or social scientists. It was her special merit to turn from the traditional subjects of study – the state or the community as a whole – progressively to concentrate on the study of industry...Her approach was to analyse the nature of the consent on which any democratic group is based by examining the psychological factors underlying it. This consent, she suggested is not static but a continuous process, generating new and living group ideas through the interpenetration of individual ideas.

(Urwick, 1956, pp.132–33)

Of course many political theorists from Plato onwards had given primacy to the social whole rather than the individual. The rise of liberal individualism in the West from the seventeenth century onwards, which had perhaps made its greatest impact in the United States, had been subject to much criticism by thinkers such as Rousseau and subsequently the German idealist philosophers including Hegel and Follett's particular favourite, Fichte. Johann Gottlieb Fichte advocated a form of nationalism under which the freedom of the individual had to be subordinated to the group. He believed that, although individuals possessed free will, they were nevertheless enmeshed in a social network to which all people were primarily committed. 'Thus an individual's ego belonged to a wider world of egos, making the ego a social one, until all swelled up into one "Great Ego" which was part of a common life among all people' (Wren, 1994, p.257).

Obviously such thinking leaves little room for conventional liberal beliefs and might even be considered dangerous given the development of fascism and Stalinism during the twentieth century and the bloodshed which they engendered. Whether Follett realised the capacity such thinking possessed for the destruction of the open society is not clear from her work. Certainly Metcalf and Urwick were prepared to give her the benefit of the doubt stating that 'her aim was quite simple: she wanted a better ordered society in which the individual could live a more satisfactory life' (Metcalf and Urwick, 1941, p.14). However, although Follett's stated purpose was to channel conflict in such a way that integration rather than domination occurred her work nevertheless often manifests an alarming mixture of mysticism and authoritarianism. This tendency grew as the world economic situation deteriorated and the USA was gripped by a depression which many identified as the final crisis of capitalism. In *Individualism in a Planned Society* (1932), the last paper Follett wrote before her death in 1933, she argued that:

We have talked of our rights. We have guarded our freedom. Our highest virtues have been service and sacrifice. Are we not now thinking of those virtues somewhat differently? The spirit of a new age is fast gripping every one of us. The appeal which life makes to us today is to the socially constructive passion in every man. This is something to which the whole of me can respond. This is a great affirmative. Sacrifice sometimes seems too negative, dwells on what I give up. Service sometimes seems to emphasize the fact of service rather than the value of the service. Yet service and sacrifice are noble ideas. We cannot do without them. Let them, however, be the handmaids of the great purpose of our life, namely, our contribution to that new world we wish to see rise out of our present chaos, that age which shall bring us individual freedom through collective control.

(Follett in Metcalf and Urwick, 1941, p.314)

Surely these words would have been as chilling to the leaders of American business, had they read them, as they would have been welcome to Joseph Stalin.

Follett's management thought

Although Follett's collectivist imperatives might be somewhat sinister if taken to their ultimate conclusions in the widest political, economic and social sense, within the constrained sphere of the business or public corporation they are amenable to a more benign interpretation. Certainly this is the interpretation which most commentators on her work have supported. One example is Wren who has observed:

if one views management as a universal phenomenon, the processes which underlie political administration would necessarily apply to business as well. The same problems of achieving unity of effort, of defining authority and responsibility, of achieving co-ordination and control, and of developing effective leadership exist. It was toward the goal of drawing this parallel that Mary Parker Follett turned her attention...She suggested that in the past an artificial line was drawn between those who managed and those who were managed. In reality, there was no line and all members of the organization who accepted responsibility for work at any level were contributing to the whole.

(Wren, 1979, p.325)

This statement has a kinship with Taylor's 'mental revolution' and reflects a long-standing and continuing ambition among management thinkers to dispose of section-alism in the interests of harmony, productive efficiency and commercial success. Further, Follett was concerned with the way in which workers respond to their work and seek to achieve identity and psychic growth through the work group, thus placing her at a transitional stage between the somewhat simplistic psychology of Taylor and the concern with the human factor pioneered by the Gilbreths and subsequently promoted by Mayo (see Chapter 11).

Follett's central interest, however, was with the achievement of integrative unity and she saw constructive conflict as a means to this end. She argued for maximum participation on the part of every worker and saw the participative worker within the organization as being tantamount to the active citizen in the polity. As she put it:

the whole matter of participation, or ways of joining the various contributions of men, is much more important in business today than it ever was before, because we have more kinds of knowledge and experience to join...I do not therefore think that participation in any social process should be one of self-sacrifice, but one of self-contribution.

(Follett in Metcalf and Urwick, 1941, pp.214–5)

Briefly, through the clash of ideas, participants in a group, enterprise or, by extension, a whole society would come to recognize their own interest in the wider interest rather than the narrow confines of the self. Of course, there is nothing new in any of this and it formed the central thrust of Rousseau's *Social Contract* (1762). Although Follett cites numerous practical examples of self-interest being overcome by the logic of collective action there is nevertheless no final way of disposing of differences of interest if the parties refuse to be persuaded by the arguments. Unless of course, recourse to coercion is taken. Certainly in the sphere of political action, although it is prudent to achieve maximum levels of consent in order to maintain legitimacy, it may still be necessary to use coercive force in the interests of the majority or, conversely, to protect a minority. Follett did not wish to resort to coercion and instead she offered insights derived from Gestalt psychology as a means of escaping from atomistic individualism and achieving wholistic understanding.

Gestalt psychology was a movement founded in 1912 by three German psychologists (*viz.* Kohler, Koffka and Wertheimer) as a reaction to the analytic approach advocated by Wilhelm Wundt. Wundt had argued that the central task of psychology was to analyse human consciousness and he claimed that consciousness could be broken down into simple, fundamental units. The Gestalt psychologists in contrast held a perceived organized whole to be greater, or at least different, than the sum of its constituent parts. As Follett put it:

> any individual psychology which has not recognized the unifying nature of experience, any social psychology which has failed to see this, has dealt not with life but with abstractions from life...Our perceptual experience, our personal experience, our social experience, is a complex structure, a unity...A number of biologists have dealt with a whole organism and another whole the constitutive elements of which are organism and environment...If dissection has been the method of traditional psychology, the study of integrative processes is surely the chief characteristic of contemporary psychology.

(Follett, 1924, pp.113–116)

Thus whereas Taylor, for example, took the individual as the key focus of analysis and worked outwards, Follett began with the organization (i.e. the complete social entity) and worked inwards. Similarly whereas many thinkers sought to treat social phenomena as static entities, Follett perceived them to be dynamic and in this she was perhaps in advance of many of her contemporaries. Her approach to the understanding of management was not, like the conventional scientific managers, based on the breaking down and analysing of tasks into their constituent parts and then attempting to artifically reconstruct them. Instead she began by accepting the complexity of social situations and focusing on the working group and the need to integrate its efforts within the productive whole. Using insights derived from Gestalt psychology, together with elements of idealist and collectivist thinking, Follett took the controversial view that organizations are ultimately characterized by unity of purpose. The role of management is to facilitate the fullest achievement of this purpose through co-ordination of effort and the promulgation of the corporate idea. The possibility of achieving lasting unity of purpose in organizations is, of course, problematical given the impact of technical, competitive and economic turbulence. Nevertheless, considerable success has been achieved, particularly in Japan and those countries which have adopted the lessons of Japanese management (see Chapter 19). Interestingly, as Clutterbuck and Crainer observe 'Follett remains, to a large extent, undiscovered in the Western world of management and business. In Japan, however, there is a Follett Society which propagates her views, believing they are as relevant in the late twentieth century as never before' (Clutterbuck and Crainer, 1990, p.38).

Critical summary

Rosenfeld and Smith have claimed that Mary Parker Follett 'connected scientific management, as advocated by F. W. Taylor and his associates, with the new social psychology of the 1920s, which made better human relations in industry a first concern of modern management' (Rosenfeld and Smith, 1966, p.33). Certainly she brought fresh insights to the study of management by emphasizing the role of the group, the significance of organizations as a whole and the dynamic nature of social interaction. Her work in the sphere of political science, together with her practical social work, provided the underpinning to her management theorizing. In philosophical terms this included idealist philosophy and Gestalt psychology. Although her writings contain many (carefully selected) practical examples of the advantages and rationality of human co-operation over conflict and the benefits of integration over competition, no final proof is offered for these assertions. Further, although she provides useful insights into the significance of the group and the role of work in creating identity, she does not allow for the phenomenon of competition between groups or the negative impact of modern technology. Her assertion of the primacy of the collective over the individual is fraught with well known dangers, although at the level of the organization rather than the state it is perhaps a reasonable one. Mary Parker Follett inhabited an entirely different intellectual universe from that of F. W. Taylor and his associates, as the following passage on the subject of creative experience (i.e. work) perfectly illustrates:

> the theory of creative experience given to us by the most profound philosophy throughout the ages, and now so happily strengthened by recent research in several fields, shows that the individual cannot create without 'transcending'. He expresses, brings into manifestation, powers which are the powers of the

universe, and thereby those forces which he is himself helping to create, those which exist in and by and through him, are ever more ready to respond, and so Life expands and deepens; fulfils and at the same moment makes possible larger fulfilment.

(Follett, 1924, p.116)

Discussion questions
1. Is the work group more important than the individual worker?
2. How successful is Follett in demonstrating that constructive conflict leads to integrative unity?
3. What is Gestalt psychology and in what ways did Follett apply its insights?
4. To what extent are organizations characterized by unity of purpose?
5. Why did Follett value worker participation?

Suggested reading
Follett, M. P. (1918) *The New State*, Longmans, Green, London.

Follett, M. P. (1924) *Creative Experience*, Longmans, Green, London.

Follett, M. P. (1937) The Process of Control in Gulick, L. and Urwick, L. (eds) *Papers on the Science of Administration*, Institute of Public Administration, Columbia University, New York.

Graham, P. (1987) *Dynamic Managing: The Follett Way*, British Institute of Management, London.

Graham, P. (1995) *Mary Parker Follett – Prophet of Management*, Harvard Business School Press, Boston, Mass.

Merril, H. (ed) (1960) *Classics in Management*, American Management Association, New York.

Metcalf, H. and Urwick, L. (eds) (1941) *Dynamic Administration: the Collected Papers of Mary Parker Follett*, Management Publications Trust, Bath.

Rosenfeld, J. and Smith, M. (1966), Mary Parker Follett: The Transition to Modern Management Thought. *Advanced Management Journal* **31**(4) 33–37.

Chapter 9

Henry Ford and mass production

Henry Ford was born in 1863 in Dearborn, Michigan where his parents were farmers. From his earliest years he was fascinated by all kinds of machinery. As he observed in his memoirs:

> Driving to town I always had a pocketful of trinkets – nuts, washers and odds and ends of machinery. Often I took a broken watch and tried to put it together. When I was thirteen I managed for the first time to put a watch together so that it would keep time. By the time I was fifteen I could do almost anything in watch repairing – although my tools were of the crudest… Machines are to a mechanic what books are to a writer. He gets ideas from them, and if he has any brains he will apply those ideas.
>
> *(Ford, 1923, pp.24–25)*

Ford left school at the age of seventeen and, ignoring his father's desire for him to become a farmer, became an apprentice – initially in the machine shop of James Flower and Brothers the valve makers and later in the engine works of the Detroit Dry Dock Company (Nevins, 1954, pp.83–85). On the completion of his apprenticeship three years later he joined the local representative of the Westinghouse Company working on the construction and maintenance of their steam-driven road engines. These were used for a variety of purposes, not only for traction, but also for driving threshing machines and sawmills. Their fastest speed on the road, however, was 12 miles an hour and the engines were very cumbersome, weighing roughly two tons. They were also expensive to purchase and to operate and thus beyond the financial reach of the smaller farmers. It was the limitations of the Westinghouse and other available steam engines which inspired Ford to build a lightweight steam tractor and also a steam car. He soon decided, however, that steam was not suitable for lightweight vehicles and abandoned the project, turning his attention instead to the internal combustion engine. During the years of his apprenticeship Ford had read an account of the 'silent gas engine' in a copy of an English journal called the *World of Science*. This was probably an account of Otto's engine and, in 1885, Ford got the opportunity of examining such an engine when he repaired one at the Eagle Iron Works in Detroit. In 1887 he constructed a four-stroke engine based on Otto's design.

Ford's father remained keen for him to return to farming and offered him 40 acres of timber land, provided he would abandon his job as a machinist. Ford provisionally and unenthusiastically agreed. It gave him the wherewithal to get married and he soon built a house on the land and began extracting the timber. However, he also built a workshop and continued his experimental work on the internal combustion engine in his spare time, constructing a double–cylinder engine in 1890. When in due course all the timber from the forty acres had been disposed of, Ford became short of money and took a job at the Detroit Electric Company as an engineer and machinist, thus decisively turning his back on agriculture. During his early months at the electricity plant Ford worked permanently on the night shift and this left him very little time for his mechanical experiments. However, when he was switched to the day shift he was able to spend every evening and much of the weekends working on a new engine. Ford continued his experiments when he left Detroit Electric and joined the Edison Illuminating Company where he rose rapidly to become chief engineer. Between 1893 and 1895 he constructed his first motor car which, although the ignition and transmission were primitive, was capable of running at two speeds – either 10 or 20 miles an hour (Ford, 1923, pp.31–34; Nevins, 1954, p.147). Ford was, of course, aware that his work was not original but given that he was working more or less in isolation he was forced to learn by his mistakes. As he moved to more advanced models of car he continued to refine the technology, incorporating improvements as he went, his work informed by natural curiosity and a high level of empirical genius.

Henry Ford was only one among a number of American pioneers working on the construction of a motor car during the 1890s. As Armytage has observed:

> From the gas buggy of Charles E. Duryea, first built in 1892, there (was) a rapid kindling of interest. Ransom E. Olds, of Lansing, Michigan, had built several steam cars before this. His Oldsmobile, manufactured in 1897, encouraged him to set up a factory in Detroit…others paced him. The Haynes, Winton, Stanley, White, Locomobile, Packard and Cadillac were becoming known. By 1904 there were 121 manufacturers assembling cars of their own organized in an association of Licensed Automobile Manufacturers.
>
> *(Armytage, 1976, p.267)*

The 'licence' refers to the fact that all these manufacturers were paying royalties to William C. Whitney's Electric Vehicle Company of Hartford. This company held a comprehensive patent, filed in 1897, for a self-propelled vehicle driven by an internal combustion engine. However, when Henry Ford began to manufacture cars on a commercial basis he refused to pay these royalties, thereby provoking (and ultimately winning) a prolonged court case. In 1899 Ford left the Edison company and went into the car business as chief engineer (and minority stock holder) of the Detroit Automobile Company. The venture was a failure and, although the company survived to become the Cadillac company, Ford left and turned his attention (somewhat reluctantly) to the construction of racing cars.

In the early years of the motor industry car racing offered a combination of publicity and attractive prize money. A successful racing driver himself, Ford teamed up with Tom Cooper, a wealthy former champion cyclist, to establish a brief winning partnership in the world of early car racing. Together they built 'The Arrow' and '999', the latter named after the New York Central train which recorded a record run from New York to Chicago and was later exhibited at the World's Fair in Chicago in 1893. The '999' was entered in a five mile event at the Grosse Pointe track outside Detroit in October 1902. It was driven by Barry Oldfield who had never driven before and whose main qualifications for the task were nerve and a strong desire to make money – as he put it 'I might as well be dead as dead broke' (Nevins, 1954, p.217). In the event Oldfield won the race, breaking the American record in the process, and launching himself on a successful career as a racing driver. Although '999' with Oldfield at the wheel improved on the American record during 1902 and 1903, Ford nevertheless severed his connection with the venture, selling his share in the car to Cooper. In fact for Ford racing was merely a means to an end rather than an end in itself. As he recalled in his memoirs:

> the idea in those days was that a first-class car ought to be a racer. I never really thought much of racing, but…the manufacturers had the notion that winning a race on a track told the public something about the merits of an automobile – although I can hardly imagine any test that would tell less. But, as the others were doing it, I too, had to do it…If an automobile were going to be known for speed, then I was going to make an automobile that would be known wherever speed was known.
>
> *(Ford, 1923, p.50)*

Thus Ford was never really committed to the manufacture of racing cars, or even luxury cars for that matter, his ultimate goal being to build what would now be termed 'volume' cars. In the Model T he was to achieve this goal with a vengeance.

The Model T and mass production methods

It (is) easier to conceive of a cheap car than to make one. Light construction and low-quality materials would merely result in a vehicle which would shake itself to pieces in a short time. What was wanted was a car light enough to keep manufacturing costs down yet durable enough to stand up under ordinary usage

- including the pounding that any vehicle took from the rough roads of the period. It also had to be simple to operate and inexpensive to maintain and repair. Meeting these specifications was a problem which baffled Ford himself for several years and completely defeated the other experiments with a popular priced car – meaning one which would sell for not over 500 dollars.

(Rae, 1959, p.105)

In the years between the establishment of the Ford Motor Company in 1903 and the emergence of the Model T in 1908, Ford produced a variety of cars, beginning with a 2-cylinder model at $800 and including 6-cylinder vehicles selling for between $2-3000. When the 4-cylinder Model N was introduced in 1906, Ford decided to abandon production of the expensive models for the time being and, instead, concentrate the company's energies on a single chassis. The popularity of the Model N, at a selling price of $600, enabled Ford to rationalize production and finance the development of a successor car. The use of vanadium steel in the new car's construction provided a solution to the problem of combining lightness with durability and was therefore central to the phenomenal success of what Rae has described as 'the Model T of imperishable memory' (Rae, 1959, p.105).

The Model T embodied all the essential features of the all purpose, volume car which Ford had long desired to produce. It was mechanically simple, which made it easy to service, and could cope with the rough road (and for that matter off road) conditions encountered in many areas of the USA. Again in the words of Rae, 'with its appearance, the manufacture of all other Ford models was terminated; for the next 20 years Ford and the Model T were to be synonymous' (Rae, 1959, pp.105–6). Having created the car Ford turned to the question of improving manufacturing techniques so that greater numbers could be produced and unit costs lowered. Part of Ford's approach was to situate as much of the manufacturing capacity on a single site, thereby reducing transport costs and dependence on outside suppliers. Another part was to hire talented individuals and deploy their gifts on the problem of meeting what rapidly became an insatiable demand for Model Ts. Among the individuals employed by Ford were Charles E. Sorensen (a Dane who originally joined Ford as a pattern maker) and Clarence Avery (a University of Michigan graduate who had taught Henry Ford's son Edsel at Detroit University School). By 1909 these men were collaborating with Ford himself on the development of the continuous flow of materials through Ford's Piquette Avenue plant in Detroit. It was here that the first experiments were made with the moving assembly track, beginning with magnetos and later extending to other parts of the Model T. In 1910 the Ford Motor Company moved into its new Highland Park plant designed by the prominent industrial architect Albert Kahn. In 1913 full scale assembly line production of Model Ts began at Highland Park and the results were astounding:

Output (leapt) from 8000 in 1907 to a quarter of a million in 1914, profits from the $1 00 0000 that the Model N earned to $27 000 000 for the first year of the mass produced Model T, and unit costs so cut that, by 1916, Ford touring cars could be sold for less than $400. This accomplishment was one of the great forward steps in the history of technology, and its has been fully acknowledged as such – to the point where the technique and organization of mass production became known in Germany as 'Fordismus' and Aldous Huxley could cast Ford in the role of deity in *Brave New World*.

(Rae, 1959, pp.107–8)

None of the elements the Ford Motor Company brought together to establish the system of mass production at the Highland Park plant was, of course, original. The three core elements were 'accuracy (which includes standardization and the inter-changeability of parts); continuity (the moving manufacturing line or assembly line, to which moving component lines are geared); and speed (which means a carefully timed correlation of manufacture, material handling, and assembly)' (Nevins, 1954, p.467). As was seen in Chapter 1 Adam Smith had identified the division of labour and increased specialization as central factors in the development of industrialization during the eighteenth century. He had also scrutinized the nature of the emerging factory system and this work had been further developed by Charles Babbage and Andrew Ure during the early nineteenth century. Eli Whitney had developed the standardization and interchangeability of components, together with the substitution of skilled labour by machines, which characterized the American system of manufac-ture. Oliver Evans, who had inspired some of Whitney's work, built a completely mechanized grain mill on Red Clay Creek, Pennsylvania between 1784 and 1785. Here grain was elevated to the top of the mill and went through the entire production process without human intervention until emerging at the bottom as flour. Further, by the mid–nineteenth century, meat packers in Cincinnati had devised an assembly line for the slaughtering, butchering and packaging of pigs which was later developed to include the use of sophisticated conveyer systems. With regard to accurate timing, the subject had of course been addressed by Babbage but it was really F. W. Taylor who made the most significant contribution to the subject, beginning with his work at Midvale Steel in the 1880s. Indeed, Nevins has shown that Taylor lectured to engineers in Detroit in 1909 and 1910, on the second occasion 'addressing more than 600 superintendents, foremen, and others drawn from industries all over the city' (Nevins, 1954, p.468). Coincidentally, Taylor published *The Principles of Scientific Manage-ment* in 1911, the year when the Model T went into production at Trafford Park, Manchester and full use began to be made of the Highland Park plant. Thus by the first decade of the twentieth century, there was a substantial body of theoretical and practical knowledge of the three core elements (i.e. 'accuracy, continuity and speed') to make a mass production system on the model created at Highland Park technically feasible given the will, the product and the capital. Henry Ford and his associates certainly had the will and the Model T was the product which generated the necessary capital.

The mass production system which evolved at the Highland Park plant was developed in a piecemeal fashion, starting in 1912 with the installation of simple conveyor belts and gravity slides for materials being transported to the machine shop. Soon an electrically operated overhead monorail was also installed in the machine shop. Meanwhile, in the foundry, an endless-chain carrier was built which passed the moulds under spouts which filled them with molten metal. Continuous conveyor belts were soon installed to transport various components to the assembly lines and it was in assembly that the greatest leap in mass production technique occurred. The Ford work study engineers, employing the approaches pioneered by Taylor and Gilbreth, timed the Model T assembly line:

> They found that in August (1913) it took 250 assemblers and 80 parts–carriers, working 9 hours a day for 26 days, to complete 6 182 chassis assemblies. Each chassis cost $12\frac{1}{2}$ man hours of labour. That was low average for motor factories. The management…installed a motor with a capstan and heavy rope and prepared to keep a line of chassis in continuous motion along the floor. Six assemblers kept pace with every chassis as it moved. From piles of parts brought up on tracks to the line, they picked out whatever was needed. At the point where the motor was to be installed, a heavy chain–fall with hooks was ready; it swung the motor directly over the frame, and the assembler lowered it into position . . . The average number of man hours needed to assemble a chassis fell to 5 hours and 50 minutes!
>
> *(Nevins, 1954, p.473)*

So the famous (some would say infamous) moving assembly track was created. By the end of 1913 the number of man hours required to assemble a chassis had been reduced to 2 hours and 38 minutes and by early 1914 it had fallen to 1 hour and 33 minutes. Meanwhile the number of assembly lines at the Highland Park plant had been increased from one to four.

The phenomenal success of the Model T gave the Ford Motor Company an immense inflow of cash and a technological and commercial lead over its rivals that for the while seemed unassailable. In addition to progressive reductions in the price of the Model T, Fords also announced that if the company sold 300 000 vehicles between 1 August 1914 and 1 August 1915 it would give each purchaser a share in the profits. In the event sales for the period were in excess of 308 000 and every buyer duly received a $50 rebate (Rae, 1959, p.109). By 1923 the Ford Motor Company held half the American automobile market with sales of 1 700 000 vehicles compared to General Motors' 800 000 and Chevrolet's 465 000. However, by 1927, Ford's had been overhauled by both General Motors and Chevrolet and were a struggling company, making losses and producing a product that no longer met the requirements of an increasingly sophisticated market. On 26 May 1927 the last of some 15 000 000 Model Ts rolled off the assembly line – the biggest selling car in history was finished. Not until 1928 did Ford's come back to the market with the Model A which served to partially restore company fortunes. However, Ford's were no longer leading the field in automobile design and production, that role having been usurped by General Motors under the guidance of its president, Alfred Sloan (see Chapter 13). Partly the decline in Ford's fortunes was caused by the decision to persist with the Model T when it had become decidedly old fashioned compared to the competition. More significantly, however, the decline stemmed from the shortcomings of the great Henry Ford himself. As Rae has commented:

> for the loss of his company's leadership, responsibility rests squarely and inescapably on the shoulders of Henry Ford. He refused to recognize that the happy-go-lucky managerial techniques which had been possible in the early days of the Ford Motor Company were not suitable for an industrial giant, so that, while General Motors was acquiring an integrated, smoothly working administrative mechanism, the Ford organization depended on the whims of one ageing individual.

> *(Rae, 1959, p.160)*

The organizational slackness that beset the Ford Motor Company during the 1920s persisted throughout the 1930s and was only arrested during the Second World War by which time Henry Ford was an ailing recluse in his eighties.

The five dollar day

By 1910 the rapid growth of the company and the concomitant expansion in its labour force meant that the workers could no longer be motivated by the personal charisma of Henry Ford alone. Instead they were placed under foremen who enjoyed the right to fire anyone they considered to be inefficient. Such a system, whilst commonplace, was not likely to generate company loyalty or high morale. The general expansion of industrial activity in Detroit had created a tight labour market and, although trade unions were weak, a climate of latent unrest existed among the workers there. One feature of this was a high level of labour turnover and constant competition among employers for good quality workers. In 1912 the employers sought to remedy the situation by agreeing to avoid competitive advertising for labour and also improving industrial training so as to ensure a ready supply of skilled workers. The bad living conditions in the city also made it difficult to produce a reliable and disciplined workforce. In the words of Nevins 'Detroit was a frontier town' (Nevins, 1954, p.518). The impact of bad living conditions on labour efficiency attracted the attention of John R. Lee who held responsibility for employment at the Ford Motor Company. He was particularly intrigued by the case of:

an experienced hammer operator (who) suddenly showed a total inability to meet moderate production standards. His health was sound; he had no grievance against the company. But an inquiry showed that his wife was ill and that as a result his children were neglected, and his debts mounting. As soon as the company removed that worry, his production rose to normal. Lee...suddenly comprehended the intimate relation between and employee's efficiency and his home life, recreations, and sense of security or insecurity.

(Nevins, 1954, p.526)

Obviously, in the face of new problems, and in the light of fresh insights, an alternative approach to labour relations than that adopted by autocratic foremen was required and Lee set about convincing Henry Ford of the need for reform.

The astounding success of the Model T gave the company plenty of financial elbow room to improve the lot of its workers. Ford himself had become immensely rich as a result of the car's success and the considerable financial rewards had spread to the company's executives, stockholders and customers. By 1913 the company had in excess of $28 million in the bank and Ford and his top management were in the mood to be generous to the workers. In January 1914 the company announced that the working day would be reduced to eight hours and the pattern of working changed from three shifts to two. More significantly they also announced that the rate of pay would be effectively doubled from $2.50 to $5.00 a day for the bulk of their workers. The impact of this announcement was immense, rapidly elevating Henry Ford beyond the status of successful industrialist to that of social guru. In the words of Nevins:

The public response was overwhelmingly approbatory...Not a few commentators perceived the underlying connection which linked high production, high wages, and high consumption, pointing out that a new economic era might find in the Ford announcement a convenient birth date. Already, by virtue of the Model T, his swift rise from overalls to millions, and his democratic expansiveness and folksiness...Ford had become something of a popular hero...That his talents in mechanics and plant organization amounted to hardly less than genius was well understood; and touches were now added which gave him the doubtful lineaments of a great philanthropist, economist, and social scientist.

(Nevins, 1954, pp.534–35)

Not surprisingly the doubling of the daily rate of pay was hugely popular with Ford's workers, the rise in their earnings and living standards marking them off as an industrial elite. However, problems also occurred. The change from two shifts to three increased Ford's labour requirements by 5000. Further, the announcement of the $5 day came at a time when economic depression was squeezing manufacturer's profits and generating unemployment. The day after the announcement was made 10 000 men gathered at the Highland Park employment office seeking work and a large force of police was required to control what soon became a restless mob. In spite of the erection of signs outside the factory announcing that the hiring of labour had been suspended, thousands of hopeful workers continued to besiege the plant. Many of those seeking work came from outside Detroit and had spent the last of their money getting to the city. Destitute, and suffering in the bitter winter weather, the jobless grew increasingly resentful of Henry Ford and his workers. By 7.30 on the morning of Monday 10 January 1914 over 10 000 men were already gathered outside the Highland Park plant:

> When employees wearing Ford badges began to push through, the sight of these privileged holders of keys to warmth, food, and security was too much for the shivering unfortunates. Tempers snapped. Isolated hoots and yells turned into a mob roar. The crowds surged against the gates, hundreds fighting past the helpless guards into the plant. More police, arriving on the run, were unable to restore order. The mob pinned them against the walls, prevented workers from entering, and threatened to break down the doors. When the fire hose was hauled out and waved threateningly…the crowd simply yelled in derision. Then somebody barked an order, and the water was poured full force into the front ranks. With the thermometer at 9 above zero, this ended the demonstration. Everyone broke for cover. As the mob disolved, many hurled stones through the multitudinous windows of the plant, while others, boiling over the lunch stands in the neighbourhood, left them wrecked and empty.
>
> *(Nevins, 1954, p.544)*

The immediate outcome of this fracas was that the company refused any longer to employ anybody who had not lived in Detroit for at least six months.

The implementation of the $5 day rendered Ford's open to the criticism that their workers would merely fritter the extra money away rather than use it for constructive purposes. To meet this criticism the company established the Sociological Department under the leadership of John R. Lee. It began with a staff of thirty but soon expanded its numbers to 150. Its central role was to undertake the investigation, counselling and instruction of Ford's employees with a view to bringing about their 'improvement'. Central to the process of 'improvement' was the inculcation of habits of prudence and economy, together with the necessary mastery of the English language, which the company construed as amounting to Americanization. At least in part the work of the Sociological Department was rendered necessary by the poor living conditions in Detroit and the backgrounds of its inhabitants. The population of the city rose rapidly during the early years of the twentieth century in response to expanding industrialisation. The promise of regular and well paid work rendered it the focus of immigration from all over Europe as well as the USA itself. Between 1910 and 1920 the population doubled from just under half a million to almost 1 million, many of the newcomers settling in their own ethnic and linguistic 'colonies'. Largely illiterate and desperately poorly housed, the immigrants were easily exploited by unscrupulous landlords and the proprietors of the city's many saloons and gambling dens. It was the Sociological Department's task to penetrate the immigrant communities, visit the homes of the company's workers, report on their welfare and, where necessary, make suggestions for improvements.

Each investigator was equipped with a car, a driver and an interpreter and was allocated a portion of the city to survey. The investigators interviewed every worker on such issues as marital status, number and age of dependants, nationality, religion and economic circumstances. All this information, together with the investigator's observations on the worker's personal habits, home conditions and neighbourhood was recorded and placed on file. On the basis of the investigators' reports every Ford employee was classified as being eligible for the $5 daily payment or not. Excessive drinking; gambling; unwholesome diet and bad personal hygiene; dirty and comfortless accommodation; inadequate family privacy through taking in too many lodgers; and too great an expenditure on foreign relatives could all result in disqualification. Workers suffering disqualification would be placed on probation and suffer financial penalties until they made the necessary improvements in their person or circumstances. Failure to meet the company's requirements within six months resulted in dismissal. However, having said this, the vast bulk of the workers succeeded in meeting the Sociological Department's requirements and even when they failed were often given a second chance.

Central to Ford's attempts to promote Americanization was the provision of English lessons for workers. The company created an English language school in May 1914 and made attendance compulsory for non-English speakers among its workforce. Classes were held before and after each shift and workers attended them for between 6 and 8 months:

> By the end of 1916, some 2,700 students were being instructed by 163 volunteer teachers...The program served several purposes in which the company was interested. It was absolutely necessary, in the long run, that all employees be able to take orders in English...In the second place, the welfare policy encouraged workers to become naturalized citizens, and for naturalization a knowledge of the language was indispensible. Federal authorities accepted a graduate of the English school as qualified for his first papers without further examination. Finally, while being taught English the workers could be indoctrinated in the ideals of the sociological department; and those who learned to read English language newspapers and magazines (including the advertisements) at once took a long step toward normal American standards of life.
>
> *(Nevins, 1954, pp.557–58)*

Critical summary

Henry Ford was the great pioneer of modern mass production. His outstanding success in combining accuracy, continuity and speed provided the necessary efficiency to enable him to reduce the price of his product whilst increasing profits. Mass production requires mass consumption and a product desirable to a mass market. In the Model T, Ford created a vehicle which exactly met the requirements of the prevailing market and for a while his company enjoyed phenomenal success. In 1913–14 Ford presided over the introduction of some of the most advanced labour policies ever implemented in large scale American industry. Nevins has compared them favourably with Robert Owen's attempts to improve the lives of his workers at New Lanark a century earlier although, to the contemporary eye, the activities of the Sociological Department appear somewhat paternalistic. Nevertheless, even Meyer, a stern critic of Henry Ford and his attempts to maintain social control in his plants, has observed that:

> the Ford Motor Company emerged in the midst of the genesis of modern management. It stood at the transition from traditional and crude forms of labor management to modern sophisticated ones. It combined the traditions of scientific management, welfare work, and personnel management…which presaged the social science approach of the Hawthorne experiments in the 1920s.
>
> *(Meyer, 1981, p.5)*

Although the Ford Motor Company only held the lead over its rivals for little more than a decade, the manufacturing techniques established by Ford remained influential, not only in the motor industry but in many other industries as well. In the event it was Henry Ford's style of leadership which proved unequal to the competition. Whereas his personal touch had been crucial in the early years it was totally inadequate for the management of a vast international enterprise. As Nevins observed 'one man control spelt danger for the Ford Motor Company' (Nevins, 1954, p.586). Nevertheless, although Ford's were overtaken by their rivals (most notably General Motors – see Chapter 13) the achievements of Henry Ford remain impressive.

Discussion questions

1. What were the advantages and disadvantages of the moving assembly track?
2. What were the three core elements of mass production?
3. To what extent was the decline in the fortunes of the Ford Motor Company during the late 1920s and 1930s a result of poor management?
4. In what ways did the introduction of the $5 day demonstrate that workers are mainly motivated by money?

Suggested reading

Ford, H. (1923) *My Life and Work*, Heinemann, London.

Meyer, S. (1981) *The Five Dollar Day: Labor Management and Social Control in the Ford Motor Company 1908–1921*, State University of New York Press, Albany.

Nevins, A. (1954) *Ford: the Times, the Man, the Company*, Charles Scribner's, New York.

Rae, J. (1959) *American Automobile Manufacturers: The First Forty Years*, Chilton, Philadelphia, chs. 7 and 10.

Chapter 10

Lyndall F. Urwick and rationalization

Lyndall Urwick was born in Malvern, England in 1891 and educated at Repton School and New College, Oxford. After graduating with a degree in history in 1913 he joined the family firm of glovemakers where he began his management training. However, with the outbreak of the First World War in 1914, he suspended his training and joined the army, subsequently winning the Military Cross. Clutterbuck and Crainer have claimed that:

> two wartime experiences proved essential in the development of his theories. He read Frederick Taylor's *Scientific Management* while in the trenches in Belgium. As a result, he began a lifetime's commitment to the principles of scientific management, although he believed that Taylor's principles were unsuited to the British industrial relations situation. The organization of the army also provided Urwick with inspiration. As an administrative staff officer, Urwick became aware of the military idea of 'staff and line', which he was later to adapt to business organization.

> *(Clutterbuck and Crainer, 1990, p.46)*

At the end of the war Urwick returned briefly to the family firm before joining the Rowntree's confectionery company in York. He worked with the social investigator and philanthropist Seebohm Rowntree, a leading advocate of advanced management thinking which combined improved working conditions for the employees with the application of the latest production techniques. Briefly, an early example of 'welfare capitalism' (see Chapter 11). From 1916 to 1918 Rowntree had been director of the Industrial Welfare Department at the Ministry of Munitions which had pioneered the application of scientific management in the British munitions industry during the war. As was noted in Chapter 8, in 1923 he succeeded his father as chairman of Rowntree's and set about reorganizing the company's York Works using the techniques of scientific management to improve productivity (Urwick, 1956, p.86). Although Urwick worked well with Rowntree, in 1928 he nevertheless 'came to the conclusion that his chances of a directorship at York were small, and left the firm' (Briggs, 1961, p.227). He joined the International Management Institute (IMI) in Geneva, becoming its director in 1929 and remaining there for the next five years. As was noted in Chapter 5, the IMI was set up in 1927 by the American retailer and philanthropist, Edward Albert Filene and was partly funded by the International Labour Organization[1]. The role of the institute was to serve as an international clearing house for the exchange of information on advanced management techniques. As its director, Urwick 'travelled widely, exchanging opinions with leading management thinkers such as Mary Parker Follett and Elton Mayo' (Clutterbuck and Crainer, 1990, p.47).

It was during his years as director of the IMI that Urwick published *The Meaning of Rationalization* which established his reputation as the leading British advocate and exponent of scientific management. However, the 1933/34 dollar crisis substantially deprived the IMI of funds, forcing it to close. Urwick returned to Britain in 1934 and took the radical step (for the time) of becoming a management consultant. As Clutterbuck and Crainer have commented he:

> established...Urwick, Orr and Partners, floated on less than £1000. By 1939 it had over 30 consultants. Orr, a Scottish engineer remained until 1945; Urwick was managing partner from 1945 to 1951 and chairman until 1961. His prophetic thinking lay behind the creation of one of the world's most prominent management consulting companies. 'Just as Shelley was the poet's poet, he seems to me to be the consultant's consultant', said Lillian Gilbreth.
>
> *(Clutterbuck and Crainer, 1990, p.47)*

During the Second World War Urwick was a consultant to the Treasury from 1940 to 1942 before joining the Petroleum Warfare Department where he held a commission as a Lieutenant Colonel. During the early post-war years he chaired the Urwick Committee which was appointed by the Minister of Education to investigate what educational facilities Britain required in order to ensure adequate training for its managers. The Committee's Report on Education for Management provided the first detailed investigation into British management training and, perhaps not surprisingly, 'concluded that Britain was seriously lacking in competent managers'.[2] During the

---

1 The International Labour Organization was established under the Treaty of Versailles with the purpose of advancing of lasting peace. Largely a British creation, and originally based in London, the ILO is charged with improving standards and conditions of work and encouraging productive employment throughout the world.
2 *The Times* 10 December 1983.

1940s and 1950s Urwick gained an international reputation as an authority on the subject of management development becoming, in 1956, advisor to the Indian government on the training of managers. In addition to consultancy work and lecturing on management issues, Urwick published widely on management topics throughout his career. In 1941 he co-edited the collected papers of Mary Parker Follett and, in 1949, wrote the introduction to Constance Storr's translation of Fayol's *General and Industrial Management*. He was also co-author of the three volume *The Making of Scientific Management* which gave the widest possible interpretation to the term 'scientific management', tracing its history back to the late eighteenth century and choosing to ignore many of the contradictions between the views of the various thinkers covered. Indeed throughout his work Urwick maintained a tone of enthusiastic advocacy for scientific management, depicting it as conducive to efficiency and prosperity, irrespective of whether an enterprise was publicly or privately owned.

In the 1960s Urwick went to live in Australia where he spent the final twenty years of his life. Scientific management became intellectually unfashionable during the 1960s and 1970s and Urwick's publications went out of print and out of mind. His contribution to management thinking was recognized in the USA (where he became the first Briton to receive the Gantt medal of the American Management Society and the American Society of Mechanical Engineers) but he was more or less forgotten in his home country. Although Urwick continued to write on management topics (developing in 1970 a theory of human behaviour which he called Theory Z – see Chapter 19) his theorizing is perhaps best seen as part of the world-wide spread of scientific management which occurred between the two world wars. Urwick died in 1983 at the advanced age of 92. As his obituarist commented, Urwick's 'contributions to the theory of management practice were influential in their day in many countries, particularly in the United States. Ironically, though a prophet of modern management techniques he was, for many years, not publicly recognized in his own country'.[3]

Urwick and the rationalization movement

At the end of the First World War the British government was justifiably hesitant about the economy. The shift from the abnormal conditions of war to a situation of peace, the run down of the munitions industries, demobilization of the armed forces and a likely growth in the level of unemployment were among the issues which, at the very least, posed considerable transitional problems. Initially the worst fears of economic dislocation, mass unemployment and wage-cutting were not justified by events. An economic boom occurred during 1919 which generated sufficient jobs to

3 *The Times* op cit.

absorb most of those leaving the forces. Further, the introduction by the government of various measures calculated to protect the most vulnerable groups of workers, avoided any tendency towards wage cutting and the re-emergence of sweated industry. However, as economic boom turned to recession during 1920 the war-expanded industries, including engineering, shipbuilding and iron and steel all experienced rapid contraction, as did cotton textiles and coalmining (both of which were hit by the collapse of the export trade). Against a background of widespread industrial unrest, organized labour was constrained to abandon long-term policies such as workers' control of industry (see Chapter 7) and concentrate instead on short-term issues such as resistance to wage cuts. Following a brief recovery in 1924 the British economy remained in the doldrums for the remainder of the 1920s with a hard core of 1 million unemployed. Unemployment, economic stagnation and a sense of national malaise stimulated a radical re-evaluation of economic and political theory in Britain and provided the context in which the rationalization movement emerged. As Hannah has explained:

> the unemployment rate rose above 10 per cent, never to fall below that figure again before the Second World War. Economic depression was…a central fact of the inter-war experience: to the labourer it meant the dole, to the employer it meant over capacity; for both it provoked a…re-evaluation of their political, social and economic beliefs and of the economic institutions they sustained…At the level of popular business philosophy, more businessmen began to question the desirability of the configuration of firms and markets which they had inherited from the pre-war era. The rationalization movement – which gained the attention of bankers, politicians and trade unionists between the wars – was an important aspect of the build up of dissatisfaction with the market mechanism and of the greater reliance on large firms for economic organization. Though the Keynesian revolution ultimately demonstrated that the malfunctioning which they witnessed also had a macro-solution, this did nothing between the wars to reduce the tenacity of the belief that the market economy was failing, and that it was the process of rationalization (essentially a micro-solution) that offered the way-out of the predicament which this posed.
>
> *(Hannah, 1976, pp.31–32)*

Although the term rationalization lacked a unitary meaning, there was nevertheless general agreement that it referred to what the politician Robert Boothby described as 'the conscious control of the production and development of industry' (Urwick, 1929, p.155). Planning, at micro –and macro–level, was to replace 'rule of thumb' methods and the vagaries of the market, thereby facilitating a closer approximation between supply and demand and the alleviation of waste. As Child has observed, 'rationalization was viewed as a quite natural extension of the principle of careful managerial regulation beyond the limited scope of individual firms to industry and distribution as a whole' (Child, 1969, p.86). In 1927 the League of Nations organized a World

Economic Conference of employers, employed and economists in Geneva. An Industrial Committee was established which produced, among other things, a series of resolutions under the title 'Rationalization' which were eventually adopted by the Conference as a whole. These resolutions defined rationalization as:

> the methods of technique and of organization designed to secure the minimum waste of either effort or material. They include the scientific organization of labour, standardization of both materials and products, simplification of processes, and improvements in the system of transport and marketing (and they recommended) that Governments, public institutions, and the general public should influence producers to direct their efforts along the channels described…and diffuse in every quarter a clear understanding of the advantages and obligations involved by rationalization and scientific management, and of the possibilities of their gradual application.
>
> *(Urwick, 1929, pp.154 and v)*

Following the World Economic Conference a meeting of interested parties was convened to examine the relevance of rationalization to the industrial situation in the UK. As a result of this meeting a committee of industrialists, engineers and academics was set up with a view to collecting evidence and producing a report on the matter. Urwick became a member of this committee by dint of his role as honorary secretary of the Management Research Groups. In the event it fell to him to produce an account of the committee's work which was published as *The Meaning of Rationalization* in 1929.

The heart of Urwick's book was the extended chapter on scientific management and its early development in the United States and beyond. Urwick described scientific management as being 'the aspect of rationalization which is of the most direct interest to the individual employer in dealing with the problems of the single business concern' (Urwick, 1929, p.54). He began by giving a brief exposition of F. W. Taylor's work (see Chapter 2) and the resistance to its application in the UK. However, he went on to note the acceptance of scientific management as a result of the production needs generated by the First World War and the official recognition given to Taylor's work by the Ministry of Munitions. Urwick was, of course, concerned with the benefits to be gained by the appropriate use of work study techniques. As he put it 'the conceptions underlying scientific management can be usefully employed in every direction where organized human effort calls for direction and control. That they should spread into every corner of business activity is in direct accord with the general intellectual tendencies of the time, and inherently in line with the march of events' (Urwick, 1929, p.77). However, he placed even greater emphasis on the advantages for industrial society as a whole to be gained from Taylor's 'mental revolution' which Urwick construed as instigating not merely the replacement of 'rule of thumb' by planning but the triumph of science and reason over habit and prejudice.

Rationalization and unemployment

Britain's economy suffered badly in the aftermath of the Wall Street Crash of October 1929. Britain's total exports fell from £839 million in 1929 to £461 million in 1931. From 1931 to 1935 the number of unemployed remained above the 2 million mark and during the worst period of the recession (i.e. the winter of 1932–33) almost 3 million people were out of work – a quarter of the insured working population. Although economic recovery began after 1933 it was slow and the percentage of unemployed workers was still over 10 per cent in 1939 (Vickerstaff and Sheldrake, 1989, pp.27–28). The incidence of unemployment was unevenly distributed throughout the country. As Pimlott has observed 'areas of expanding industry...suffered relatively little (but) where the old, declining industries – coal, iron and steel, engineering, shipbuilding, textiles – were concentrated, a bad situation became suddenly, dramatically worse, and worklessness and the dole became a way of life' (Pimlott, 1986, p.10). Such was the impact of long-term unemployment on the national consciousness that a potent myth of the inter-war years as a period of unmitigated misery was born and has persisted. In such a situation the arguments for rationalization, including the replacement of obsolescent equipment and the displacement of workers in the interests of efficiency, became readily associated with the creation of greater levels of unemployment. As Booth and Pack have observed there was a:

> widely held view in the trade union movement that rationalization, whether in the form of industrial reorganization by amalgamation or of the introduction of new techniques and machinery, had resulted simultaneously in increased output and the displacement of labour. The Trades Union Congress therefore demanded that the new developments in industrial efficiency should be used to improve the conditions of labour in the affected branches of production, rather than create employment.
>
> *(Booth and Pack, 1985, p.106)*

Individuals such as Urwick who continued to advocate rationalization were placed on the defensive. In 1938, in an article in the *British Management Review* he challenged the notion that rationalization might be a cause of long-term unemployment, claiming that 'there is a good deal of evidence that over all and in the long run it increases the volume of employment' (Urwick, 1938, p.29).

   In his defence of rationalization Urwick deployed similar arguments to those used by F. W. Taylor before the Special House Committee some 35 years earlier (see Chapter 2). Although a minority of displaced workers might be disadvantaged in the short-term, improved efficiency would stimulate economic activity and growth leading to greater benefits for the majority. In any case, Urwick argued, managers could not afford to shrink from the prospect of change in the hope that problems would merely go away. As he put it:

management must recognize its responsibility, not only to its shareholders and consumers, but to its workers and the community, to maintain the enterprise for which it is accountable at the maximum economic effectiveness. Whatever the objections to the system, we live in a competitive world. And however painful and difficult constant readjustments may be, it is our bounden duty to face them, whenever they are necessary to improve the relative position of our undertaking. Because we may be quite certain that if we do not adopt improvements, others will. And the consequences of a weakening of our competitive position are likely to be far more serious for those dependent on the economic success of the company, than any consequences which will accrue from readjustment.

(Urwick, 1938, p.23)

Urwick did not advocate a callous approach by management with regard to questions of staff reductions. On the contrary he called for the greatest tact, sympathy and, where possible, support such as re-training. Nevertheless he believed that management must above all show leadership whatever the short-term difficulties and however burdensome the task. As he observed 'we have assumed the responsibilities of management. And, having assumed those responsibilities...we cannot do less than face them fairly to the best of our ability. One of the first responsibilities is to lead those dependent on us to face squarely and in time the changes of a changing world' (Urwick, 1938, p.30).

Critical summary

Lyndall Urwick was arguably Britain's foremost management thinker. His many works included the consideration of such issues as leadership and, as has been seen, rationalization. However, perhaps his most significant contributions were as an interpreter of the work of others, rather than as an original thinker in his own right. In particular he succeeded in publicising the ideas of Taylor, Fayol and Follett to a trans-Atlantic audience.

Discuss questions

1. How would you account for the emergence of planning in all its forms during the inter-war years?
2. In what ways was rationalization linked to scientific management?
3. How convincing was Urwick's argument that rationalization would create jobs rather than destroy them?
4. Why did Urwick consider that managers must, above all things, provide leadership?

Suggested reading

Booth, A. and Pack, M. (1985) *Employment, Capital and Economic Policy: Great Britain 1918–1939*, Basil Blackwell, Oxford.

Child, J. (1969) *British Management Thought: A Critical Analysis*, Allen & Unwin, London.

Gulick, L. and Urwick, L. (eds) (1937) *Papers on the Science of Administration*, Institute of Public Administration, Columbia University, New York.

Hannah, L. (1976) *The Rise of the Corporate Economy*, Methuen, London, ch.3.

Urwick, L. (1929) *The Meaning of Rationalization*, Nisbet, London.

Urwick, L. (1938) Rationalization. *British Management Review*, **3** 13–30.

Urwick, L. (ed) (1956) *The Golden Book of Management*, Newman Neane, London.

Vickerstaff, S. and Sheldrake, J. (1989) *The Limits of Corporatism: The British Experience in the Twentieth Century*, Avebury, Aldershot, ch.3.

Chapter 11

Elton Mayo and the Hawthorne experiments

George Elton Mayo was born in Adelaide, the capital of South Australia, in December 1880. Mayo's paternal grandfather became the leading surgeon in South Australia, a Fellow of the Royal College of Surgeons, a lieutenant colonel in the Adelaide Regiment and a pillar of the local community. Mayo's father, while not achieving great social or professional prominence, nevertheless enjoyed sufficient success in the real estate business to provide his wife and several children with a comfortable, middle class life style. Mayo's early education was provided at home by a governess and it was not until the age of 12 that he was sent to Queen's School in North Adelaide where he remained for the next three years. Between 1896 and 1898 he studied at St Peter's College, a private school for Christian gentlemen, of which his grandfather had been a co-founder and where his father had also studied. Mayo's parents were ambitious for their children and they strongly encouraged him to study medicine. Accordingly, in 1899, he became a medical student at the University of Adelaide. The course lasted five years and at the end of his first year Mayo did well in the examinations, sharing top place with two others. However, at the end of his second year he failed his examinations and was required to leave Adelaide, his parents sending him to Scotland where he resumed his medical studies at Edinburgh University. In 1901 he left Scotland and entered the small medical school at St George's Hospital in London. He also enrolled to take the joint examinations of the Royal College of Physicians and the Royal College of Surgeons. In spite of all this, however, by 1903 Mayo's enthusiasm for medicine had become minimal and he only continued his studies for fear of disappointing his parents and losing face among his peers in South Australia. Eventually his distaste for the subject became so great that, in December 1903, he finally abandoned medicine and persuaded his father to pay him a small allowance while he sought an alternative career. In the event he joined the Ashanti Mining Company, which mined gold in Obuassi, West Africa. Both his grandfather and father before him had embarked on youthful adventures before settling in their chosen professions and to some extent therefore Mayo was continuing a tradition. Unfortunately, to his bitter disappointment, his health failed and he was forced to return to England in March 1904.

Mayo returned to South Australia in 1905 and worked in a printing firm where his parents had acquired a partnership for him. In 1907 he resumed his university studies, this time reading philosophy and psychology, and eventually graduating in 1911. He decided to pursue an academic career and obtained a foundation lectureship in logic, psychology and ethics at the newly established University of Queensland in Brisbane. Mayo enjoyed considerable success at Queensland, becoming lecturer in charge of the Department of Philosophy and marrying into one of the state's prominent families. In 1919 he published *Democracy and Freedom* a monograph on the political problems of industrial society, in which he criticized the contemporary system of representative democracy based on parties. Deploying insights from the psychologists Sigmund Freud and Carl Jung he argued that politicians 'stimulate unconscious emotional fears . . . attach them to social and industrial problems, and then profess the cure' (Trahair, 1984, p.97). Not for the last time in his writings, he was at pains to emphasize the elements that bind a society together rather than those which divide it. Party politics, he argued, through their artificially stimulated conflicts, are inevitably divisive and can deliver neither social harmony nor individual autonomy (Mayo, 1919, p.20). In order for democracy to be constructive rather than destructive there is a need for political education and enlightened leadership so that rational thought and understanding might replace irrationality and prejudice. Antagonism towards all things tending to political conflict, together with the desire to achieve social harmony, became constant themes in Mayo's work. For example, in his essay *Modernization of a Primitive Community*, produced in 1947, he observed that 'a society is a co-operative system; a civilized society is one in which the co-operation is based on understanding and the will to work together' (Mayo, 1949, p.115). In the years between the production of these two works Mayo increasingly depicted the workplace as the focus of individual identity and the key to social cohesion.

In spite of his professional and personal successes in Brisbane, Mayo was not satisfied with his situation. As Gillespie has commented:

Mayo found the atmosphere in sub-tropical Brisbane physically and intellectually stifling; throughout his 11 years there he constantly sought means of escape, either back to England or to a position in Melbourne or Sydney. At the end of 1921, failing to find alternative employment, he took one year's leave from the university (although he had little intention of returning to Brisbane). He spent several months in Melbourne and then set sail for the United States, arriving in San Francisco in August 1922, now 42 years old.

(Gillespie, 1991, p.97)

Mayo arrived in the United States with some letters of introduction and just £50 in cash. Given his financial situation he was constrained to take employment in a variety of jobs, ranging from university research to personnel work for Standard Oil. His best opening, however, came when he met Vernon Kellogg, the secretary of the National Research Council (NRC). Kellogg was intrigued by Mayo's views on industrial relations and proposed that Mayo should visit him in Washington for further discussions. Once in Washington Mayo was at pains to impress the leaders of the NRC and also the recently formed Personnel Research Foundation which operated under its auspices. He succeeded in presenting himself as a man untramelled by disciplinary boundaries and thus able to operate beyond the conventional categories of psychology, psychiatry and sociology. Mayo travelled on to New York where he met, and impressed, Beardsley Ruml the director of the Laura Spelman Rockefeller Memorial foundation. The recently appointed Ruml was eager to promote research in the social sciences and considered Mayo's ideas for promoting industrial harmony as suitable for funding. Ruml succeeded in obtaining a temporary research post for Mayo in the University of Pennsylvania's Department of Industrial Research in Philadelphia where he began work in the beginning of 1923.

In Philadelphia Mayo began referring to his ideas on industrial psychology as 'psychopathology', thereby associating his work with that of Freud and Jung and also the growing mental hygiene movement. He depicted industrial conflict as deriving from psychological rather than economic causes. Thus:

> every individual suffered from irrationalities and reveries, which, while they did not affect the well integrated individual, might interact with the reveries of others to cause a 'breakdown' in industry or society. Strikes and the political disturbances of mass democracy therefore were not rational attempts to gain an increase in wages or the acceptance of a political programme. They were expressions of underlying reveries, and it was these reveries that had to be addressed, not the political demands or 'symptoms'.

> *(Gillespie, 1991, pp.104–5)*

If this explanation of industrial conflict was correct then presumably the psycho-pathologist could improve labour relations by diagnosis and therapy. At Continental Mills, makers of woollen fabrics, Mayo had the opportunity to turn theory into practice when he was invited to investigate the high level of labour turnover in the spinning department. He found that although working conditions in the department were poor, they were no worse than those in other parts of the plant and did not therefore explain the huge disparity in turnover. Mayo claimed that the problem stemmed from the awkward posture which the spinners were forced to adopt in order to carry out their work. He further claimed that the physical fatigue the spinners suffered influenced their mental state giving rise to pessimistic reveries and leading to poor levels of productivity and high labour turnover. Mayo's proposed remedy for the problem was simple enough consisting of the institution of rest periods in order to reduce the level of fatigue and enable the workers to come out of their reveries and relax. Of course, there was nothing particularly novel in the notion of rest breaks. F. W. Taylor, for example, had introduced them at Simonds Rolling Machine Company (see Chapter 2). Further, the Gilbreths had investigated fatigue and there also existed 'a substantial body of literature on industrial fatigue written by physiologists and psychologists in the United States, Britain and Germany (and) in particular . . . the reports of the British Industrial Fatigue Research Board' (Gillespie, 1991, p.108). However, in claiming a definite link between fatigue and pessimistic reveries, Mayo was going beyond experimental evidence into the realms of mere speculation. Not for the last time he claimed rather more for his work than his research results justified and it is worth bearing in mind Trahair's caution that 'Mayo was not interested in the niceties of research design or the techniques and procedures of data collection or analysis' (Trahair, 1984, p.352). Nevertheless, in the case of Continental Mills he did succeed in reducing labour turnover and improving productivity and the results were sufficiently impressive to prompt Ruml to recommend that Rockefeller fund Mayo's research for the next three years. In September 1926 Mayo was appointed associate professor and head of the Industrial Research Department in the Harvard Business School. The post, to be fully funded by the Laura Spelman Rockefeller Memorial foundation, was initially for a five year period but in the event Mayo remained at Harvard until his retirement in 1947. Although Elton Mayo had lived in the United States for many years and was Australian by birth, he considered England to be his home. Following his retirement from Harvard he and his wife lived in a private apartment in the National Trust's manor house, Polesden Lacey, near Guildford in Surrey where he died in 1949. Of course, Mayo's reputation, one might almost say fame, rests on his association with the Hawthorne experiments and it is to a consideration of these that we now turn.

The Hawthorne experiments

In *Manufacturing Knowledge*, his history of the Hawthorne experiments, Richard Gillespie observes that:

> although it is now more than half a century since they were conducted (they) are still among the most frequently cited and most controversial experiments in the social sciences. Generations of students in the social sciences have committed to memory the findings of the experiments. They are acclaimed as a landmark study in both sociology and psychology and have acquired the status of a creation myth in such sub-disciplines as industrial sociology, the social psychology of work, industrial psychiatry, and the anthropology of work. Surveys of the key developments in organization and management theory consistently note the seminal contribution of the experiments to their field.

> *(Gillespie, 1991, p.1)*

Without doubt the perceived significance of the experiments is at least partially due to Elton Mayo's ability as a publicist and his use of them for propaganda purposes in support of his views on industrial society. As Rose has commented in this context, Mayo 'was a natural communicator with a flair for propaganda' (Rose, 1988, p.122). Certainly consideration of the Hawthorne experiments figures prominently in Mayo's two major works *The Human Problems of an Industrial Civilization* (1933) and *The Social Problems of an Industrial Civilization* (1949). However, Mayo's purpose in the essays contained in these books was less concerned with exposition than with interpretation on the basis of his pre-conceived prejudices. Again, in the words of Rose, 'at no time in his life did Mayo show either the patience or scepticism which most social research demands . . . his treatment of the Hawthorne material . . . was thoroughly uncritical' (Rose, 1988, p.122). Indeed the classic accounts of the Hawthorne experiments are not to be found in the writings of Mayo himself but in Whitehead's *The Industrial Worker: A Statistical Study of Human Relations in a Group of Manual Workers* (1938) and F. J. Roethlisberger and William J. Dickson's *Management and the Worker: An Account of a Research Program Conducted by the Western Electric Company, Hawthorne Works, Chicago* (1939).

The Hawthorne experiments were conducted at the Hawthorne Works of the Western Electric Company in Chicago between 1927 and 1932. Western Electric was the manufacturing subsidiary of the American Telephone and Telegraph Company and the Hawthorne Works was an example of advanced American industrial production. Organization of the production processes was based on the application of the scientific management and mass production methods pioneered by F. W. Taylor and Henry Ford. However, these were tempered by an enlightened approach to personnel management that can be characterized as 'welfare capitalism'. Briefly this was an attempt to reduce worker dissatisfaction and resist trade union influence by the putting in place of a paternalistic package of social and recreational benefits calculated to sustain workers' loyalty. The package of benefits at the Hawthorne Works was, by contemporary international standards, impressive and included a pension scheme, sickness and disability benefits, a share purchase plan, a system of worker representation, a medical department and hospital. Further:

in 1921 an athletic field consisting of six baseball diamonds, thirteen tennis courts, and a running track was constructed; and in 1927 the Albright Gymnasium was built in memory of the first factory superintendent. The Hawthorne Club...organized social activities, vacations, sports competitions (including a baseball league, gun, golf, and swimming clubs, and a women's basketball team called the 'Ruthless Babes'), evening classes, a club store, a savings and loan association, and even beauty contests...All these activities were co-ordinated through the *Hawthorne Microphone*, a bi-monthly magazine combining factory and company news with social activities and paternalistic messages from works managers.

(Gillespie, 1991, pp.19 and 20)

At the time the Hawthorne experiments were started there were almost 30 000 workers employed at the plant, many of whom were immigrants including Czech Poles, Italians and Germans.

The Hawthorne experiments had their origins in a series of tests on the appropriate intensity for industrial lighting. At the end of the nineteenth century a struggle took place concerning the comparative efficiency of gas and electric lighting which was ultimately resolved in favour of the latter. The introduction of tungsten lamps to replace the less efficient carbon lamps enabled industrial users to obtain similar levels of illumination using less electricity. The electricity companies, fearing that their revenues would be threatened by this trend, began to campaign for increased levels of industrial lighting as a means of sustaining demand. In 1918, as Wrege has observed, 'these campaigns were replaced by industrial illumination tests sponsored by the electric industry, which continually indicated that more illumination increased productivity' (Wrege, 1976, p.12). Not surprisingly managers were sceptical about the validity of the results of these tests. In 1923 the General Electric company proposed that an extensive programme of research on industrial illumination should be carried out under the auspices of the National Research Council. This proposal led directly to the establishment of the Committee on Industrial Lighting which was chaired by D. C. Jackson, professor of electrical engineering at the Massachusetts Institute of Technology (MIT), and had Thomas A. Edison, the father of the electricity industry, in the symbolic position of honorary chairman. Although electrical manufacturers and utilities would finance the research they would be distanced from its actual conduct and unable to influence its results. As Gillespie has commented 'by channeling the research through a public organization such as the NRC and attaching Edison's prestige to the research, the electrical industry was seeking to ensure that the research would be viewed as disinterested and objective' (Gillespie, 1991, p.39).

However, notwithstanding the desire for objectivity, Western Electric had close connections with the NRC through their vice-president of research, Frank B. Jewett who chaired the NRC's Division of Engineering and Industrial Research. Jewett approached Clarence G. Stoll, the works superintendent of Western Electric's Hawthorne Works, and secured his agreement to allow some of the Committee on Industrial Lightings illumination tests to be carried out at the plant. Stoll also agreed that Western Electric would bear the costs of installing the necessary lighting equipment, together with the maintenance of production records. The Committee on Industrial Lighting enthusiastically accepted Stoll's offer and illumination tests commenced at the Hawthorne Works in November 1924 and continued intermittently until April 1927. The tests were supervised by Charles E. Snow, a recent graduate of MIT and a protégé of Professor D. C. Jackson. Snow was assisted by Homer Hibarger (a

Hawthorne piecerate analyser) and supported by works superintendent Stoll and technical superintendent George Pennock. Commenting on the team which carried out the Hawthorne Illumination Tests (HIT) Gillespie has discounted any suggestion of naivety on their part observing that Stoll and Pennock were:

> both members of the general directive board of the Committee on Industrial Lighting...(while) at MIT Jackson was assisted by Joseph W. Barker, an electrical engineer who acted as chief research assistant to the entire industrial lighting programme, and Vannevar Bush, a professor of electrical engineering who would go on to become one of the most (eminent) scientists in the United States and director of scientific research during the Second World War. The Hawthorne lighting tests were thus controlled by an elite group of academic and industrial engineers.
>
> *(Gillespie, 1991, p.42)*

The HIT results for the first series of experiments carried out between November 1924 and April 1925 showed no direct relationship between the intensity of illumination and the rate of output. Although levels of output had indeed improved among the groups tested, the researchers suspected that this was due to factors ancillary to the illumination tests such as the inevitable increase in the level of supervision. When the tests were resumed in February 1926, therefore, the experimentors sought to make allowance for the influence of non-experimental variables (the so-called 'Hawthorne effect') by isolating any ancillary factors affecting output. The results from this set of tests confirmed the experimentors suspicions that the effects of increased supervision, together with psychological factors relating to work under test conditions, were of far greater moment in improving output than levels of illumination. As Gillespie has observed 'in contrast to the inflated claims of the lighting industry, the researchers concluded that no increase in production could be definitely credited to the illumination increases. Medium levels of lighting...seemed sufficient for regular tasks; any higher levels could not be expected to return their investment' (Gillespie, 1991, p.43).

Having satisfied themselves that securing improvements in output was not a matter of merely increasing the levels of illumination, the experimentors turned their attention to the impact on productivity of reducing illumination levels. Between September 1926 and April 1927 a series of experiments were carried out in order to measure the effect on output of low levels of artificial lighting. Natural lighting was therefore excluded from the test rooms where the experiments were conducted. Two groups of workers were selected, one of which acted as a control group working under a steady illumination of 11 foot-candles. Meanwhile, a test group was subjected to progressively lower levels of lighting, the level reducing steadily from 11 foot-candles down to 1.4 foot-candles, at which point the workers complained bitterly about the lack of light. As the experimentors had expected, the output of both groups improved, the test group out-performing the control group in spite of the reduced levels of illumination. Failure to show a positive correlation between increased levels of illumination and improved output was disappointing to the electricity industry. Further, the information on the significance of supervision gathered as a result of the HIT was of little or no interest to the Committee on Industrial Lighting. However, to the team of scientists and engineers directly involved in the HIT the results pointed the direction for further research way beyond the narrow confines of illumination. As Wrege has noted:

> Between April 11 and April 15 Hibarger reviewed the results of ...the 1926–27 HIT...his conclusions were: 1. Illumination intensity had a minor influence on a worker's output. 2. Supervision had an effect, yet unknown on output. (He also) raised three questions: 1. If worker output increased under low levels of illumination, why didn't it increase under shop conditions (were they restricting output?). 2. If fatigue was surveyed and the findings systematically applied to the group, would output increase? 3. If workers were placed in a small room... and their habits carefully studied, could reasons for increased/decreased output be ascertained? Hibarger reported these observations to Pennock stating that at a modest cost he could ascertain what influenced employee output...Pennock approved this plan and on May 10 1927...initiated the first stages of the Relay Assembly Test Room (experiments) based on procedures devised by Snow.
>
> *(Wrege, 1976, p.15)*

Thus although the HIT were now concluded what were to become known as the Hawthorne experiments were about to begin.

Relay assembly was selected for study because it involved the type of extreme repetitive work with which fatigue was most commonly associated. In order to be proficient a relay assembler needed manual dexterity and also the capacity to repeat the same operation for almost every minute of a nine hour day for five and a half days a week. As Gillespie has observed:

> the assembly of a relay required the simultaneous use of both hands to place pins, bushings, springs, terminals, and insulators between plates, insert a coil and armature, then screw the assembly together. A motion analysis of the operations required to put together the 32 parts of a R-1498 relay identified 32 separate operations for each hand.
>
> *(Gillespie, 1991, p.51)*

Six young women were selected to take part in the Relay Assembly Test Room (RATR) experiments, ranging in age from 15 to 28. They were drawn from the ethnic communities of Chicago, the four youngest from the local Polish community, one from a Bohemian family and the eldest a Norwegian who had arrived in the United States some three years before. The young women were all working in order to provide additional income for their families as well as financial independence for themselves until they married. Prior to entering the test room the women's individual production levels were monitored in order to provide a yardstick for anticipated output in the

RATR. Further, the women were invited to technical superintendent Pennock's office where 'the purpose of the study was carefully explained to them, their comments were sought and some changes made in the experimentor's plans as a result' (Landsberger, 1958, p.9). Work began in the test room during May 1927 and continued until June 1932. From June 1927 the women were placed on a special group rate of bonus which effectively marked them off from their peers in the main workshop by providing access to higher levels of earnings. In the RATR five relay assemblers sat side by side at a bench while a sixth worker (the layout operator) sat along side them preparing trays of parts for the others to assemble. Each completed relay was dropped down a shute in the bench, triggering a device which recorded output by punching a hole in a moving paper tape. Homer Hibarger sat in the test room combining the dual role of supervisor and scientific observer, responsible both for maintaining the flow of materials and monitoring output. Part of Hibarger's task was 'to create and maintain a friendly atmosphere in the test room' (Roethlisberger and Dickson, 1939/1964, p.22). In August 1927 rest periods were introduced signalling the beginning of a series of changes in the women's work routine that included the provision of free snacks, a shorter working day and a reduced working week.

Although often referred to in patronising terms as 'girls' the women workers involved in the RATR experiments were by no means mere passive recipients of the changes in work patterns introduced by the investigators. Prior to each stage in the experiments the women were involved in discussions with Hibarger and his colleagues in Pennock's office. The women were well aware of their unique status in the works and this was enhanced by the regular medical examinations that were instituted as part of the monitoring of the women's mental and physical welfare. Young, semi-skilled female production workers at the Hawthorne Works, or anywhere else for that matter, were not normally consulted about issues relating to their work and welfare. Further, the relationship of the women to the higher managers involved in the experiments meant that the women could more or less ignore the customary discipline imposed by first line supervisors. As Gillespie has commented:

> privileged status and a modicum of control over work days brought about a strong identification with the test room among the workers. At their own initiative they requested prints of a photograph taken of the test room and its occupants...In time the friendly and co-operative Homer Hibarger became 'Hi' ...With the introduction of refreshments during the morning rest period, the women's status soared higher still.
>
> *(Gillespie, 1991, p.59)*

Nevertheless everything did not run smoothly in the RATR and confrontations soon occurred between two of the women, Adeline Bogatowicz and Irene Rybacki, and the experimentors concerning the issue of talking. Talking was prohibited during working hours in the main workshops but, in the relaxed atmosphere of the small group situation of the RATR, it became almost impossible to prevent. Attempts by the experimentors to stop what they saw as excessive talking, or to make a record of the conversations, prompted threats from Bogatowicz and Rybacki to go on strike. As relations between the two women and Hibarger and Pennock continued to deteriorate, Rybacki became particularly strident about criticisms of her work and behaviour. On his part, Pennock did not relish being answered back by a very junior member of his staff. Briefly, the experimentors' declared objective of maintaining worker co-operation without sanctions was not viable if the individual worker's temperament proved insufficiently compliant. Ultimately, in January 1928, 'the showdown came when Hibarger obtained some direct evidence that Bogatowicz was restricting output' (Gillespie, 1991, p.61). Bogatowicz and her close friend Rybacki were removed from the RATR and replaced by Mary Volango, an 18 year old Polish woman, and Jennie Sirchio, a 20 year old Italian. The replacement of the two women had a dramatic effect on production in the test room. As Gillespie has observed:

> output in periods 2 through 7, covering 37 weeks, had risen 12.3 per cent over the starting level; now, in the 7 weeks of period 8, it jumped a further 12 per cent. There appear to be two reasons for this extraordinary change. First, the two new workers were much faster than the women they replaced...Second, the removal of the two women constituted an explicit threat to the remaining workers of their own removal from the privileged conditions of the test room...Sirchio...quickly took on the role of leader, even driver, of the team.
>
> *(Gillespie, 1991, p.63)*

By June 1929 output in the RATR was 30 per cent higher than the base period started in May 1927 (Rose, 1988, p.108). Meanwhile, a further series of experiments had been started including a Second Relay Assembly Group (which ran from August 1928 to March 1929) where five relay assemblers were placed in a special room, paid a group rate, but not given rest periods; a Mica Splitting Group (which ran from October 1928 to September 1930) where an attempt was made to parallel the RATR, with similar changes, but using an individual piecework payment system; and a Typewriting Group (which ran briefly during February 1929) where women typists were paid a weekly salary with increases based primarily on output; output being determined by an automatic recording device on the typewriter indicating the number of keys struck. Further, a plant-wide interview programme began in September 1928 and continued until 1930. Initially the interviews were formal and relatively structured in nature 'gradually, however, a more open-ended approach to interviewing emerged. Respondents were allowed to talk about those issues which pre-occupied them (and), an interviewing technique close to therapeutic counselling was devised to explore these "social sentiments" in depth' (Rose, 1988, p.111). Finally, in November 1931 a study was established by W. Lloyd Warner, an industrial anthropologist from Harvard, which aimed to parallel the RATR but using men. This study, the Bank Wiring Observation Room, monitored the social relations of 14 male workers involved in the wiring, soldering and inspection of banks of telephone switch gear. As Greenwood,

Bolton and Greenwood have observed 'it became a sociological study, often reported in the literature for its study of the action of cliques as they developed in this industrial environment' (Greenwood, Bolton and Greenwoood, 1983, p.230).

Mayo and the Hawthorne experiments

In March 1928 T. K. Stevenson, director of personnel at Western Electric, sent Elton Mayo an interim report of the results of the experiments conducted in the RATR. Stevenson 'had been impressed by a speech Mayo had given five months previously to a luncheon of personnel directors from large corporations entitled *What Psychology Can Do for Industry in the Next Ten Years* (Gillespie, 1991, p.70). Mayo read the report with interest and arranged to visit the Hawthorne plant in April 1928, accompanied by his assistant, Emily Osborne. As well as wishing to scrutinize the RATR at first hand, Mayo also wanted to carry out a series of blood pressure measurements on the workers as part of his study of industrial fatigue. His interest in blood pressure had been stimulated by his association with a Harvard colleague, Lawrence Henderson, who held the Lowell Professorship of Chemistry there and had written a book on the subject of blood. Henderson was at this time in the process of absorbing the sociological writings of Vilfredo Pareto. In the early 1930s he established a seminar at Harvard known as the 'Pareto Circle' which included Mayo and was highly influential in the development of management theory (see Chapter 12). During their visit to the Hawthorne Works Mayo and his assistant took the blood pressure and pulse rate measurements of the five relay assemblers in the RATR and also of three women in the Coil Winding Department. Although the measurements did indicate some correlation between the provision of rest periods and the improvements in production in the RATR they were by no means conclusive. On one issue, however, Mayo did feel able to speak with certainty. While examining the medical record of Irene Rybacki he noticed that she was anaemic and he had no hesitation in citing this as the reason for what he termed her 'paranoid' and 'bolshevik' behaviour. Mayo conveniently ignored the case of Adeline Bogatowicz whose blood counts were normal. As Gillespie has commented 'Mayo's account of Rybacki's removal from the test room demonstrates a persistent tendency in (his) work to transform any challenge by workers of managerial control into evidence of psychotic disturbance.' (Gillespie, 1991, p.73).

Mayo spent the summer of 1928 in Britain where he was able to scrutinize the recent work of the Industrial Fatigue Research Board. When he visited the Hawthorne Works again in October 1928 to take further blood pressure readings he was approached by technical superintendent George Pennock and asked to give a presentation on the experiments to a meeting of personnel directors of corporations in New York. The presentation was a success and, early in 1929, Pennock offered Mayo the role of director of the Hawthorne interview programme. Mayo refused, offering instead to maintain his connection with the experiments by making the occasional visit to the

Hawthorne Works and providing expert advice as necessary. From 1929 to 1933 Mayo received an annual retainer of $2 500 from Western Electric and increasingly filled the role of official interpreter of the Hawthorne experiments to the academic world. In the words of Gillespie:

> Mayo was able to orchestrate the writing of the official accounts and the popularization of the experiments by drawing on the institutional and academic resources of Harvard and the financial resources of his Rockefeller grant. Whereas the development of the research had always been under the control of the company researchers, with the academics only advising the researchers, publication came under the control of Mayo and his Harvard colleagues, a shift that had a significant impact on the type of knowledge produced and on its subsequent influence.
>
> *(Gillespie, 1991, p.75)*

In December 1931 Mayo gained the approval of Clarence Stoll (by now the vice-president of Western Electric) to write an official account of the Hawthorne experiments. The outcome was *The Human Problems of an Industrial Civilization* published in 1933. The book, consisting of eight chapters originally given as Lowell Lectures at Harvard, did not provide a continuous narrative of the Hawthorne experiments. Instead, in the brief compass of 180 pages, it addressed the much broader question of how social equilibrium might be achieved and maintained in industrial society. In the first two chapters Mayo examined the subject of fatigue and monotony, claiming that both phenomena sprang from 'a disequilibrium within the individual and between him and his work' rather than from the nature of the work itself. Apparently boring tasks could be rendered satisfying if the work were to be organized so as to remove any imbalance in workers' psychological adjustment. The next three chapters of the book were devoted to an interpretation of the Hawthorne experiments which placed the maximum emphasis on the correlation between the vastly improved levels of output in the RATR and the development of a highly cohesive working group operating under a managerial regime that was both enlightened and supportive. In making his interpretation Mayo chose to discount the significance of financial incentives which on the face of it was an odd oversight. In many ways the women in the RATR were as 'hungry' as the labourers in the yard at Bethlehem Steel and the immigrant workers at the gates of Ford's Highland Park plant. Certainly when a team of academics interviewed some of the surviving participants in the RATR experiments during the 1980s, they had no hesitation in confirming that money was the major source of their motivation (Greenwood, Bolton and Greenwood, 1983, pp.217–221).

In chapter 6 of his book Mayo significantly widened the scope of his study, moving from the narrow confines of the Hawthorne Works to industrial society at large. In particular he was concerned with the breakdown of community as a result of rapid urbanization and industrialization and the resultant high incidence of delinquency and crime. Observing that the two were intimately connected, Mayo turned for an initial explanation to the work of the French sociologist, Emile Durkheim, and his concept of anomie. As Mayo put it, Durkheim's:

> central claim is, first, that a small society lives in an ordered manner such that the interests of its members are subordinated to the group…an individual (is) born as a member of the community (and) can, during infancy and adolescence, see ahead of him the function he will unquestionably fulfil for the group when he is adult. This anticipation regulates his thought and action in the developing years and in adulthood culminates in satisfaction and a sense of function for, and necessity to, the society. He is throughout his life solidaire with the group. Modern development…has brought to an end this life of satisfactory function for the individual and the group. We are facing a condition of anomie, of planlessness in living, which is becoming characteristic both of individual lives and of communities…individuals increasingly are lapsing into restless movement, planless self-development – a method of living which defeats itself because achievement has no longer any criterion of value; happiness always lies beyond any present achievement. Defeat takes the form of ultimate disillusion – a disgust with the 'futility of endless pursuit'.
>
> *(Mayo, 1933/1960, pp.124–25)*

In addition to Durkheim's work Mayo also appropriated insights from the work of Sigmund Freud claiming that 'the maladjustment of the neurotic is a social maladjustment; neurotic disability is not an individual but a social problem . . . any social situation which shows extensive disorganization will also show a higher tendency to obsession in its individual members than an ordered society' (Mayo, 1933/1960, pp.127–8).

In the last two chapters of his book Mayo returned to the problems of maintaining social equilibrium that he had examined previously in *Democracy and Freedom*. Drawing on insights derived from political theory, anthropology, sociology and child psychology he claimed that the development of modern industrial society had 'brought relative annihilation to the cultural traditions of work and craftsmanship (whilst) the development of a high labor mobility and a clash of cultures has seriously damaged the traditional routine of intimate and family life. Generally the effect has been to induce everywhere a degree of social disorganization' (Mayo, 1933/1960, p.159). Political action alone, he observed, could never restore the social harmony of earlier times. As he put it, 'political action in a given community presumes the desire and capacity of individuals to work together; the political function cannot operate in a community from which this capacity has disappeared' (Mayo, 1933/1960, p.160). How then might social harmony be restored and individuals freed from the feelings of anomie that characterized contemporary life? Partly at least the answer was to be found in the workplace and its proper ordering in accordance with the insights provided by the Hawthorne experiments. The vastly increased levels of production achieved in the RATR had demonstrated the beneficial impact of group cohesiveness under enlightened supervision. Deploying Pareto's elite theory Mayo claimed that the existing managerial elite were preoccupied with technical and economic considerations. However, contrary to the claims of the scientific managers, 'the industrial worker...does not want to develop a blackboard logic which shall guide his method of life and work. What he wants is more nearly described as, first, a method of living in social relationship with other people and, second, as part of this an economic function for and value to the group. The whole of this most important aspect of human nature we have recklessly disregarded in our "triumphant" industrial progress' (Mayo, 1933/1960, p.173). Above all, for Mayo, the Hawthorne experiments had demonstrated that the industrial managers of the future had a significant role to play in restoring social equilibrium and should therefore be educated accordingly. Wren has correctly observed that in *The Human Problems of an Industrial Civilization* Elton Mayo:

> had set the stage for the social person by seeking a new leadership, buttressed by social and human skills, that would overcome anomie and social disorganization. In its very essence Mayo's theory espoused the same goal as that of Taylor, collaboration and co-operation in industry. The means to this goal differed but the end that both anticipated was the recognition of a mutually beneficial relationship between the worker and management.
>
> *(Wren, 1994, p.250)*

Critical summary

Central to Mayo's work was his antipathy to social conflict and possible social dislocation. His belief that industrial unrest sprang from personal problems, both physiological and psychological, strongly coloured his analysis of industrial society. It prompted him, for example, to construe industrial unrest as arising from the pessimistic reveries of individual workers rather than legitimate economic or sectional interests. Challenges to management were therefore depicted by Mayo as evidence of psychic disturbance rather than part of the normal rough and tumble of industrial life. Further, in his interpretation of the RATR experiments, Mayo chose to willfully disregard the significance of financial incentives on the behaviour of the participants, and to emphasize instead, the impact of group cohesiveness and benign supervision. Although Mayo's association with the Hawthorne experiments was, of necessity, pitched at the micro-level, his preferred focus was the macro-level of society and what he saw as the dire consequences of anomie. He was thus tempted to extrapolate from the apparent 'success' of the RATR experiments to the wider society, thereby allocating to industrial managers a significant role in the restoration and maintenance of social equilibrium. Just as the ideas of scientific management coalesced around the work and reputation of F. W. Taylor so the notions of human relations and the social person took shape in relation to the work of Elton Mayo, in the process consumating a new era in management theory. Ironically, considering that Mayo's ideas are often placed somewhat artificially in opposition to those of Taylor by academic commentators, the two men were seeking much the same goals, namely industrial harmony and an end to antagonism between management and workers.

Discussion questions

1. What were the origins of the Hawthorne experiments?
2. How would you account for the increased productivity levels in the RATR?
3. 'Mayo's main function in connection with the Hawthorne experiments was that of publicist'. Is this a fair assessment?
4. Why did Mayo consider that industrial managers of the future would have a significant role to play in maintaining social equilibrium?

Suggested reading

Aron, R. (1967/1990) Emile Durkheim. *Main Currents in Sociological Thought Volume 2*, Penguin Books, Harmondsworth.

Gillespie, R. (1991) *Manufacturing Knowledge: A History of the Hawthorne Experiments*, Cambridge University Press, Cambridge.

Henderson, L. J., Whitehead, T. N. and Mayo, E. (1937) The Effects of Social Environment in Gulick, L. and Urwick, L. (eds) *Papers on the Science of Administration*, Institute of Public Administration, Columbia University, New York.

Mayo, E. (1919) *Democracy and Freedom: An Essay in Social Logic*, Macmillan, Melbourne.

Mayo, E. (1933) *The Human Problems of an Industrial Civilization*, Viking Press, New York.

Mayo, E. (1949) *The Social Problems of an Industrial Civilization*, Routledge & Kegan Paul, London.

Roethlisberger, F. and Dickson, W. (1939/1964) *Management and the Worker: An Account of a Research Program Conducted by the Western Electric Company, Hawthorne Works, Chicago*, Wiley & Sons, New York.

Rose, M. (1988) *Industrial Behaviour: Research and Control*, Penguin Books, Harmondsworth, chs. 11, 12 and 13.

Trahair, R. (1984) *The Humanist Temper: The Life and Work of Elton Mayo*, Transaction Books, New Brunswick, New Jersey.

Whitehead, T. N. (1938) *The Industrial Worker: A Statistical Study of Human Relations in a Group of Manual Workers*, Harvard University Press, Cambridge, Mass.

Whyte, W. F. (1987) From Human Relations to Organizational Behavior: Reflections on the Changing Scene. *Industrial and Labor Relations Review*, **40**(4) 487–499.

Wrege, C. (1976) Solving Mayo's Mystery: The First Complete Account of the Origin of the Hawthorne Studies – The Forgotten Contributions of C. E. Snow and H. Hibarger. *Academy of Management Proceedings 12–16*.

Chapter 12

Chester Barnard and the functions of the executive

Chester I. Barnard was born in Malden, Massachusetts in 1886. When he was five years old his mother died and Barnard went to live with his maternal grandparents. Although the family was short of money the atmosphere was one of intellectual endeavour, with great importance given to discussion and reading. Lack of money meant that Barnard was unable to go to college when he completed his schooling. Instead, utilizing his gift for music, he became apprenticed as a piano tuner earning $3 a week. While practicing his trade, however, Barnard was able to prepare himself for prep school, eventually attending the prestigious Mount Hermon School. In 1906 he entered Harvard, majoring in economics, and studying government under A. Lawrence Lowell. During his three years in college he supported himself financially by working in the evenings on such tasks as typing student dissertations and conducting a dance orchestra. Although he successfully completed his studies at Harvard he failed, on a technicality, to obtain a degree. Nevertheless when he left in 1909, he managed, through a family contact, to obtain a job as a statistician with American Telephone and Telegraph (AT&T).

During his time at Harvard Barnard studied languages, mastering German, French and Italian. At AT&T he became involved in a world-wide review of telephone rates and his ability as a linguist was put to good use. In 1915 he was promoted to the post of commercial engineer and, in 1922, became assistant vice-president and general manager of the Bell Telephone Company of Pennsylvania. At this time he wrote a short article for the house journal dealing with some of the issues that were later covered in *The Functions of the Executive*. His theme was the improvement of functional organization and, as Wolf has noted:

> He argued that improvement must proceed along three lines. First, a
> co-operative attitude between functional units must be maintained; second,

117

adequate inter-departmental instruction must be established; and, third, the cross-training of personnel should be promoted to ensure an adequate supply of executives.

(Wolf, 1974, p.11)

In 1925 Barnard delivered a paper at Pennsylvania State College on the *Development of Executive Ability*. Again his paper contained many of the themes pursued in his later work, including what he considered to be the six universal qualifications of executives, these being 'the ability to determine the desirable results to be accomplished in any business or activity; ability to organize; ability to state intelligibly the things required of the organization; ability to secure enthusiastic co-operative action; balance; and flexibility' (Wolf, 1974, p.11). Here his concerns are close to those of Fayol, particularly in the sphere of management development and the need to blend innate ability with formal training (see Chapter 5).

Barnard continued his upward rise through the ranks of AT&T, becoming president of the New Jersey Bell Telephone Company at the age of 41. Further, he developed his activities into voluntary, public service including work with the New Jersey Emergency Relief Administration and the New Jersey Reformatory. During the Second World War he was president of the United Service Organization. When he finally retired from AT&T after nearly 40 years service in 1948 he became president of the Rockefeller Foundation. Chester Barnard died in 1961.

Barnard and the Harvard Pareto Circle

The concepts of social system and social equilibrium have been key ideas in sociological theory and have been debated from pre-Comtian times to the present. But these concepts enjoyed a special importance during the 1930s and early 1940s for a group of scholars at Harvard. These men were interested in Vilfredo Pareto, whose sociological writings were based on a...model of society as a system of mutually interacting particles which move from one state of equilibrium to another.

(Heyl, 1968, p.316)

Among this group, known as the Harvard Pareto Circle, were Elton Mayo (see Chapter 11), the sociologists George Homans and Talcott Parsons, the historian Crane Brinton, the economist Joseph Schumpeter, and the physiologist Lawrence Henderson. At least part of the attraction of Pareto's ideas for these men was their apparent utility as a plausible counter to Marxism. As Homans admitted many years later:

I took to Pareto because he made clear to me what I was already prepared to believe. I do not know all the reasons why I was ready for him, but I can give one. Someone has said that much modern sociology is an effort to answer the arguments of revolutionaries. As a Republican Bostonian who had not rejected his comparatively wealthy family, I felt during the thirties that I was under personal attack, above all from the Marxists. I was ready to believe Pareto because he provided me with a defense.

(Homans, 1962, p.4)

The emphasis placed on social system and social equilibrium in Pareto's writings offered a conservative bulwark against Marxist notions of social revolution. This need was particularly felt in the years of economic depression following the Wall Street Crash of 1929, when communist ideas were gaining wider influence and the Soviet Union was emerging from international isolation. The central figure in the group was Lawrence Henderson who held the Lowell Professorship of Chemistry at Harvard and was also chairman of the Society of Fellows. Between 1926 and 1932 Henderson read the bulk of Pareto's work and became fully convinced of its significance. Early in the academic year of 1932 he decided to establish a seminar on Pareto and began recruiting faculty members as participants. Those attending the seminar responded to their exposure to Pareto's ideas in various ways. In the case of Homans, for example, the seminar was crucial in shifting his academic interests from English literature to sociology. One outcome of the Harvard Pareto Circle was a substantial body of publications inspired by, or concerned with, aspects of Pareto's work. In 1934 Homans and Charles Curtis (a Boston lawyer, Harvard Fellow and close friend of Henderson) published *An Introduction to Pareto: His Sociology* while Henderson himself published *Pareto's General Sociology* in 1935. In 1937 Talcott Parsons published *Structure of Social Action* which contained a close analysis of Pareto's theories while, in 1938, Brinton applied a conceptual framework derived from Pareto for the study of four revolutions contained in his *Anatomy of Revolution*. Not surprisingly, perhaps, all these works place an emphasis (in larger or smaller measure) on the themes of social system and equilibrium and the counter-revolutionary propensity of social systems, when disturbed by external events, to restore themselves.

It was through contact with Lawrence Henderson that Chester Barnard came to write *The Functions of the Executive*. The two men were introduced by Wallace Brett Donham, Dean of the Harvard Graduate School of Business, and found that they had a mutual interest in Pareto. Indeed Barnard had read Pareto's work extensively in French translation before it had been discovered by Henderson. Although heavily engaged in his business activities, Barnard had been active as a guest speaker at conferences at the Wharton School of Finance and Commerce of the University of Pennsylvania and served on a number of visiting committees at Harvard. He also found time to collaborate with Henderson on the development of a sociology course for the Harvard Business School. Henderson became much impressed by Barnard's intellectual capacities and practical experience and also his capacity to blend the two constructively. He therefore approached the president of Harvard, A. Lawrence Lowell, who was a close friend and suggested that Barnard might be asked to give a course of public lectures. Lowell readily agreed and Barnard chose to give eight lectures on the general topic of the functions of the executive, which were given at the Lowell Institute in Boston during November and December 1937. Although very few people actually attended them, Barnard was nevertheless approached by the Harvard University Press and asked to turn the lectures into a book. When it appeared in 1938 much of its initial popularity was with Henderson and his Pareto Circle associates at Harvard. In February 1939 Barnard was invited to discuss *The Functions of the Executive* at a Conference of the Committee on Work in Industry of the National Research Council of which Henderson was the chairman, Homans the secretary and Mayo a member. Henderson died in 1945 and Barnard undertook the onerous task of editing his papers. Although, after considerable effort, he completed the task and also prepared an introduction, publication never took place. Wolf, who personally tackled Barnard on the issue in an interview, has noted that:

> In reply to the question of why he had not released these materials Barnard stated there were 'various reasons'. One which he enlarged was that (Henderson) got himself into a polemic position where he was fighting everybody all of the time on behalf of Pareto...in his ardor of behavior regarding Pareto, he was off balance considerably.
>
> *(Wolf, 1974, p.23)*

Self-evidently, at least with hindsight, Barnard did not share Henderson's uncritical passion for Pareto. Nevertheless the fact that the two men were close friends and that Barnard was brought into regular contact with leading members of the Harvard Pareto Circle is significant in establishing the context in which *The Functions of the Executive* was produced. Further, that figures such as Henderson, Homans and Mayo admired Barnard's work is a clear indication that a substantial identity of opinion existed between the Harvard academics and the 'philosopher-practitioner' from AT&T.

The functions of the executive

As has been seen Barnard had already sketched out his views on the subject in papers produced during the 1920s. However, in *The Functions of the Executive* these sketches were expanded into a complex text of some 330 pages. Indeed Barnard's book was from the very first criticized both for its length and opacity. The first 200 or so pages were concerned with what the author termed co-operative systems, and that particular form of co-operative system which we refer to as the formal organization. It was only in the final 50 or so pages that Barnard closely considered the topic contained in the title. He thus began by establishing the primacy of formal organizations in modern society. As he put it:

formal organization is that kind of co-operation among men that is conscious, deliberate, purposeful...Moreover, much of what we regard as reliable, foreseeable and stable is so obviously a result of formally organized effort that it is readily believed that organized effort is normally successful, that failure of organization is abnormal.

(Barnard 1938, p.5)

He went on, however, to observe that the latter was not in fact the case and that in reality most formal organizations fail. Thus what we observed are the successful survivors. As he put it, 'failure to co-operate, failure of co-operation, failure of organization, disorganization, disintegration, destruction of organization and re-organization – are characteristic facts of human history' (Barnard, 1938, p.5). Although he was willing to concede that some organizations failed owing to internal defects, Barnard argued that the main source of failure derived from what he termed 'forces outside'. Thus 'the survival of an organization depends upon the maintenance of an equilibrium of complex character in a continuously fluctuating environment...which calls for readjustment processes internal to the organization'. He continued 'we shall be concerned with the nature of the external conditions to which adjustment must be made, but the centre of our interest is the processes by which it is accomplished' (Barnard, 1938, p.6).

The formal organization as Barnard conceived of it was thus dynamic rather than static and was poised in constant interaction with outside forces. The formal organization was constrained to embark on a process of continuous adaptation if it was to survive in an ever changing environment. Barnard's notion of the organization itself was novel in that he did not limit its boundaries to the conventional one of 'a definite group of people whose behaviour is co-ordinated with reference to some explicit goal or goals' (Barnard, 1948, p.112). Instead he included a much wider range of what would now be termed 'stakeholders' including investers, suppliers, customers and clients. The functions of the executive in the process of organizational adaptation and survival were involved with control, management and administration on the model more or less set forth by Fayol (see Chapter 5) but, pre-eminently, they were concerned with communication. It was in the sphere of communication that Barnard noted the existence of informal organization within the formal structure of an organization. As he put it 'the communication function of executives includes the maintenance of informal executive organization as an essential means of communication' (Barnard, 1938, p.224).

The starting point for Barnard's analysis of the organization was the individual. Individuals chose to co-operate with others to undertake tasks that they could not achieve alone. However, by choosing to co-operate they were constrained to accept the goals of the group which might, of course, differ somewhat from their own. Thus organizational constraints were placed upon individuals which might be at variance with their own desires and this disparity Barnard referred to as incompatability. He claimed that the persistence of co-operation depended on two conditions as follows:

> its effectiveness; and its efficiency. Effectiveness relates to the accomplishment of the co-operative purpose, which is social and non-personal in character. Efficiency relates to the satisfaction of individual motives, and is personal in character. The test of effectiveness is the accomplishment of a common purpose or purposes; effectiveness can be measured. The test of efficiency is the eliciting of sufficient individual wills to co-operate.
>
> *(Barnard, 1938, p.60)*

Thus Barnard identified a clear dichotomy between organizational and personal motives. When an organization succeeded in its declared objective it was said to be effective. However, the extent to which the personal desires of the individuals concerned had also been satisfied was not a matter of organizational effectiveness but efficiency. As he put it:

> co-operative efficiency is the resultant of individual efficiencies, since co-operation is entered into only to satisfy individual motives...The efficiency of the co-operative action is the degree to which these motives are satisfied. The only determinant of this efficiency is the individual, since motives are individual.
>
> *(Barnard, 1938, p.44)*

In making this dichotomy between organizational and personal goals, Barnard highlighted a perennial problem. If individuals do not feel that the organization satisfies their desires over time they will tend to withold part of their effort or ultimately leave. Organizational efficiency is thus the capacity of the organization to meet the goals of the individuals associated in it and thereby maintain effectiveness. Of course the organization can respond actively by seeking to modify the motivations of the individuals in line with the goals of the organization, or by replacing disaffected individuals with others who either possess the appropriate motives or are willing to adopt them. Nevertheless in order to remain effective (indeed, in order to survive) an organization must sustain the 'ability to continue to offer enough inducements to satisfy individual motives in the pursuit of group purposes' (Wren, 1994, p.267).

The possible problems posed by the variation in individual motivations, together with the need to sustain unity of organizational purpose, led Barnard to a consideration of authority. He defined authority as follows:

> authority is the character of a communication (order) in a formal organization by virtue of which it is accepted by a contributor or 'member' of the organization as governing the action he contributes; that is, as governing or determining what he does or is not to do so far as the organization is concerned. According to this

definition, authority involves two aspects: first, the subjective, the personal, the accepting of a communication as authoritative, and, second, the objective aspect – the character in the communication by virtue of which it is accepted.

(Barnard, 1938, p.163)

On this model the source of organizational authority is rooted not in those who give the instructions but in those who either accept or reject them. This was a radical suggestion for its time and injected an element of uncertainty into the conventional view of the relationship between the various tiers of an organizational hierarchy. As Daiute has observed:

the gist of the theory is that the subordinate decides for himself whether he will obey an order or not...The superior must face the reality of authority and cope with it. Why are orders obeyed? An order is followed if the recipient (1) understands the order, (2) feels it will further his personal interests, (3) feels it will further the organization's interests, and (4) has the physical and mental ability to comply. In a particular organization many people will accept orders because they do not want responsibility for making decisions but prefer to 'delegate upward' this responsibility. Also, many subordinates have a range of alternative orders which they will accept; that is, they are relatively indifferent whether they are told to do this or that, since all four conditions are met by this or that. They possess a zone of indifference. Furthermore, situations can be found in which the personal interests of others will be served by the particular subordinates obeying the order; hence the others exert social pressure on him to conform even though he believes his own personal interests are not furthered. The prudent superior does not issue orders he thinks will be rejected.

(Daiute, 1964, pp.46–7)

Barnard provided a revision of the conventional view of authority proposed, for example, by Fayol. The objective aspect of authority is closer to the conventional view whereby instructions are passed 'down' the formal organization in the form of orders backed by sanctions. However, the subjective aspect introduces elements of choice, interpretation and uncertainty into the situation. Whilst the formal organization, with of course the threat and actuality of sanctions, serves to reinforce the legitimacy of authority it is often the informal organization which comes into play when instructions are actually carried out. Again in the words of Daiute, 'in the final analysis...the informal organization is crucial in the giving and accepting of orders' (Daiute, 1964, p.47). Unlike the formal organization, which is merely an abstract depiction of various relationships, the informal organization is dynamic and held together above all by networks of communication. Good communications are, according to Barnard, facilitated by individuals possessing a close affinity of outlook derived from socialization and training. Obviously such conformity is somewhat inimical to contemporary views on diversity. Nevertheless it is self-evident that the success of an informal organization must largely depend on the individuals involved 'seeing eye to eye'.

Having dealt extensively with the nature of organizations and the role of the individual within them, Barnard turned to the specific functions of the executive. As he put it:

> it might be said…that the function of executives is, to serve as channels of communication so far as communications must pass through central positions. But since the object of the communication system is co-ordination of all aspects of organization, it follows that the functions of executives relate to all the work essential to the vitality and endurance of an organization, so far, at least, as it must be accomplished through formal co-ordination.
>
> *(Barnard, 1938, p.215)*

However, he went on to observe that much of the work carried out by executives did not relate to the essential function of co-ordinating the work of others. Hence 'executive work is not that of the organization, but the specialized work of maintaining the organization in operation' (Barnard, 1938, p.215). On this basis the conventional view of an executive as being mainly concerned with managing a group of people is clearly inadequate, or at least inaccurate. Further, Barnard did not accept the role of executives as being to manage the system of co-operative efforts, which he saw as being largely self-managed. Instead, as he put it:

> the functions with which we are concerned are like those of the nervous system, including the brain, in relation to the rest of the body. It exists to maintain the bodily system by directing those actions which are necessary more effectively to adjust to the environment, but it can hardly be said to manage the body, a large part of whose functions are independent of it and upon which it in turn depends.
>
> *(Barnard, 1938, pp.216–17)*

In summary the functions of the executive according to Barnard covered three broad areas:

1. Developing and maintaining a system of communication, including staff selection and the offering of incentives; various techniques of control aimed at promoting effectiveness such as promotion, demotion and dismissal; and, finally, the nurturing of the informal organization.
2. Promoting the supply of what would now be termed human resources, including the attracting of suitable individuals to the organization and their effective motivation during their subsequent career.
3. Formulating and defining the purposes, objectives and ends of the organization, including, as Barnard terms it, indoctrinating 'those at the lower levels with

general purposes, the major decisions, so that they remain cohesive and able to make the ultimate detailed decisions coherent' (Barnard, 1938, p.233).

This final function obviously involved aspects of what would now be termed organizational culture and, of course, leadership. Barnard believed that the greatest personal attributes an executive could bring to an organization were loyalty and belief. If the executives lacked these core attributes it was not likely that they could communicate the purposes of the organization with sufficient conviction to sustain coherence of organizational action. The executive must therefore be a positive value-shaper and, by extension, leader. In 1940 Barnard gave two extensive lectures on the subject of leadership which were later published as an essay *The Nature of Leadership*. Again he took communication to be the key element observing that the leader must be 'at times a mere centre of communication' (Barnard, 1948, p.86). Nevertheless the leader must also have the capacity to arbitrate convincingly between various opinions and inspire followers. In Barnard's view there was no simple formula for achieving successful leadership. Instead he saw it as being dependent upon a combination of the individual concerned, the followers and the conditions. With regard to the production of leaders he commented that they 'are made quite as much by conditions and by organizations and followers as by any qualities and propensities which they themselves have. Indeed, in this connection, I should put much more emphasis upon the character of organizations than upon individuals' (Barnard, 1948, p.42). On this basis leaders are the product of the organizations they serve (and whose values they share, promulgate and manage) rather than the product of innate ability, training and expertise suggested by Fayol.

Critical summary

Barnard's work covered much of the ground already examined by Fayol. This is hardly surprising given the two men's careers which both included a rise from the junior ranks of their respective organizations to the 'heights' of chief executive. However, Barnard appears to have been ignorant of Fayol's writing even though, as a linguist, he would have found no difficulty in reading *Administration, industrielle et générale* in the original. Further, although both men dealt with the formal organization, Barnard placed greater emphasis on the networks of communication which he termed the informal organization. He also took a wider view of the organization itself than Fayol, or indeed Weber or Taylor and the scientific managers, by including not only employees and managers but investors, suppliers, customers and clients. Barnard's conception of authority was equally novel, residing not in the post or the person but in those who are nominally 'under' authority. Thus an executive's authority is always limited by the extent to which those receiving the instructions are willing to obey them. Instructions are liable to interpretation by subordinates and the skilful executive will realise the limits of authority. Barnard claimed that the organization had a dual role concerned partly with meeting its declared objectives and partly with satisfying the desires of those who participated in its operation. An organization which failed to satisfy its contributing members would not be effective and therefore unlikely to survive. In the words of Wren, 'this attempt to bridge the requirements of the formal organization with the needs of the socio-human system was a landmark in management thought that stands to this day' (Wren, 1994, p.267). Although Barnard was aware of the strength of the organization in forming and sustaining the attitudes and motivations of its members, unlike Follett he was not attracted by collectivism. Instead, he placed great emphasis on individual autonomy and the freedom of the individual to quit the organization. Having said this, however, Barnard argued the need for a shared set of values in an organization and saw the executive as the repository of these values and a conduit through which these values could be communicated to others. Barnard's debt to Pareto can be discerned in the theoretical underpinning of his work, particularly those parts concerned with the social system and the maintenance of social equilibrium. Not surprisingly, perhaps, he was hostile to trade unions; like Mayo he saw them as competing sources of loyalty and values and thus a threat to equilibrium. Barnard placed the greatest emphasis on good communications and saw their maintenance as the central function of the executive. Ironically, in terms of communication, his own writings are extremely difficult to read and are best absorbed in small portions.

Discussion questions

1. What did Barnard consider to be the six universal qualifications of executives?
2. What was the significance of the Harvard Pareto Circle to the development of management theory?
3. How convincing is Barnard's view that the formal organization is dynamic rather than static?
4. What does Barnard mean when he speaks of the informal organization?
5. How convincing is Barnard's view that leaders are mainly the products of the organizations they serve?

Suggested reading

Aron, R. (1967/1990) Vilfredo Pareto. *Main Currents in Sociological Thought Volume 2*, Penguin Books, Harmondsworth.

Barnard, C. (1938) *The Functions of the Executive*, Harvard University Press, Cambridge, Mass.

Barnard, C. (1948) *Organization and Management: Selected Papers*, Harvard University Press, Cambridge, Mass.

Daiute, R. (1964) *Scientific Management: Ideas, Topics and Readings*, Holt Rinehart & Winston, New York.

Heyl, B. (1968) The Harvard "Pareto Circle". *Journal for the History of the Behavioural Sciences* **4** 316–333.

Wolf, W. (1974) *The Basic Barnard: An Introduction to Chester I Barnard and His Theories of Organization and Management*, Cornell University, Ithaca, New York.

Wren, D. (1994) *The Evolution of Management Thought*, Wiley & Sons, Chichester, ch. 14.

Chapter 13

Alfred Sloan and General Motors

Alfred P. Sloan was born in New Haven, Connecticut in 1875 and graduated from the Massachusetts Institute of Technology, with a degree in electrical engineering, in 1895. His first job was as a draughtsman at the Hyatt Roller Bearing Company in Harrison, New Jersey. The company had been founded a few years before Sloan joined by John Wesley Hyatt in order to manufacture a bearing which Hyatt had invented. Sloan soon left the company, however, spending the next two years working for a firm which manufactured refrigerators. Meanwhile, Hyatts went through a difficult period financially and was on the brink of going out of business. Alfred Sloan's father and a group of associates raised enough money to keep the company going while Alfred, who had re-joined the firm, and a young book-keeper named Peter Steenstrup tried to turn things round. As Rae has commented:

> this, of course, they succeeded in doing, and in the process Sloan acquired a comprehensive education in business management. Steenstrup looked after finances until he left the company in 1909; Sloan had charge of everything else – engineering, design, production, sales. Simultaneously, he was learning the meaning of mass production. He took charge of the Hyatt Roller Bearing Company just in time to find in the automobile industry the principal market for his products, and keeping pace with its expanding and varied demands was an invaluable educational experience.
>
> *(Rae, 1959, p.113)*

In the spring of 1916 William C. Durant, the founder of the General Motors Corporation (GM), proposed to Sloan that Hyatt be sold to a holding company – United Motors Corporation. United Motors had been organized by Durant for the purpose of buying out a number of leading components makers:

129

including Hyatt Roller Bearing Company and New Departure Manufacturing Co., both major producers of ball bearings, Remy Electrical Company, and the Dayton Engineering Laboratories Company, known as Delco, both makers of starting, lighting, ignition and other electrical equipment, and the Perlman Rim Corporation. Not only did these purchases help assure a steadier volume of essential supplies from different sources, but they also brought a number of able men into the General Motors orbit.

(Chandler, 1962/1993, p.123)

Among these 'able men', of course, was Alfred Sloan. Sloan's initial reaction to Durant's proposal had been one of scepticism. Hyatt's customers included Ford's and GM and, under Sloan's guidance, the company had successfully achieved the combination of large scale production and accuracy essential to meet the demands of the burgeoning American automobile industry. Nevertheless, on reflection Sloan realized that 'Hyatt had paradoxically become too big to be independent' (Rae, 1959, p.113). The company had geared itself up to mass production and could only operate profitably in a stable market the size of Ford's or GM. However, if either of these companies decided to manufacture their own bearings then Hyatts would be left in a difficult situation. Thus Durant's proposal was accepted and Sloan became the president of United Motors and a major stockholder in the company. When United Motors was later absorbed into General Motors in 1918, Sloan combined the jobs of vice-president of GM with that of president of United Motors.

General Motors was created by Durant from what Wren has described as 'an amalgam of motor car and parts producers' (Wren, 1994, p.212). Durant was apparently incapable of imposing an orderly structure on the enterprise he had created and this weakness was cruelly exposed by the crisis of 1920. At the end of the First World War the American economy, like that of Britain (see Chapter 10), enjoyed a brief boom which engendered a general mood of optimism among automobile manufacturers. As Chandler has observed 'both demand and prices were…rising, and new automobiles continued to be in short supply' (Chandler, 1962/1993, p.128). However, during the spring of 1920 demand began to fall and continued to decline during the summer until manufacturers, starting with Fords, were forced to cut prices. In the event the depression was brief and has been described by Rae as 'short, sharp and quickly forgotten'. Nevertheless, 'to the automobile industry…the crash of 1920 was an event of far-reaching importance. It found most of the manufacturers badly over extended and necessitated sweeping reorganizations that had lasting effects on the structure of the industry' (Rae, 1959, p.136). This was certainly the case at GM where the fall in demand for their cars soon caused serious cash-flow problems. In spite of Sloan's demand to cut prices, Durant refused and by October 1920 the company's managers were struggling even to find sufficient cash to meet immediate needs such as invoices and pay rolls. Meanwhile the value of the company's stock collapsed and Durant made a reckless attempt to sustain its value by buying GM stock on credit. The attempt failed and on 20 November 1920 Durant was forced to resign as president of the company he had founded. In the event the company was saved from the brink of collapse by a huge infusion of money from the Du Pont Company which held a major financial stake in GM. Pierre du Pont came out of semi-retirement to become president of GM, one of his first acts being to name Alfred Sloan as his successor. Sloan became chief executive and president of GM in 1923 and was elected board chairman in 1937. He became honorary chairman in 1956 and continued in that capacity until his death in 1966.

The Sloan structure

The situation at GM in the aftermath of Durant's departure was later described by Sloan in the following terms:

> at the close of the year 1920 the task before General Motors was reorganization. As things stood, the corporation faced simultaneously an economic slump on the outside and a management crisis on the inside. The automobile market had nearly vanished and with it our income. Most of the plants and those of the industry were shut down or assembling a small number of cars out of semi-finished materials in the plants. We were loaded with high-priced inventory and commitments at the old inflated price level. We were short of cash. We had a confused product line. There was a lack of control and of any means of control in operations and finance, and a lack of adequate information about anything. In short, there was just about as much crisis, inside and outside as you could wish for if you liked that sort of thing.
>
> *(Sloan, 1963, p.42)*

When Sloan joined United Motors in 1916 he had begun devising an appropriate organizational structure. As each of the constituent companies was in capable hands, Sloan was able to concentrate his energies on establishing a general office capable of co-ordinating and expanding the operations of each company as appropriate. Among the innovations Sloan introduced were uniform accounting procedures and a marketing organization. He also worked to ensure that GM's dealers received a reliable supply of spare parts and accessories. As Chandler has commented, 'this...was an invaluable asset, since the ability to give good, quick servicing and repairing was becoming an increasingly important competitive weapon' (Chandler, 1962/1993, p.131). However, although Sloan was successful in organizing United Motors, he became increasingly concerned about GM's lack of structure and system. He had no idea, for example, how United Motors fitted into GM at large. Further, he was not certain of how the various operating divisions of GM itself supplemented or complemented each other. At the end of 1919 he began working on an 'Organization Study' which embodied 'the concept of decentralization and effective delegation of authority that subsequently became basic to his philosophy of industrial management' (Rae, 1959, p.139). At the beginning of 1920 he submitted his plans for the reorganization of GM to Durant who broadly approved of them but showed no appetite for arranging their implementation. With the arrival of Pierre du Pont, however, a wholly new approach was adopted and Sloan's 'Organization Study' rapidly became 'the foundation of management policy in the modern General Motors' (Sloan, 1963, p.45).

The core of Sloan's new structure for GM was the principle of decentralization. In one sense this was easy to achieve, given the lack of company-wide cohesion during the Durant years. Sloan's notion of organization involved the development of co-ordination without sacrificing whatever benefits accrued from the existing decentralization. As Rae has observed:

> essentially, Sloan gave General Motors the staff-line pattern of a military organization. The separate companies were transformed into operating divisions, each under an executive with virtually complete responsibility for its management. The staff functions, such as research, financial policy, and sales policy, were organized separately, with their services available to the whole General Motors family but without direct authority over the operating divisions...Alfred P. Sloan made it possible for General Motors to be transformed from a loose conglomeration of automotive and other enterprises into a coherent and co-ordinated business structure, combining to a unique degree the advantages of concentration with the flexibility of decentralization.
>
> *(Rae, 1959, p.140)*

The new structure was put in place at GM during the years 1921 to 1925 and one of the earliest tasks undertaken by Sloan and his executives was to define the boundaries for the activities of each division. As well as failing to produce a coherent organizational structure, Durant had not really attempted to create a rational product line. The various divisions of GM competed against each other rather than their external competitors. Under Sloan's direction, however, the product line became more or less defined by 1923. As Chandler has commented 'Cadillac sold in the highest price position, Buick the next, followed by Oakland and then Olds, with Chevrolet in the largest-volume, lowest-price market' (Chandler, 1962/1993, p.143). In 1925 GM produced the six-cylinder Pontiac to fill the gap in its range between the Oldsmobile and the Chevrolet. Also in 1925 the company purchased the Yellow Cab Manufacting Company of Chicago, merging it with its own truck division to form the Yellow Truck and Coach Manufacturing Company. Further, GM began to acquire foreign subsidiaries including Britain's Vauxhall Motors in 1925 and Germany's Adam Opel Company in 1929.

With the new structure in place and GM's product range under process of rationalization, Sloan began to plan an attack on the tough but profitable low-price car market. This market, as Sloan put it:

was then practically monopolized by the Ford (Model T) and we were trying to invade it…General Motors (could) not attempt to build and sell a car of the precise Ford level, as the Ford sold at the lowest price…Instead the corporation should market a car much better than the Ford…We did not propose to compete head to head with Ford, but to produce a car that would be superior to the Ford, yet so near the Ford price that demand would be drawn from the Ford…and lifted to the slightly higher price in preference to Ford's then utility design.

(Sloan, 1963, p.68)

As was seen in Chapter 9, GM soon succeeded in overhauling Ford's. While Henry Ford persisted with the increasingly dated Model T, GM's more stylish (as well as technically superior) Chevrolet grew ever more popular with the consumers. By 1927 Chevrolet was the best selling car, the Model T was finished and GM had become the world's leading automobile manufacturer.

Critical summary

The decentralized organizational structure which Alfred Sloan devised for General Motors was hugely influential and was subsequently emulated throughout the industrialized world. Decentralized operations with centrally co-ordinated control, enabled the separate elements of GM to work effectively towards a common goal. As Kennedy has commented 'where Fayol had achieved the organizational solution for the single-product manufacturing business, Sloan accomplished it for the large, complex manufacturing business of the mass production age' (Kennedy, 1991, p.156).

Discussion questions

1. 'Decentralization and effective delegation of authority'. Is this an accurate description of Sloan's philosophy of industrial management?
2. Why were decentralized operations with centrally co-ordinated control particularly appropriate to General Motors?

Suggested reading

Chandler, A. (1962/1993) *Strategy and Structure: Chapters in the History of the American Industrial Enterprise*, MIT Press, Cambridge, Mass, ch. 3.

Kennedy, C. (1991) *Guide to the Management Gurus*, Century, London, ch. 31.

Rae, J. (1959) *American Automobile Manufacturers: The First Forty Years*, Chilton, Philadelphia.

Sloan, A. (1963) *My Years with General Motors*, Sidgwick &Jackson, London.

Chapter 14

Abraham Maslow and the hierarchy of needs

Abraham Maslow was born in Brooklyn, New York in 1908. He trained as a psychologist at the University of Wisconsin, became Carnegie Fellow of the College Teachers' College in 1935 and was subsequently associate professor of psychology at Brooklyn College. During the mid-1930s he began work on what was eventually to become his major text – *Motivation and Personality* – which was published in 1954. As Maslow put it, 'my effort was to synthesize the holistic, the dynamic and the cultural emphases which…excited so many young psychologists of the time. I felt that they were intrinsically related to each other, and that they were sub-aspects of a single, larger encompassing whole' (Maslow, 1954, ix). Maslow embarked on a long intellectual quest, studying Gestalt psychology under Max Wertheimer and Kurt Koffka at the New School for Social Research and learning psychoanalysis from, among others, Erich Fromm. He also underwent psychoanalysis and continued his studies of psychology with Alfred Adler. He studied anthropology with Ruth Benedict and Margaret Mead and undertook a field trip to the Northern Blackfoot Indians. In 1943 he published his papers *A Preface to Motivation Theory* and *A Theory of Human Motivation* in which he formulated a positive theory of motivation which he described as 'general-dynamic'. Between 1947 and 1949 Maslow broke his academic career to work in the family business, the Maslow Cooperage Corporation. However, during these years he maintained his academic links and continued to publish articles in learned journals. On his return to academic life he became an associate professor and later full professor and head of department at Brandeis University in Massachusetts. Maslow's later work became increasingly utopian and even mystical. Like Lyndall Urwick (see Chapter 10) he formulated a Theory Z in response to McGregor's Theory X and Theory Y (see Chapter 16). Commenting on the various formulations of Theory Z in a consideration of Ouchi's work (see Chapter 19) Wren has commented that 'where Urwick referenced Taylor, Maslow cited

Taoism; where Urwick was pragmatic, Maslow was romantic; and where Urwick wrote of individuals in organizations, Maslow saw them as transcendent beings' (Wren, 1994, p.375). Abraham Maslow died in 1970.

The hierarchy of needs

According to Maslow 'human needs arrange themselves in hierarchies. That is to say, the appearance of one need usually rests on the prior satisfaction of another, more prepotent need. Man is a perpetually wanting animal' (Maslow, 1943, p.370). Maslow identified five sets of goals which he termed basic needs. These were physiological needs, safety needs, love needs, the need for self-esteem and, finally, the need to achieve self-actualization. The hierarchical arrangement of these needs or goals meant 'that the most prepotent goal will monopolize consciousness and will tend of itself to organize the recruitment of the various capacities of the organism. The less prepotent needs are minimized, even forgotten or denied' (Maslow, 1943, pp.394–95). At the base of the hierarchy Maslow placed physiological needs, most obviously the need for food. As he put it:

> undoubtedly...physiological needs are the most prepotent of all needs. What this means specifically is, that in the human being who is missing everything in life in an extreme fashion, it is most likely that the major motivation would be the physiological needs rather than any others. A person who is lacking food, safety, love, and esteem would most probably hunger for food more strongly than for anything else...The urge to write poetry, the desire to acquire an automobile, the interest in American history, the desire for a new pair of shoes are, in the extreme case, forgotten or become of secondary importance. For the man who is extremely and dangerously hungry, no other interests exist but food. He dreams food, he remembers food, he thinks about food, he emotes only about food, he perceives only food and he wants only food...Freedom, love, community feeling, respect, philosophy, may all be waived aside as fripperies, which are useless since they fail to fill the stomach. Such a man may fairly be said to live by bread alone.
>
> *(Maslow, 1943, pp.373–74)*

Maslow observed that in the United States and other developed societies such chronic, extreme hunger was rare. Further, he claimed that what most individuals experienced as hunger was merely appetite. Indeed in the developed societies the experience of sheer life and death hunger was likely to occur only by accident. Similarly the other physiological needs such as air and water were also generally satisfied. As Maslow commented:

it is quite true that man lives by bread alone – when there is no bread. But what happens to man's desires when there is plenty of bread and when his belly is chronically filled? At once other (and 'higher') needs emerge and these, rather than physiological hungers, dominate the organism. And when these in turn are satisfied, again new (and still 'higher') needs emerge and so on. This is what we mean by saying that the basic human needs are organized into a hierarchy of relative prepotency...The organism is dominanted and its behaviour organized only by unsatisfied needs. If hunger is satisfied, it becomes unimportant in the current dynamics of the individual.

(Maslow, 1943, p.375)

If then, Maslow argued, the physiological needs were relatively well gratified, a new set of needs would emerge, namely the safety needs. As he put it 'all that has been said of the physiological needs is equally true, although in lesser degree of these desires. The organism may equally well be wholly dominated by them. They may serve as the almost exclusive organizers of behaviour, recruiting all the capacities of the organism in their service, and we may then fairly describe the whole organism as a safety seeking mechanism' (Maslow, 1943, p.376). Maslow illustrated his notion of safety needs by examining the child's desire for security and also the behaviour of neurotic or near neurotic adults who were, in many ways, like the insecure child in their desire for safety. Nevertheless, as in the case of the physiological needs, Maslow argued, that 'the healthy, normal, fortunate adult in our culture is largely satisfied in his safety needs...in a very real sense, he no longer has any safety needs as active motivations. Just as a sated man no longer feels hungry, a safe man no longer feels endangered' (Maslow, 1943, pp.378–79). If both the physiological and the safety needs are fairly well gratified then, claims Maslow, the needs for love, affection and belongingness will emerge and the whole cycle described for physiological and safety needs is repeated. Thus 'the person will feel keenly, as never before, the absence of friends, or a sweetheart, or a wife, or children. He will hunger for affectionate relations with people in general, namely, for a place in his group, and he will strive with great intensity to achieve this goal. He will want to attain such a place more than anything else in the world and may even forget that once, when he was hungry, he sneered at love' (Maslow, 1943, pp.380–81). Unlike the physiological and safety needs, however, the needs for love, affection and belongingness are not so readily gratified in modern society. As Maslow puts it 'the thwarting of these needs is the most commonly found core in cases of maladjustment and more severe psychopathology' (Maslow, 1943, p.381). Again, when these needs are sufficiently satisfied, esteem needs emerge. In the words of Maslow:

all people in our society (with a few pathological exceptions) have a need or desire for a stable, firmly based, (usually) high evaluation of themselves, for self respect, or self-esteem, and the esteem of others. By firmly based self-esteem, we mean that which is soundly based upon real capacity, achievement and respect from others…Satisfaction of the self-esteem needs leads to feelings of self-confidence, worth, strength, capability and adequacy of being useful and necessary in the world. But thwarting of these needs produces feelings of inferiority, of weakness and of helplessness.

(Maslow, 1943, pp.382–83)

The final, and highest point in the hierarchy of needs, Maslow describes as self-actualization. Even if the physiological, safety, love and esteem needs are all more or less satisfied 'we may still often (if not always) expect that a new restlessness will soon develop, unless the individual is doing what he is fitted for. A musician must make music, an artist must paint, a poet must write, if he is to be ultimately happy. What a man can be, he must be. This need we may call self-actualization…the desire to become more and more what one is, to become everything that one is capable of becoming' (Maslow, 1943, p.382). Maslow readily concedes that self-actualization needs will vary greatly from individual to individual. He also observes that the emergence of self-actualization needs rests upon the prior satisfaction of the physiological, safety, love and esteem needs. As he described the situation, 'we shall call people who are satisfied in these needs basically satisfied people, and it is from these that we may expect the fullest (and healthiest) creativeness. Since, in our society, basically satisfied people are the exception, we do not know much about self-actualization, either experimentally or clinically. It remains a challenging problem for research' (Maslow, 1943, p.383).

The managerial implications of the hierarchy of needs

Maslow was careful not to claim too much for his theory. He was, for example, ready to concede that the hierarchy of needs might be subject to variation depending upon individual circumstances. In some cases the drive for the higher needs might be entirely lacking. As Maslow put it, 'in certain people the level of aspiration may be permanently deadened or lowered. That is to say, the less prepotent goals may simply be lost, and may disappear for ever, so that the person who has experienced life at a very low level…may continue to be satisfied for the rest of his life if only he can get enough food' (Maslow, 1943, p.386). Further, some variation in the extent and order of needs was likely to occur as a result of cultural variations between societies. Thus, 'in any particular culture an individual's conscious motivational content will usually be extremely different from the conscious motivational content of an individual in another society' (Maslow, 1943, p.389). Nevertheless, having said all of this, Maslow remained confident that the hierarchy of needs contained some valuable element of truth concerning human motivation.

As has been seen 'man is a perpetually wanting animal'. According to Maslow, 'the average member of our society is most often partially satisfied and partially unsatisfied in all of his wants. The hierarchy principle is usually empirically observed in terms of increasing percentages as we go up the hierarchy...Also it has been observed that an individual may permanently lose the higher wants in the hierarchy under special conditions...Any thwarting or possibility of thwarting of these basic human goals...is considered to be a psychological threat...A basically thwarted man may actually be defined as a 'sick' man' (Maslow, 1943, p.395). For much of the world's history the bulk of work was perforce concerned with fulfilling the physiological and other lower needs – the words 'subsistence agriculture' accurately describe the situation. However, modern technology, together with political, economic and educational changes, freed the bulk of workers in the advanced societies from the narrow concerns of subsistence and raised their aspirations accordingly. Unless these workers were to be conditioned by bitter experience (such as prolonged unemployment or social breakdown) to 'lose the higher wants', they would rapidly encounter frustration as they found their needs for self-esteem and self-actualization 'thwarted' by the prevailing structures of work organization. As Rose observed, commenting on the work of Maslow's follower, Chris Argyris:

> An organization usually takes the form of a pyramid. Yet these structures conflict directly with the individual needs of their members. Individuals and organizations are strongly opposed...As we grow up we are encouraged to proceed from a state of dependence to independence...In short, we progress from irresponsible childhood to responsible adulthood, and learn to associate lack of responsibility with childishness, and its possession with maturity. Yet a person's condition in most work situations is one of dependence and constraint...usually associated with this are directive leadership, and managerial control measures such as budgets, quality control, time and motion study and rates setting. As we descend the organizational hierarchy the more severe the constraints stemming from these sources become.
>
> *(Rose, 1988, pp.203–4)*

Self-evidently the organizational arrangements which followed from the widespread introduction of scientific management and the implementation of mass production techniques, such as the moving assembly track, left limited scope for the higher needs such as self-esteem and self-actualization. The imperatives of efficiency and control required workers to merely do as they were told by management. Sponteneity, creativity and innovative action were all banished; not only for blue collar workers on the line but increasingly for white collar staff employed in bureaucracies. Of course, F. W. Taylor had been aware of the desire for self-esteem and had injected an element of status and competition into his various schemes. Further, he had argued for a careful matching of people to jobs and some opportunity for career progression as a means of overcoming the worst effects of 'thwarted' ambition (see Chapter 2). However, by the time Maslow's work began to make an impact during the 1950s and

1960s there was a growing consensus that condemning workers to apparently futile jobs was bad both for them and for business. As Argyle has commented, 'it is noteworthy that complaints about boring work became most vocal in the USA, in particular, in the 1950s and 1960s, while many job improvement schemes were brought in from 1964 to 1976. This was a period of relatively full employment, and perhaps a period when many American workers had satisfied their material needs, described by Maslow as 'lower-order needs' (Argyle, 1972/1989, pp.33–34).

During the 1960s a new emphasis developed in management thinking which was aimed at enlarging jobs and developing alternative work arrangments as a means of enhancing the intrinsic interest of work. Thinkers such as Rensis Likert and Douglas McGregor examined the attitudes of supervisors and managers and the impact of their particular management style on the workers under their control. Both Likert and McGregor proferred prescriptions for improvement. Likert, for example, argued that:

> supervisors with the best record of performance are found to focus their attention on the human aspects of their subordinates' problems, and on building effective work groups which are set high achievement goals. These supervisors are 'employee-centred'. They regard their jobs as dealing with human beings rather than with the work; they attempt to know them as individuals. They see their function as helping them to do the job efficiently. They exercise general rather than detailed supervision, and are more concerned with targets than methods. They allow maximum participation in decision making. If high performance is to be obtained, a supervisor must not only be employee-centred but must also have high performance goals and be capable of exercising the decision-making process to achieve them.
>
> *(Pugh and Hickson, 1989, pp.156–57)*

Briefly, the workers under Likert's ideal form of supervision would be enabled to deploy their abilities to an extent that would be impossible under the tight constraints of 'old fashioned' foremanship with its traditional emphasis on keeping subordinates busy at narrowly specified tasks. Workers would be enabled to fulfil both their need for self-esteem and, hopefully, even achieve self-actualization through identification with the goals of the group. Although organizations might not be able to allow every musician in its employ to make music or every artist to paint, they could at least take positive steps to ameliorate some of the frustrations among their workers caused by under achievement and boredom. At the same time, by encouraging workers to internalize the goals of the organization, they could encourage them to put forward their best efforts voluntarily rather than under duress.

Critical summary

As a theory Maslow's hierarchy of needs presents a number of problems. In the words of Rose, 'the status of the needs hierarchy concept is uncertain. If we assume that needs are real how can their existence be proved? As with all such psychological constructs, no direct method of doing so is available. We are obliged to resort to indirect methods. We can say, for example, that if a man is observed to pursue status, that suggests he has a need for status. But this is unsatisfactory…We can argue just as well that if status is sought, it is not necessarily as an end in itself, but as a means to other ends, such as more wealth and power. How many needs are there in fact?' (Rose, 1988, p.205). Maslow himself considered that, in addition to the five basic needs, there might also be an aesthetic need. Moreover, Kakabadse, Ludlow and Vinnicombe, in their consideration of group dynamics, assert that individuals possess a need for power and that this can be facilitated through participation in the group. As they put it, 'one more need can be added to the needs identified by Maslow. Needs for power can…be satisfied in groups: either power over the other members of the group, or by using the power leverage of the group to effect the changes in the organization which individual members, by themselves, cannot achieve' (Kakabadse, Ludlow and Vinnicombe, 1988, p.161). Confusion regarding the number of needs is matched by concern over the universality of Maslow's hierarchy. Although he conceded that the ordering of needs might vary between individuals and across cultures he was nevertheless confident that the hierarchy was true for most people, in most places, for most of the time. However, his claims for universalism are far from convincing. Above all Maslow appears to be describing the observed behaviour patterns of middle class, American men in the mid-twentieth century. Nevertheless, having said all of this, Maslow's work was highly influential and this is reflected in the writing of such thinkers as Argyris, Likert, Herzberg (see Chapter 15) and McGregor (see Chapter 16). As Wren has observed 'Maslow paved the way for the humanist psychologists who argued for better employee mental health through improved organizational practices' (Wren, 1994, p.371).

Discussion questions

1. How convincing is Maslow's view that the human being is a perpetually wanting animal?
2. What did Maslow mean by the hierarchy of needs?
3. In what ways might the constraints of modern organizations frustrate the fulfilment of the higher needs?

Suggested reading

Argyle, M. (1972/1989) *The Social Psychology of Work*, Penguin Books, Harmondsworth.

Maslow, A. (1943) A Theory of Human Motivation, *Psychological Review* **50** *370–96.*

Maslow, A. (1954) *Motivation and Personality*, Harper and Row, New York.

Maslow, A. (1965) *Eupsychian Management*, Richard Irwin, Homewood, Illinois.

Maslow, A. (1971) *The Farther Reaches of Human Nature*, Viking Press, New York.

Rose, M. (1988) *Industrial Behaviour: Research and Control*, Penguin Books, Harmondsworth, ch.19.

Wren, D. (1994) *The Evolution of Management Thought*, Wiley and Sons, Chichester, ch.15.

Chapter 15

Frederick Herzberg and the motivation to work

Frederick Herzberg was born in Lynn, Massachusetts in 1923. He attended the City College of New York where he studied history and psychology. In his final year at college he ran short of money and decided to enlist in the American army. He was posted to Dachau concentration camp when it was liberated – an experience which provided the inspiration for his later academic work. As he put it:

> from my World War II military experiences, particularly at Dachau concentration camp, I concluded that a society does not go insane because of the insane. Every society has at least an estimated 15 per cent that are mentally deranged for one reason or another. But they account for only a minute amount of the pathologies than can grip any society. I believed at Dachau as an American soldier in 1945 and believe now...more than ever, that a society goes insane when the sane go insane and, in truth, more problems are created by the sane who are inept or unethical than by the acknowledged insane and criminal. My emphasis in teaching my students has been how they could contribute to our organizations by keeping the sane people sane.

> *(Herzberg, 1993, p.xi)*

At the end of the war Herzberg completed his studies in New York and later gained Masters and PhD degrees at the University of Pittsburgh. As part of his doctoral programme, he studied quantitative methods with John Flanagan. Flanagan had developed what he termed the 'Critical Incident' method for selecting individuals with the necessary capacities to function as pilots, bombadeers and gunners in the Army Air Corps during the war. Herzberg was much impressed by the manner in which Flanagan's work focussed 'on real happenings in individual lives' rather than mere statistical analysis. As Herzberg put it, Flanagan's approach 'had external validity built in' (Herzberg, 1993, p.xii). Herzberg later spent a year at the Pittsburgh Graduate School of Public Health, during which time he wrote a thesis entitled *Mental Health is Not the Opposite of Mental Illness*. In the mid-1950s he became research director of Psychological Service of Pittsburgh, a non-profit-making psychological consulting company. There he carried out numerous job attitude surveys as a means of gauging working morale and became increasingly intruiged by the contradictory information gathered from such surveys. With funding from the Buhl Foundation and local industries, Herzberg 'brought together a classification of the problem areas of job-attitudes in a review of almost two thousand writings – virtually everything that had been published on the subject from 1900 to 1955' (Herzberg, 1993, p.xiii). As Herzberg later explained:

> the goal of the study was to definitively answer the question, 'What do workers want from their jobs?' A total of 155 research studies published between 1920 and 1954, purported to present data in answer to this question. It was disturbing to find that this accumulated research provided evidence for all possible answers to the question. Results were contradictory. The first obvious explanation was the vast differences in methods and quality of research designs. Even slight changes in phrasing of questions for eliciting job-attitude responses repeatedly demonstrated major effects on the information obtained. I began to suspect the premise that feelings of job satisfaction and dissatisfaction could validly be measured on the same rating scale. Could this assumption have mislead previous researchers?
>
> *(Herzberg, 1993, p.xiii)*

Following his study of the literature, Herzberg formed the view that some of the factors relating to an individual's job-attitude could be described as 'satisfiers' whereas other, not necessarily opposite factors, could be described as 'dissatisfiers'. This was consistent with the approach he had taken in *Mental Health is Not the Opposite of Mental Illness* and from it Herzberg derived the basic hypothesis for the research study which was published as *The Motivation to Work* in 1959. This research will be examined in the next section but, for the moment, it is sufficient to observe that it generated what Herzberg called the 'motivation-hygiene' theory which provided the basis for his subsequent publications. In 1966 he published *Work and the Nature of Man*, which summarized the first ten replications of the original research study. In 1968 his article *One More Time: How Do You Motivate Your Employees?* appeared in the *Harvard Business Review* and became 'that journal's biggest selling article, with well over a million re-printed copies sold' (Kennedy, 1991, p.62). Motivation-hygiene theory, together with his ideas for job-enrichment, brought Herzberg immense celebrity as an academic (he became Distinguished Professor of Management in the University of Utah) and also as a consultant to major corporations, including AT&T, ICI, Texas Instruments, British Petroleum and Shell. Ease of international travel, together with the use of films, turned Herzberg into perhaps the first truly international management guru. As he later commented, 'all in all, I consulted or gave seminars in over 30 countries, 275 different industrial, governmental and social organizations, 175 professional societies, and 100 universities. *The Motivation to Work* and subsequent books and articles literally kept me in the air' (Herzberg, 1993, p.xiv).

What do people want from their jobs?

The Motivation to Work (1959) presented the findings of a study of job motivation undertaken by Herzberg and two of his colleagues at the Psychological Service of Pittsburgh, namely Bernard Mausner and Barbara Snyderman. The data used in the study were gathered from a variety of companies operating in the Pittsburgh area which the authors had selected to provide a representative sample of local industrial activity. Following two pilot studies, Herzberg and his colleagues decided that the major study should consist of approximately 200 interviews and also that two groups of workers should participate. As Herzberg explained:

> we decided to concentrate…on engineers and accountants…It was apparent in the results of (the) second pilot study that engineers were able to give exceptionally vivid accounts of their work experiences…A sample limited to one profession would have yielded results of doubtful generality. To develop findings independent of the peculiar circumstances of the engineer, we needed to study a comparable group. Accountants were chosen because their jobs, like those of engineers, are rich in technique…By covering accountants and engineers, we examined the job attitudes of two of the most important staff groups in modern industry.
>
> *(Herzberg et al, 1959/1993, p.32)*

In the interviews, the respondents were asked to think of a time when they felt exceptionally good or exceptionally bad about their present job or any other job they had done. Such questions as 'did the consequences of what happened at this time affect your career?' and 'did what happened change the way you felt about your profession?' were posed. Further, the respondents were asked to estimate 'how seriously were your feelings (good or bad) about your job affected by what happened?' and to rate the intensity of their feelings on a numerical scale. When Herzberg and his colleagues analysed their findings they discovered that the experiences which made the individuals surveyed feel good or bad were not polar opposites of the same phenomenon. Instead, they sprang from two quite different sets of phenomena. As Herzberg observed many years later, 'people are made dissatisfied by bad environment, the extrinsics of the job. But they are seldom made satisfied by what I called the hygienes. They are made satisfied by the intrinsics of what they do, what I call the motivators' (Herzberg, 1993, pp.xiii–xiv).

In chapter 12 of *The Motivation to Work* Herzberg and his colleagues summarized their answer to the question 'what do people want from their jobs?' in the light of motivation-hygiene theory. Lack of motivation they observed was:

> not associated with the job itself but with the conditions that surround the doing of the job. These events suggest to the individual that the context in which he performs his work is unfair or disorganized and as such represents to him an unhealthy psychological work environment. Factors involved in these situations we call factors of hygiene. Hygiene operates to remove health hazards from the environment of man. It is not a curative; it is, rather, a preventive...when there are deleterious factors in the context of the job, they serve to bring about poor job attitudes. Improvements in these factors of hygiene will serve to remove the impediments to positive job attitudes.
>
> *(Herzberg et al, 1959/1993, p.113)*

Among the 'hygiene factors' identified by Herzberg and his colleagues were supervision, interpersonal relations, physical working conditions, remuneration, company policies and administrative procedures, benefits and job security. When any of these deteriorated to a level the employee considered unacceptable, then job dissatisfaction could be expected to ensue. However, Herzberg and his colleagues argued, 'the reverse does not hold true. When the job context can be characterized as optimal, we will not get dissatisfaction, but neither will we get much in the way of positive attitudes' (Herzberg *et al*, 1959/1993, pp.113–14). Thus, although the provision of proper hygiene is necessary to ensure a satisfied worker, it does not ensure a motivated worker.

In seeking to differentiate the factors which generated motivation from those which caused dissatisfaction, Herzberg and his colleagues turned to the work of Maslow (see Chapter 14). As they put it 'the factors that lead to positive job attitudes do so because they satisfy the individual's need for self-actualization in his work' (Herzberg *et al*, 1959/1993, p.114). The context in which an employee works does not possess the potential to provide self-actualization:

> It is only from the performance of a task that the individual can get the rewards that will reinforce his aspirations...Factors in the job context meet the needs of the individual for avoiding unpleasant situations. In contrast to this motivation by meeting avoidance needs, the job factors reward the needs of the individual to reach his aspirations. These effects on the individual can be conceptualized as actuating approach rather than avoidance behaviour. Since it is in the approach sense that the term motivation is most commonly used, we designate the job factors as the 'motivators', as opposed to the extra-job factors, which we have labelled the factors of hygiene. It should be understood that both kinds of factors meet the needs of the employee; but it is primarily the 'motivators'

that serve to bring about the kind of job satisfaction…the kind of improvement in performance that industry is seeking from its workforce.

(Herzberg et al, 1959/1993, p.114)

Notwithstanding the limited nature (numerically, geographically and socially) of their sample, Herzberg and his colleagues were sufficiently confident of the universality of motivation-hygiene theory to make a number of generalizations concerning work and motivation in industrial society. They were particularly scathing about the impact of bureaucracy on the individual worker (see Chapter 6). As they put it, 'the profoundest motivation to work comes from the recognition of individual achievement and from the sense of personal growth in responsibility. It is likely that neither of these can…flourish in a bureaucratic situation' (Herzberg et al, 1959/1993, p. 125) The main reason they gave for this was that bureaucracies are governed by rules and that the opportunity to exercise personal judgement and initiative are therefore severely constrained. As the rigidity and complexity of bureaucracy increases there will thus be a concomitant 'decrease in the available amount of motivation'. Herzberg and his colleagues were similarly hostile to the attempts to motivate workers through the use of financial incentives, such as the piecework and premium payments associated with scientific management. Economic incentives alone, they claimed, did not motivate workers but merely compensated them for enduring the tedium of their jobs. Even in cases where financial incentives and bonus schemes had apparently succeeded in motivating employees, improvements often resulted as much from increases in job content and responsibility as increases in pay. Herzberg and his colleagues were not impressed either with attempts to employ the human relations lessons derived from the Hawthorne experiments (see Chapter 11). For example, criticizing the contemporary fashion for training supervisors in improved inter-personal skills, they observed that:

supervisory training in human relations is probably essential to the maintenance of good hygiene at work. This is particularly true for the many jobs…in which modern industry offers little chance for the operation of the motivators. These jobs are atomized, cut and dried, monotonous. They offer little chance for responsibility and achievement and thus little opportunity for self-actualization. It is here that hygiene is exceptionally important. The fewer the opportunities for the 'motivators' to appear, the greater must be the hygiene offered in order to make the work tolerable.

(Herzberg et al 1959/1993, p.115)

Thus, like money, sympathetic supervision could not fully compensate for lack of intrinsic interest in the work itself. Neither, for that matter, could the packages of 'company newspapers and athletic teams,…feeding facilities, and…lush working surroundings' associated with 'welfare capitalism'. Enlightened management and attractive fringe benefits might fulfil workers' hygiene requirements but nothing more.

Having thus, as they saw it, disposed of the conventional approaches to motivating workers, Herzberg and his colleagues put forward their own suggestions. Above all 'jobs must be restructured to increase to the maximum the ability of workers to achieve goals meaningfully related to the doing of the job' (Herzberg *et al*, 1959/1993, p.132). In advocating the need for what Herzberg later described as job-enrichment he and his colleagues were seeking to reverse a tendency to 'degrade' work that had lasted for well over a century. The American system of manufacturing had sought as far as possible to replace craft skill with machinery (see Chapter 1). Similarly, scientific management had attempted to draw a clear distinction between the planning and execution of work (see Chapters 2 and 3). Finally, mass production had encouraged the combination of extreme division of labour and machine paced work, most fully realized in the moving assembly tracks of the automobile industry (see Chapter 9). As Herzberg and his colleagues commented 'the individual should have some measure of control over the way in which the job is done in order to realize a sense of achievement and of personal growth. Clearly, most assembly line workers cannot have such control' (Herzberg *et al*, 1959/1993, p.132). However, they were cautious about merely re-designing jobs to make them 'broader' in the hope that this might lead to improved motivation. Instead they called for something rather more subtle. As they put it, 'jobs themselves have to be set up in such as way that, interest or no, the individual who carries them out can find that their operations lead to increased motivation' (Herzberg *et al*, 1959/1993, p.134). Having said this, however, they also asserted the need for careful staff selection. Thus 'if one structures the jobs properly, one must also structure the selection process properly...This demands a continued close analysis of the actual kinds of abilities needed for each job and an equally close analysis of the potential abilities of applicants for work (Herzberg *et al*, 1959/1993, p.134).

In deploying the attitudes of professional and managerial workers to interpret the putative attitudes of clerical and production workers, Herzberg and his colleagues made a huge, and perhaps indefensible, leap. Professional and managerial workers had been specifically chosen for study because pilot studies had shown that they 'were more verbal, showed a quicker grasp of the technique, and gave more and better delineated sequences of events than the clerical and production groups' (Herzberg *et al*, 1959/1993, p.32). This suggests that the kinds of people who made up the two groups were very different and, in all probability, had equally different sources of motivation. Or if not different sources then certainly differing attitudes and differing perceptions of achievement. Indeed Herzberg and his colleagues went some way to conceding this very point when they observed (in their discussion of selection) that 'there should be some recognition of the fact that in many jobs...there are numerous combinations of abilities and temperaments that will lead to success in the same job for different reasons' (Herzberg *et al*, 1959/1993, p.134). In addition to doubts concerning the validity of making the leap from one class of workers to another, there were grounds for justifiable scepticism regarding the validity of motivation-hygiene theory itself. Among the sceptics was Victor Vroom who, whilst congratulating Herzberg and his colleagues 'for directing attention towards the psychological effects of job content,' declared that:

> even if (subsequent) research were to perfectly replicate the Herzberg, Mausner and Snyderman findings on widely different populations, their influence concerning a qualitative difference between satisfiers and dissatisfiers could not be unequivocally accepted. It is still possible that obtained differences between stated sources of satisfaction and dissatisfaction stem from defensive processes within the individual respondent. Persons may be more likely to attribute the causes of satisfaction to their own achievements and accomplishments on the job. On the other hand, they may be more likely to attribute their dissatisfaction not to personal inadequacies or deficiencies, but to factors in the work environment, i.e. obstacles presented by company policies or supervision.
>
> *(Vroom, 1964, p.129)*

Vroom went on to observe that this was exactly the conclusion reached by Guin, Veroff and Feld in their 1960 study *Americans View their Mental Health*. Herzberg proved impervious, however, to attempts to refute motivation-hygiene theory. In *Work and the Nature of Man* (1966) he was at pains to show that replications of the Pittsburgh study had all served to reinforce its findings. On the specific point of Vroom's criticism, which he quoted without attribution, he was particularly dismissive. As he put it 'the supposition that people would prefer to blame hygiene factors rather than the motivators for their job unhappiness in order to make themselves look good is naive. It does not take too much experience with job-attitude data to find that the opposite is more often true' (Herzberg, 1966/1974, p.130).

Adam and Abraham

In *Work and the Nature of Man* Herzberg sought to represent motivation-hygiene theory as springing from human nature itself. Although, as has been noted, the core of this book was an account of ten replications of the Pittsburgh study, he now placed the narrowly empirical material in the context of wide-ranging speculation concerning the historical development of work and industrial relations. Adapting the Old Testament figures of Adam and Abraham to his purpose, Herzberg claimed they signified two discrete sets of human desires. Adam stood for the human being's animal nature. As Herzberg put it, the 'overriding goal as an animal is to avoid the pain inevitable in relating to the environment. This avoidance nature is determined by man's biological inheritance' (Herzberg, 1966/1974, p.168). Adam thus represented the hygiene factors in motivation-hygiene theory. By contrast Abraham stood for the human being's desire 'to determine, to discover, to achieve, to actualize, to progress and add to his existence' (Herzberg, 1966/1974, p.168). Abraham was thus associated with the motivational concerns of motivation-hygiene theory. According to Herzberg, Adam and Abraham (like hygienes and motivators) were two essentially independent aspects of human nature. Furthermore:

> each aspect has a system of needs that operate in opposing directions. Meeting the needs of one facet of man has little effect on the needs of the other facet...This theory of motivation opens the door wide for reinterpretation of industrial relations phenomena...job attitudes must be viewed twice: What does the employee seek? What makes him happy? Then a separate question arises that is not deducible from the first: What does he wish to avoid? What makes him unhappy? Industrial relations that stress sanitation as their *modus operandi* can serve only to prevent dissatisfactions and the resultant personnel problems. Of course, attention to hygiene is important, for without it any organization will reap the consequence of unhappy personnel. The error lies in assuming that prevention will unleash positive feelings and the returns of increased creativity, productivity, lowered absenteeism and turnover, and all the other indecies of manpower efficiency.
>
> *(Herzberg, 1966/1974, p.169)*

Such was the universality claimed by Herzberg for motivation-hygiene theory that he claimed the Adam/Abraham dichotomy to be present in everyone. However, he offered a refinement of this rather crude position by suggesting that individuals possessed a propensity or disposition to be either 'hygiene seekers' or 'motivation seekers'. Whereas, for example, a hygiene seeker would be 'motivated by the nature of the environment' a motivation seeker would be 'motivated by the nature of the task'. Similarly, whereas a hygiene seeker would realize 'little satisfaction from accomplishments' the motivation seeker would realize 'great satisfaction from accomplishments'. The hygiene seeker, according to Herzberg, was dominated by the animal insecurities associated with Adam and possessed an essentially negative outlook. Such people would be those who indulged in what F. W. Taylor described as 'soldiering' (see Chapter 2). Although hygiene seekers might appear to be good at their jobs, in Herzberg's view they could never be relied upon to 'come through' when things got tough. As he put it 'I believe that hygiene seekers will let the company down when their talents are most needed. They are motivated only for short times and only when there is an external reward to be obtained. It is just when an emergency situation arises, and when the organization cannot be bothered with hygiene, that these key men may fail to do their jobs' (Herzberg, 1966/1974, p.89). Furthermore, a hygiene seeker in a managerial position could have a dire impact on the organization's future. Thus:

> if we accept the notion that one of the most important functions of a manager is the development of future managers, the teaching of hygiene motivators becomes a serious defect to the company. This, I believe, is one of the major implications that the motivation-hygiene theory has for modern personnel

practices. Previous research knowledge has strongly indicated that the effectiveness of management development is attuned to its congruence with the company atmosphere, as it is manifested in the supervisor's beliefs and behaviour. The superior who is a hygiene seeker cannot but have an adverse effect on management development which is aimed at the personal growth and actualization of subordinates.

(Herzberg, 1966/1974, p.91)

Apparently too much association with Adam could blunt Abraham's desire for achievement and lead him to settle back into a placid acceptance of the hygiene factors.

In Herzberg's view conventional industrial relations practices only addressed the Adam/hygiene factors of human motivation. Incremental improvements in the hygiene factors could not bring lasting benefits in terms of staff motivation. After a brief 'feel good' period workers would once again feel a sense of dissatisfaction, 'primarily because of (the) endless nature of hygiene requirements'. If workers could not derive their motivation from the work itself then managements could expect a constant battle to sustain productivity. In order to obviate this situation Herzberg made the ambitious proposal that a separate unit be created within every organization to deal with the Abraham/motivator factors, taking as its central concern the psychological growth of the personnel. This 'motivator division' would have three essential tasks, namely, educating workers to adopt a motivator orientation; organizing the process of job-enrichment; and taking the necessary 'remedial or therapeutic actions'. The first of these sprang from Herzberg's belief that negative job attitudes were often derived from socialization and could be adjusted through education. The second sprang from his notion that work could be re-designed to provide a greater sense of achievement. The third sprang in part from his awareness of the need to re-train workers whose skills were rendered obsolete through technological change, and in part from his controversial belief that hygiene seekers were suffering from mental illness. As he put it:

a hygiene seeker is not merely a victim of circumstances, but is motivated in the direction of temporary satisfaction. It is not that his job offers little opportunity for self-actualization; rather, it is that his needs lie predominantly in another direction, that of satisfying avoidance needs. He is seeking positive happiness via the route of avoidance behaviour, and thus his resultant chronic dissatisfaction is an illness of motivation. Chronic unhappiness, a motivation pattern that ensures continual dissatisfaction, a failure to grow or to want to grow – these characteristics add up to a neurotic personality.

(Herzberg, 1966/1974, p.81)

As in the case of Elton Mayo and his insistence that industrial conflict derived from psychological rather than economic causes (see Chapter 11) Herzberg was unwilling to accept that workers might be motivated merely by their 'lower order needs'. Put crudely, in Herzberg's view workers ought to desire 'growth achievements' and if they did not then they must be sick.

Critical summary

Herzberg's work was produced at a time when economic boom was producing tight labour markets in the United States and the rest of the industrialized West. There was a general consensus among academics and practitioners that a mismatch between personal aspirations and job content was leading to worker frustration and low productivity and morale. Herzberg condemned the progressive degradation of work in industrial societies and, like Braverman (see Chapter 18), he accepted the views of Karl Marx on the impact of capitalism on the labour process. Unlike Braverman, however, he rejected the economic and political implications of Marxism, focusing instead on the psychological effects of capitalism and the impact of 'alienation'. Herzberg was close to Maslow in believing that human beings possessed a natural desire to aspire, achieve and self-actualize. Taking the business corporation to be the 'dominant institution of modern times', Herzberg convincingly argued that the bulk of people must seek feelings of achievement through their paid employment. He deployed motivation-hygiene theory to explain why generous packages of pay and conditions apparently failed to motivate workers. Motivation derived from the job itself and if the job failed to generate a sense of achievement then, according to Herzberg, improving pay and conditions would not generate motivation.

In spite of legitimate doubts concerning the research basis of motivation-hygiene theory, and the suspicion that it was in any case based on a false dichotomy, Herzberg's work was highly influential. The growing acceptance that the excessive division of labour associated with scientific management and mass production was self-defeating created a situation in which Herzberg's message was welcomed. There had long been concern about the lack of job satisfaction in much contemporary work and Herzberg offered a glib justification for changes that many executives were in any case already contemplating. Herzberg's ideas were rendered doubly attractive by the fact that they were, on the face of it, readily intelligible and offered the possibility of improved profits. Herzberg has claimed that motivation-hygiene theory is 'perhaps the most heuristic theory in industrial psychology' (Herzberg, 1993, p. xviii). Certainly motivation-hygiene theory does illuminate the behaviour of at least some people in the work situation. Above all, however, Herzberg shows in his work how to sustain a successful management theory – make it simple, say it often and never accept a refutation.

Discussion questions

1.   What did Herzberg mean by the term 'motivation–hygiene theory'?

2. Why did Herzberg advocate careful staff selection?
3. Why did Herzberg argue for job-enrichment?
4. How convincing is Herzberg's view that workers are not mainly motivated by money?

Suggested reading

Herzberg, F., Mausner, B. and Snyderman, B. (1959/1993) *The Motivation to Work*, Transaction Publishers, New Brunswick, New Jersey.

Herzberg, F. (1966/1974) *Work and the Nature of Man*, Crosby Lockwood Staples, London.

Kakabadse, A., Ludlow, R. and Vinnicombe, S. (1988) *Working in Organizations*, Penguin Books, Harmondsworth, ch.5.

Pugh, D. and Hickson, D. (eds) (1989) *Writers on Organizations*, Penguin Books, Harmondsworth, ch.5.

Pugh, D. (ed) (1990) *Organization Theory: Selected Readings*, Penguin Books, Harmondsworth, ch.21.

Vroom, V. (1964) *Work and Motivation*, Wiley & Sons, New York.

Chapter 16

Douglas McGregor and the human side of enterprise

Douglas McGregor was born in 1906. He received his doctorate in psychology from Harvard and subsequently taught there for several years before moving to the Massachusetts Institute of Technology (MIT) in 1937. At MIT he helped establish the Industrial Relations section before leaving, in 1948, to become president of Antioch College where he stayed until 1954. In that year he returned to MIT as the first Sloan Fellows Professor, remaining with the institution until his death in 1964. During the early 1950s McGregor began to formulate his ideas on management which were eventually published in his single major work *The Human Side of Enterprise* in 1960.[1] As he put it in the preface to that book:

> some years ago during a meeting of the Advisory Committee of MIT's School of Industrial Management, Alfred Sloan raised some questions related to the issue of whether managers are born or made...The discussion...served to sharpen certain interests I had had for some time in a systematic examination of the many common but inconsistent assumptions about what makes a manager. In 1954 the Alfred P. Sloan Foundation made a grant to me to explore some of these ideas more fully.
>
> *(McGregor, 1960/1987, vii)*

---

1 At the time of his death McGregor was working on a new book. The manuscript was edited by Caroline McGregor and Warren Bennis and published by McGraw-Hill in 1967 under the title *The Professional Manager*.

McGregor's research led him to the view that the key question for top management was, 'what are your assumptions (implicit as well as explicit) about the most effective way to manage people' and he added 'from the answer to this question flow the answers to the questions Mr. Sloan raised...as well as the answers to many other questions which perplex and confound management as it seeks to achieve more successfully the economic objectives of enterprise' (McGregor, 1960/1987, viii). In *The Human Side of Enterprise*, McGregor expanded on his notion that behind every managerial decision or action there lay assumptions about human nature and human behaviour which were central in determining each individual manager's style of operation. He divided these assumptions into two broad categories which he termed Theory X and Theory Y. These will be examined in detail in the two sections which follow.

Theory X: the traditional view of direction and control

McGregor claimed that the assumptions of Theory X pervaded most of the existing literature on organizations and were also implicit in the bulk of current managerial policy and practice. The first assumption he identified was that 'the average human being has an inherent dislike of work' (McGregor, 1960/1987, p.33). McGregor traced this assumption back to biblical times and claimed that it was evidenced in the stress placed by management on productivity and the much publicized evils of output restriction. Further, the contemporary emphasis on rewards for individual perform-ance reflected 'an underlying belief that management must counteract an inherent human tendency to avoid work'. The second assumption, McGregor claimed, fol-lowed from the first and held that 'because of this human characteristic of dislike of work, most people must be coerced, controlled, directed, threatened with punishment to get them to put forth adequate effort toward achievement of organizational objec-tives' (McGregor, 1960/1987, p.34). Thus, although various rewards might be offered, workers would not necessarily complete the required tasks. Only the threat of punishment would suffice, the underlying assumption being 'that people will only work under external coercion and control'. The third assumption identified by McGre-gor was that 'the average human being prefers to be directed, wishes to avoid responsibility, has relatively little ambition, wants security above all' (McGregor, 1960/1987, p.34). Although the prevailing American political and social values might, McGregor observed, pay lip service to the 'ideal of the worth of the average human being', the majority of managers actually believed in the 'mediocrity of the masses'. As he put it, 'paternalism has become a nasty word, but it is by no means defunct managerial philosophy' (McGregor, 1960/1987, p.34). Having identified the three central assumptions of Theory X, McGregor was at pains to show that it accurately represented current management practice and was not merely an intellectual construct. As he explained, 'Theory X is not a straw man for purposes of demolition, but is in fact a theory which materially influences managerial strategy in a wide sector of American industry today. Moreover, the principles of organization which comprise the bulk of the literature of management could only have been derived from assumptions such as those of Theory X. Other beliefs about human nature would have led to quite different organizational principles' (McGregor, 1960/1987, p.35).

McGregor was, of course, willing to concede that Theory X did provide an explanation of some human behaviour in industry. However, in broad terms he considered Theory X to be inadequate, particularly in the light of recent developments concerning the understanding of human motivation. Freely adapting the words of Abraham Maslow (see Chapter 14) he claimed that:

> man is a wanting animal – as soon as one of his needs is satisfied, another appears in its place. This process is unending. It continues from birth to death. Man continuously puts forth effort – works, if you please – to satisfy his needs.... A satisfied need is not a motivator of behaviour! This is a fact of profound significance. It is a fact which is unrecognized in Theory X and is, therefore, ignored in the conventional approach to the management of people.
>
> *(McGregor, 1960/1987, p.36)*

According to McGregor, managers were well aware of the validity of the hierarchy of needs but chose to construe it as a threat rather than a meaningful insight into human behaviour. For example, numerous studies had indicated 'that the tightly knit, cohesive work group may, under proper conditions, be far more effective than an equal number of separate individuals in achieving organizational goals. Yet management, fearing group hostility to its own objectives, often goes to considerable lengths to control and direct human efforts in ways that are inimical to the natural 'groupiness' of human beings' (McGregor, 1960/1987, pp.37–38). McGregor omitted to add, of course, that there was also plenty of evidence to show that the 'tightly knit, cohesive work group' was just as likely to restrict output as facilitate it. However, he was not greatly interested in counter arguments, preferring instead to emphasise the problems which sprang from inhibiting the 'natural' desire to work in groups. As he put it, 'when man's social needs – and perhaps his safety needs, too – are thus thwarted, he behaves in ways which tend to defeat organizational objectives. He becomes antagonistic, unco-operative. But this behaviour is a consequence, not a cause' (McGregor, 1960/1987, p.38).

In McGregor's view the 'typical industrial organization' offered very limited opportunities to workers to satisfy their higher needs. As he observed, 'the conventional methods of organizing work, particularly by mass production, give little heed to these aspects of human motivation…We will be mistaken if we attribute his resultant passivity, or his hostility, or his refusal to accept responsibility to his inherent "human nature". These forms of behaviour are symptoms of illness – of deprivation of his social and egoistic needs' (McGregor, 1960/1987, pp.38–39). In such circumstances, McGregor argued, managers should not be surprised if increased wages failed to produce improved productivity. Given that their work lacked intrinsic interest and provided no sense of self-fulfilment, workers could use extra financial rewards to pursue the satisfaction of their higher needs only outside of work when they resumed their private life. Workers thus came to resent their work and, as McGregor put it, 'it is not surprising...that for many wage earners work is perceived as a form of punishment which is the price to be paid for various kinds of satisfaction away from the job. To the extent that this is their perception, we would hardly expect them to undergo more of this punishment than is necessary' (McGregor, 1960/1987, p.40).

Given that McGregor was writing at the height of the long post-war economic boom he was able to claim, with some plausibility, that employers had 'provided relatively well for the satisfaction of physiological and safety needs'. As a result of this, however, workers' desires had shifted 'upwards' to their unfulfilled higher needs. Frustration of the higher needs manifested itself in worker dissatisfaction and led management to respond by applying a combination of financial rewards and punishment – i.e. 'carrot and stick'. As McGregor put it:

> Unless there are opportunities at work to satisy...higher-level needs, people will be deprived; and their behaviour will reflect this deprivation. Under such conditions...the mere provision of rewards is bound to be ineffective, and reliance on the threat of punishment will be inevitable...People will make insistent demands for more money under these conditions. It becomes more important than ever to buy the material goods and services which can provide limited satisfaction of the thwarted needs. Although money has only limited value in satisfying many higher-level needs, it can become the focus of interest if it is the only means available...The 'carrot and stick' theory of motivation...works reasonably well under certain circumstances...But...does not work at all once man has reached an adequate subsistence level and is motivated by primarily higher needs.... People deprived of opportunities to satisfy at work the needs which are now important to them, behave exactly as we might predict – with indolence, passivity, unwillingness to accept responsibility, resistance to change, willingness to follow the demagogue, unreasonable demands for economic benefits.
>
> *(McGregor, 1960/1987, pp.40–42)*

For McGregor Theory X provided an explanation of the 'consequences' of a specific management strategy which he identified with the scientific management approach. Whereas, for example, in the sphere of child rearing it had become commonplace to progressively modify parental strategies in order to adapt to the changed abilities and attitudes of the developing infant, Theory X assumed no capacity for development in the worker. Instead a tacit assumption was made that 'the average human being is permanently arrested in development in early adolescence. Theory X is built on the least common denominator – the factory 'hand' of the past...So long as the assumptions of Theory X continue to influence management strategy, we will fail to discover, let alone utilize, the potentialities of the average human being' (McGregor, 1960/1987, p.43).

Theory Y: the integration of individual and organizational goals

Having outlined and criticised the assumptions of Theory X, McGregor turned to the assumptions of Theory Y. He claimed that 'the expenditure of physical and mental effort in work is as natural as play or rest' (McGregor, 1960/1987, p.47). The average human being was not necessarily averse to work but would see it as either a source of satisfaction or punishment 'depending upon controllable conditions'. Further, 'external control and the threat of punishment are not the only means for bringing about effort toward organizational objectives' (McGregor, 1960/1987, p.47). In fact, argued McGregor, it was self-evident that workers would exercise both self-direction and self-control, provided they were sufficiently committed to organizational objectives. Such commitment 'is a function of the rewards associated with their achievement' and the most significant rewards (such as the satisfaction of self-esteem and self-actualization needs) could be 'direct products of the effort directed toward organizational objectives' (McGregor, 1960/1987, p.48). Contrary to the assumptions underpinning Theory X, 'the average human being learns, under proper conditions, not only to accept but to seek responsibility' (McGregor, 1960/1987, p.48). The observed reluctance of some workers to accept responsibility, together with their apparent lack of ambition and emphasis on security, 'are generally consequences of experience, not inherent human characteristics' (McGregor, 1960/1987, p.48). In fact the capacity to 'exercise a relatively high degree of imagination, ingenuity, and creativity in the solution of organizational problems is widely, not narrowly, distributed in the population' (McGregor, 1960/1987, p.48). On this basis it was a clear mistake to pursue the stark division between planning and execution of work that was inherent in scientific management. Such an approach inevitably wasted the bulk of workers' abilities and at the same time reduced them to mere drudges. As McGregor put it, 'under the conditions of modern industrial life, the intellectual potentialities of the average human being are only partially utilized' (McGregor, 1960–1987, p.48).

According to McGregor the assumptions of Theory Y offered 'sharply different' implications for management than those of Theory X. They were, for example, dynamic rather than static and they suggested the strong possibility of human growth and development within the context of the work situation. On the basis of Theory Y the workforce became 'a resource which has substantial potentialities' (McGregor, 1960/1987, p.48). McGregor argued that the insights derived from Theory Y suggested that the limits of human collaboration in an organizational setting sprang not from inherent human nature but from managerial failure. Theory X provided management with a ready means of rationalizing such failure by enabling them to blame the nature of the human resources with which they were constrained to work. Theory Y, 'on the other hand, places the problems squarely in the lap of management. If employees are lazy, indifferent, unwilling to take responsibility, intransigent, uncreative, unco-operative, Theory Y implies that the causes lie in mangement's methods of organization and control' (McGregor, 1960/1987, p.48). Whereas the central principle of organization which derived from Theory X was direction and control, the central principle which derived from Theory Y was that of integration. Integration placed the responsibility upon management to create circumstances 'such that the members of the organization can achieve their own goals best by directing their efforts toward the success of the enterprise' (McGregor, 1960/1987, p.49). Self-control would thus replace external control, the goals of the organization would be internalized by the workers and the achievement of these goals would satisfy the workers' needs for self-esteem and self-actualization. As McGregor expressed it, 'integration means working together for the success of the enterprise so we all may share in the resulting rewards' (McGregor, 1960/1987, p.53). Having said all of this McGregor did not, of course, believe that the assumptions of Theory Y were 'finally validated'. Instead, he saw it rather as a potent challenge to the prevailing orthodoxy of Theory X – that is as an 'invitation to innovation'.

Critical summary

McGregor's Theory Y was a logical extension of Maslow's hierarchy of needs. If Maslow's categories were accurate then it followed that prevailing patterns of work could not be satisfying the human needs for self-esteeem and self-actualization. Theory X assumptions led to direction rather than integration and control rather than commitment. As Wren has commented:

> managers who accepted the Y image of human nature would not structure, control or closely supervise the work environment. Instead, they would attempt to aid the motivation of subordinates by giving them wider latitude in their work, encouraging creativity, using less external control, encouraging self-control, and motivating through the satisfaction that came from the challenge of work itself. The use of the authority of external control by management would be replaced by getting people committed to organizational goals because they perceived that this was the best way to achieve their own goals. A perfect integration was not possible, but McGregor hoped that an adoption of Y assumptions by managers would improve existing industrial practice.
>
> *(Wren, 1994, p.374)*

Of course, although a manager might have the disposition to adopt a Theory Y approach, this would not be sufficient of itself to change the attitudes of workers. The jobs themselves might have to be re–designed in order to yield greater opportunity for creativity (see Chapter 15). Equally the nature of the production process might prove hostile to the implementation of Y assumptions. Nevertheless McGregor indicated the direction in which management style might constructively evolve if sufficient trust between management and workers could be developed and sustained.

Discussion questions

1. What were the main assumptions of Theory X?
2. What were the main assumptions of Theory Y?
3. Why did McGregor consider that direction in organizations must be replaced by integration?

Suggested reading

McGregor, D. (1960/1987) *The Human Side of Enterprise*, Penguin Books, Harmondsworth.

Pugh, D. and Hickson, D. (eds) (1989) *Writers on Organizations*, Penguin Books, Harmondsworth, ch.5.

Rose, M. (1988) *Industrial Behaviour: Research and Control*, Penguin Books, Harmondsworth, ch.19.

Wren, D. (1994) *The Evolution of Management Thought*, Wiley & Sons, Chichester, ch.20.

Chapter 17

Fritz Schumacher and small is beautiful

Fritz Schumacher was born in Bonn, Germany in 1911 where his father was professor of economics at the university. Schumacher was educated at the Arndt Gymnasium in Berlin and also at the universities of Berlin and Bonn. In 1930 he came to England as a Rhodes Scholar and studied philosophy, politics and economics for two years at New College, Oxford. He spent the third year of his scholarship at the school of banking at Columbia University in the USA. By the time Schumacher returned to Germany the Nazis were in power and, unwilling to come to terms with Hitler's regime, he decided to leave Germany and return to England. When the Second World War began in 1939 Schumacher's academic abilities saved him from being interned as an 'enemy alien'. Instead he spent five years as an agricultural labourer in Oxfordshire, immersing himself in the works of Marx and also attending regular meetings with economic and financial experts in Whitehall. From 1946 to 1950 Schumacher was a member of the British section of the Control Commission in Western Germany – a post which involved him in renouncing his German nationality and becoming a naturalized British citizen. His work with the Control Commission won him the notice of such notables as Sir Stafford Cripps and Lord Keynes, and resulted in his appointment to the post of economic advisor to the National Coal Board (NCB) in 1950. Schumacher retained the post for the next 20 years, enjoying a particularly close working relationship with Lord Robens when the latter became chairman of the NCB in 1961.

In 1960 Schumacher's wife Ann Maria, whom he had married in 1936, died quite suddenly of cancer. This event precipitated a period of deep reflection in Schumacher's life which led him to question his economic and philosophical beliefs. Drawn to mysticism and eastern religions in general he was particularly drawn to Buddhism. The acceptance of an offer to become economic advisor to the Burmese government provided him with the opportunity to visit a Buddhist country and study the impact of Buddhist beliefs on the nature of work. He subsequently used the insights gathered in Burma to criticise contemporary western approaches to work. As he wrote:

> the Buddhist point of view takes the function of work to be at least threefold: to give a man a chance to utilize and develop his faculties; to enable him to overcome his egocentredness by joining with other people in a common task; and to bring forth the goods and services needed for a becoming existence . . . the consequences that flow from this view are endless. To organize work in such a manner that it becomes meaningless, boring, stultifying, or nerve-racking for the worker would be little short of criminal; it would indicate a greater concern with goods than with people, an evil lack of compassion and a soul-destroying degree of attachment to the most primitive side of this worldly existence.
>
> *(Schumacher, 1973/1993, pp.40–41)*

However, having said all of this, Schumacher ultimately rejected Buddhism as a viable system of belief for the Westerner. Instead, together with his second wife and his daughter, he was eventually received into the Roman Catholic church. Typically, in his eclectic way, he absorbed Catholic doctrine (specifically that of subsidiarity) into his arguments for the peaceful improvement of industrialized and industrializing societies.

During the 1960s and 1970s Schumacher became the leading propagandist of 'intermediate' or 'appropriate' technology – an idea he originally set out in a report prepared for the Indian Planning Commission in 1963. He claimed that intermediate technology was more productive for the people of developing nations than the indigenous technologies while also being far cheaper and environmentally benign than advanced technology. Moreover, intermediate technology enabled access and control to reside at the level of the village, thereby sustaining rather than destroying communities. In 1966 Schumacher became founder-chairman of the Intermediate Technology Development Group and subsequently travelled widely lecturing on his ideas for small-scale, environmentally friendly technology. He also served as President of the Soil Association (Britain's largest organic farming organization) and as Director of the Scott-Bader Company (a chemical company which pioneered industrial common ownership). Schumacher retired from the NCB in 1970 and was appointed CBE in 1974. Like many of the theorists mentioned in this book, Schumacher spent his 'retirement' proselytising for his ideas. He was always ready to meet with groups, of whatever kind or size, provided they were willing to act upon his ideas. Crowded schedules and excessive travel probably hastened Schumacher's death – at the height of his celebrity in September 1977 he was taken ill and died while travelling by train through Switzerland to attend a conference.[1]

---

1 Much of the biographical information contained in this chapter is based on Schumacher's entry in *The Dictionary of National Biography 1971–1980* Oxford University Press, Oxford, 1986.

Small is beautiful

Schumacher published his major work *Small is Beautiful: A Study of Economics as if People Mattered* in 1973. Consisting of 19 chapters and an epilogue it brought together various articles, essays and lectures which he had produced from the mid-1960s to the early 1970s. The material contained in the book demonstrated the width of Schumacher's interests, ranging from education to nuclear energy and from Buddhist economics to the problem of unemployment in India. It also displayed the vast variety of sources from which Schumacher had gleaned his inspiration. As Jonathon Porritt has commented:

> Fritz Schumacher was a great synthesizer, bringing many disparate concerns within the same frame of reference. He was the first of the 'holistic thinkers' of the modern Green Movement. Re-reading *Small is Beautiful* one has a very strong sense of the rich tradition from which Schumacher gained so much. He is the natural inheriter of the insights of William Morris on the crucial significance of giving people access to good work, of Lady Eve Balfour and Henry Doubleday on organic farming and the importance of maintaining soil fertility, of Lewis Mumford on technology and the Industrial Revolution, of Gandhi, Kropotkin, Tawney and Galbraith. All these and many more were stirred into Schumacher's pot to produce a work of wonderful vitality and originality.
>
> *(Porritt in Schumacher, 1993, pp.vii–viii)*

Although Schumacher's contributions to management theory were substantially contained in three chapters (i.e. 'A Question of Size', 'Technology With a Human Face' and 'Towards a Theory of Large-Scale Organization') allusions to management issues were nevertheless scattered throughout the book.

Central to Schumacher's thinking was the question of size and his sustained criticism of the propensity of organizations to get ever larger. As he put it, 'I was brought up on the theory of "economics of scale" – that with industries and firms, just as with nations, there is an irresistible trend, dictated by modern technology, for units to become ever bigger' (Schumacher, 1973/1993, p.48). He characterized the notion that organizations must go on getting larger as 'the idolatory of large size' and termed the whole phenomenon 'giantism'. According to Schumacher, giant organizations, for all that they might provide a necessary element of stability, were almost bound to result in stultifying bureaucracy, anonymity and sickness. In his own words:

> nobody really likes large-scale organization; nobody likes to take orders from a superior who takes orders from a superior who takes orders…Even if the rules devised by bureaucracy are outstandingly humane, nobody likes to be ruled by

rules, that is to say, by people whose answer to every complaint is; 'I did not make the rules: I am merely applying them'.

(Schumacher, 1973/1993, p.203)

Notwithstanding his hostility to large–scale organization, however, Schumacher was not sufficiently naive to consider that every modern industry could be re-structured as a small-scale, face-to-face enterprise. In fact he readily conceded that 'large-scale organization is here to stay' but added crucially that 'the fundamental task is to achieve smallness within large organization' (Schumacher, 1973/1993, p.203). Examples of 'smallness within large organization' were, in Schumacher's view, already in existence and included the NCB. As he saw it, Alfred Sloan's greatest achievement at General Motors (see Chapter 13) had been 'to structure this gigantic firm in such a manner that it became, in fact, a federation of fairly reasonably sized firms' (Schumacher, 1973/1993, p.48).

Thus Schumacher's strong prejudice was in favour of smallness – as he put it in his most quoted (if somewhat facile) phrase, 'man is small, and, therefore, small is beautiful' (Schumacher, 1973/1993, p.131). Nevertheless he recognized that the need for operational coherence, order, stability, efficiency and even competitiveness often tended in the direction of excessive organizational size. He therefore saw his role as offering a corrective and desired to establish a compromise between his ideal of small-scale organization and the technological imperatives driving things towards giantism. This led Schumacher to postulate a theory of large-scale organization in the form of five guiding principles as follows:

1. The Principle of Subsidiarity or the Principle of Subsidiary Function – this derived directly from the Papal Encyclical *Quadragesimo Anno* which stated, *inter alia*, that 'a community of a higher order should not interfere in the internal life of a community of a lower order, depriving the latter of its functions, but rather should support it in case of need and help to co-ordinate its activity with the activities of the rest of society, always with a view to the common good'.[2] Schumacher was, of course, aware that the idea of subsidiarity was addressed to society at large. However, he argued that the idea was equally applicable to the various strata within a large organization. As he put it, 'the higher level must not absorb the functions of the lower one, on the assumption that, being higher, it will automatically be wiser and fulfil them more efficiently ... The Principle of Subsidiary Function teaches us that the centre will gain in authority and effectiveness if the freedom and responsibility of the lower formations are carefully preserved' (Schumacher, 1973/1993, p.205).

---

2 Quoted in *Catechism of the Catholic Church (Pocket Edition)*, Geoffrey Chapman, London, 1995, p.414.

In order to achieve this structure Schumacher proposed that large organizations consist of many semi-autonomous units or 'quasi-firms'. Each of these, he claimed, should be given the largest amount of operational freedom so as to maximize the opportunities for creativity and what he termed 'entrepreneurship'. In his own words:

> the structure of the organization can then be symbolized by a man holding a large number of balloons in his hand. Each of the balloons has its own buoyancy and lift, and the man himself does not lord it over the balloons but stands beneath them, yet holding all the strings firmly in his hand. Every balloon is not only an administrative but also an entrepreneurial unit. The monolithic organization, by contrast, might be symbolized by a Christmas tree, with a star at the top and a lot of nuts and other useful things underneath. Everything derives from the top and depends on it. Real freedom and entrepreneurship can exist only at the top.
>
> *(Schumacher, 1973/1993, pp.205–6)*

2. The Principle of Vindication – in order for central control to be meaningful in a situation where subsidiarity is applied, the quasi-firm must be 'able to know without doubt whether or not it is performing satisfactorily'. The central authority in the organization must therefore set clear performance targets or criteria for the subsidiary units. Provided these are met the central authority must be prepared to vindicate (i.e. 'defend against reproach or accusation') the subsidiary units at all times. As Schumacher observed:

> in its ideal application, the Principle of Vindication would permit only one criterion for accountability in a commercial organization, namely profitability. Of course, such a criteria would be subject to the quasi-firm's observing general rules and policies laid down by the centre. Ideals can rarely be attained in the real world, but they are none the less meaningful. They imply that any departure from the ideal has to be specially argued and justified. Unless the number of criteria for accountability is kept very small indeed, creativity and entrepreneurship cannot flourish in the quasi-firm.
>
> *(Schumacher, 1973/1993, p.208)*

3. The Principle of Identification – required that each subsidiary unit or quasi-firm had a profit and loss account and a balance sheet. Each operating unit required its own balance sheet in order that its financial contribution to the organization as a whole might be readily identified. Again in Schumacher's words:

> a unit's success should lead to greater freedom and financial scope for the unit, while failure – in the form of losses – should lead to restriction and disability. One wants to reinforce success and discriminate against failure. The balance sheet describes the economic substance as augmented or diminished by current

results. This enables all concerned to follow the effect of operations on substance. Profits and losses are carried forward and not wiped out. Therefore, every quasi-firm should have its separate balance sheet, in which profits can appear as loans to the centre and losses as loans from the centre. This is a matter of great psychological importance.

(Schumacher, 1973/1993, p.208–9)

4. The Principle of Motivation – required that the entire organizational structure be designed with regard to the individual motivation of its workforce. Schumacher offered little practical advice on how this was to be achieved beyond reciting the well known fact that 'for a large organization, with its bureaucracies, its remote and impersonal controls, its many abstract rules and regulations, and above all the relative incomprehensibility that stems from its very size, motivation is the central problem' (Schumacher, 1973/1993, p.209). Not surprisingly Schumacher rejected the notion that people work simply for money and called for what he termed, in another context, 'good work' i.e. work that combined financial incentives, challenge and satisfaction with intrinsic worth.

5. The Principle of the Middle Axiom – according to Schumacher all real human problems arose from the 'antinomy' (i.e. the contradiction) between order and freedom. Top management, for example, were caught between the responsibility for directing the organization while simultaneously nurturing creative freedom. As he wrote:

the centre can easily look after order; it is not so easy to look after freedom and creativity. The centre has the power to establish order, but no amount of power evokes the creative contribution. How, then, can top management at the centre work for progress and innovation? Assuming that it knows what ought to be done; how can the management get it done throughout the organization? This is where the Principle of the Middle Axiom comes in. An axiom is a self-evident truth which is assented to as soon as annunciated. The centre can annunciate the truth it has discovered – that this or that is the right thing to do. (However, having made this discovery, how is the centre to proceed? According to Schumacher,) it can, of course, preach the new doctrine . . . but it incurs the valid criticism that 'they only talk and do not do anything'. Alternatively, the centre can issue instructions but, being remote from the actual scene of operations, the central management will incur the valid criticism that 'it attempts to run the industry from headquarters' . . . Neither the soft method of government by exhortation nor the tough method of government by instruction meets the requirements of the case. What is required is something in between, a middle axiom, an order from above which is yet not quite an order.

(Schumacher, 1973/1993, pp.210–211)

Critical summary

Schumacher's guiding principles concerning the advantages of small-scale organizations, the disadvantages of giantism, together with the need to develop smallness within bigness, have become part of the received management wisdom. Although some of Schumacher's notions, such as his interpretation of life at the now defunct National Coal Board, seem somewhat quaint, his work nevertheless remains influential, not least in the sphere of enablement. As Kennedy has observed, although his 'prescriptions did not go much beyond...broad brush statements...his approach...struck a resonant chord that reverberated long after the contents of his modest essays were forgotten. He was ahead of his time by about 15 years in advising the recognition of people's need to be involved in decision-making in small units' (Kennedy, 1991, p.150).

Discussion questions

1. Why was Schumacher critical of bureaucracy?
2. How convincing is Schumacher's contention that small is beautiful?
3. In what ways did Schumacher deploy the concept of subsidiarity?
4. What did Schumacher mean when he spoke of good work?

Suggested reading

Clutterbuck, D. and Craner, S. (1990) *Makers of Management: Men and Women Who Changed the Business World*, Macmillan, London, ch.7.
Kennedy, C. (1991) *Guide to the Management Gurus*, Century, London, ch. 30.
Schumacher, E. F. (1973/1993) *Small is Beautiful: A Study of Economics as if People Mattered*, Vintage Books, London.
Schumacher, E. F. (1979) *Good Work*, Jonathan Cape, London.
Wood, B. (1984) *Alias Papa: A Life of Fritz Schumacher*, Jonathan Cape, London

Chapter 18

Harry Braverman and the degradation of work

Harry Braverman was born in 1920 and began his working life by serving a four year apprenticeship as a coppersmith in a naval shipyard. In total he spent seven years in the shipyard a place where, as he later put it:

> almost all the mechanic crafts which had arisen in the course of (two centuries) were practiced in...close association with each other. Because of this propinquity and the interlocking processes practiced by the crafts, and also because of the gathering together of apprentices of all crafts in a trade school for semi-weekly sessions, I learned not only my own trade but gained a concrete understanding of most of the others.
>
> *(Braverman, 1974, p.5)*

The decline of employment opportunities in his trade made it difficult for Braverman to find work as a coppersmith as he moved from job to job around the USA. However, using the skills he had gained in the shipyard he was able to turn his hand to pipefitting and sheet metal work. Again, in his own words, 'I did work of these sorts for another seven years; in a railroad repair shop, in sheet metal shops, and especially in two plants which fabricated heavy steel plate and structural steel into equipment for the basic steel industry, including blast furnaces' (Braverman, 1974, p.5). During his years as a manual worker Braverman was active in the American socialist movement and became a Marxist. His political commitment led him into radical journalism and eventually employment in book publishing, initially as an editor but subsequently 'as an operating executive in two publishing houses'. He spent over 12 years in publishing gaining 'first hand experience of some of the most typical office processes of our times...at the moment when they were beginning to undergo rapid changes...this

171

experience twice included the transition from conventional to computerized office systems' (Braverman, 1974, p.7).

The central insight which Braverman claimed to have gained from his working life was the constant erosion of craft skills and the concomitant 'degradation of work'. As he explained:

> I had the opportunity of seeing at first hand...not only the transformation of industrial processes but the manner in which these processes are reorganized; how the worker systematically robbed of craft heritage, is given little or nothing to take its place. Like all craftsmen, even the most inarticulate, I always resented this.
>
> *(Braverman, 1974, p.6)*

Braverman's response to what he saw was one of 'social outrage' and 'personal affront'. As a Marxist he construed the attack on craft skills to be more than merely a combination of inevitable technological progress and the laudable pursuit of increased efficiency. Instead he took it to be part of a conspiracy implicit in the capitalist system whereby the owners of the means of production (i.e. the capitalists) and their hired agents (i.e. the managers) sought to dispossess and dominate the workers (i.e. the proletariat). He set forth his analysis of the impact of the modern capitalist economy on the organization of work in *Labor and Monopoly Capital: the Degradation of Work in the Twentieth Century* which was published in 1974. Harry Braverman died in 1976.

The defence of craft

Laying aside for the moment Braverman's Marxist approach, his defense of craft prerogatives stood in a long tradition stretching back at least as far as the Luddites. As was seen in Chapter 1, Adam Smith had noted the probable baleful consequences of the division of labour for the workers involved. Also, as we have seen, workers who saw their livelihood extinguished by technical changes in the British cotton and woollen textile industries during the early nineteenth century, waged an unsuccessful campaign of resistance through direct action. Nevertheless, as Belchem has noted, 'industrialization in Britain did not necessarily entail the de-skilling of labour' (Belchem, 1990, p.43). Instead craft skills were broken down, re-defined and often protected through trade unionization as technology developed. Again in the words of Belchem:

> the experience of work varied dramatically amid the combined and uneven development of the industrial revolution. Some occupations (engineering is the best studied example) were transformed and expanded by new technology and

industrial change. At the other extreme were the poor handloom-weavers, victims of technological redundancy.

(Belchem, 1990, p.43)

Engineering was, perhaps, the paradigm case where the notion of 'the craftsman' was constantly reformulated whilst being as far as possible protected by apprenticeship (which limited entry to the trade) and trade unions (which offered a defence against both employers and the inroads of the unskilled). Although in the British case employers would, depending on the vagaries of trade, from time to time attack craft prerogatives, an accommodation was nevertheless sustained between employers and unions which has endured to the present day. Ironically, it was the British craft unions, and particularly the engineers, that Lenin characterized as being the 'aristocracy of labour' a decidedly non-revolutionary element within the working class (Price, 1986, pp.7 and 84).

In spite of the obstacles to the erosion of craft prerogatives provided by apprenticeship and trade unions, technological change nevertheless made significant inroads in the majority of industries during the nineteenth century. In the American case trade unions were slow to develop. As Bendix has commented, 'in the United States, workers began to organize on a mass basis only in the 1890s, hampered as they were by the willingness of immigrants to work at lower wages' (Bendix, 1956/1974, p.255). Further, there was a conscious and prolonged effort by American manufacturers to replace craft skill by using standardized components and the techniques of scientific management and mass production. In such a situation there were both winners and losers among the workers as former 'labour aristocrats' were brushed aside (or pushed down) and their places taken by semi-skilled or unskilled replacements. This displacement was often painful for the groups involved, requiring surrender of their control over the labour process, financial penalty and damaged self-esteem. Although the impact of change was most obvious in engineering, similar restructuring took place, for example, in coal mining. In 1925 Carter Goodrich (see Chapter 7) who had traced the attempts by British trade unions during the First World War to shift the frontier of control in industry, published *The Miners' Freedom: A Study of the Working Life in a Changing Industry*. This book provided an account of the impact of changing technology and working methods on the life of American coal miners. Similarly the impact of technological developments and concomitant de-skilling was felt in boot and shoemaking and it is this industry, in the American case, which generated a precursor of Braverman's work in a classic study of a harmonious community shattered by the process of change.

The study was produced as part of the so-called Yankee City studies carried out by the Harvard industrial anthropologist W. Lloyd Warner and his associates during the early 1930s, although not published until the 1940s. Warner was a pupil of the British functionalist anthropologist (and devotee of Durkheim) Radcliffe-Brown and before going to Harvard he had produced a study of Australian aborigines which he published

in 1937 under the title *Black Civilization: A Social Study of an Australian Tribe*. Warner's approach to research was to apply the techniques of anthropology he had utilized in studying pre-industrial people to the investigation of industrial situations. In 1931 he established the Bank Wiring Observation Room experiment at the Hawthorne Works which generated a highly influential study of small group behaviour at work. However, tensions between the Business School at Harvard and the Department of Anthropology there eventually prompted Warner to leave and join the University of Chicago. In Chicago he became the leader of the group of academics who formed the influential Committee on Human Relations in Industry which was committed to 'picking up the neglected leads from the Bank Wiring Room case...(and) studying industrial life in its natural settings' (Whyte, 1987, p.489). Warner was closely associated with Elton Mayo during his years at Harvard and the latter went out of his way to praise the Yankee City studies in his book *The Human Problems of an Industrial Civilization*. Yankee City was in fact Newburyport, a small town on the coast of Massachusetts, and the studies (which eventually ran to six volumes) focused on the determinants of co-operation in a modern community. As Rose has observed 'Warner was primarily interested in Yankee City as a community, especially its class, status and ethnic ranking systems' (Rose, 1988, p.149). These matters were substantially covered in the first three volumes of the series *The Social Life of a Modern Community* (1942); *The Status System of a Modern Community* (1942) and *The Social Systems of American Ethnic Groups* (1945). However, in 1947 Warner, together with his associate J. O. Low, published *The Social System of the Modern Factory* which provided a detailed account of a strike that occurred during 1933. In the words of Rose:

> the immediate cause of the strike was unemployment in the shoe industry, on which Yankee City had depended for over a century...In March 1933 the previously deferential, 'unorganizable' shoe workers began to strike, spontaneously, against further wage cuts and redundancies. Their solidarity was virtually complete, crossing previously wide ethnic, religious, sex and skill divisions...This explosive change, Warner and Low concluded had to be viewed against a backcloth of long-run economic and technological change. In the chapters that trace this change they often sound like 'Bravermaniacs'.
>
> *(Rose, 1988, p.150)*

In chapter 9 of his book Warner examined the problems caused by the emergence of an industrial proletariat in the United States. In the case of Yankee City, he argued, the destruction of craftsmanship (together with the loss of opportunities for upward social mobility) had served to increase worker solidarity and stimulate trade union membership. The erosion of craft-based differences between workers 'had made them more alike, with common problems and common hostilities against management (and) increasingly motivated to act together because their new occupational status had contributed to their downward orientation in the community' (Warner and Lowe, 1947, p.171). Warner claimed that this was a new situation for the United States, a country where workers had traditionally been reluctant to accept class labels. The proletarianisation of the workforce in Yankee City was being repeated across America, and indeed the entire industrialized world, and was becoming a menace to social stability. As he saw it 'the growing conflict between the opposing forces of managers and workers in the United States (is) causing intense and widespread anxiety' (Warner and Lowe, 1947, p.181). The destruction of craft in many industries was destroying workers' hopes of upward social mobility. Instead they were being driven downwards, losing both skill and self-esteem. Further, the opportunities available for the children of the workers were also being diminished as the better positions were increasingly taken by the children of wealthy Americans who were better able to afford education and better placed to ensure their children got the best jobs. Warner feared that a society which had traditionally been 'open to the talents' was fast becoming stratified into two mutually hostile camps of the 'haves' and the 'have nots'. His solution to this phenomenon was the development of a corporate state where big government could control the contending forces of big business and big labour. As he put it:

> the referee between the two great conflicting forces of workers and management must necessarily be endowed with great social power and be able to apply sanctions with sufficient force to maintain moderate collaboration between the two for the good of all the people. As long as the governmental, labor and management systems remain separate, the partial or full integration of American society can only be maintained by the subjugation of one of the contestants by the other, by the destruction of the power of one of them by the government, or by the government's treating the whole matter as a combat between two equal forces where each side can score a little but not too much. This latter condition will probably remain with us in America until a time when our country's social system re-integrates itself and the opposing forces now focused in the conflict of capital and labor are controlled or express themselves in some other form.

> *(Warner, 1947, p.194)*

Finally Warner moved beyond national boundaries to argue the need for supra-national governmental agencies capable of grappling with what is now termed the globalization of capital and the rise of multi-national cartels. Warner's use of his observation of events in the limited circumstances of Yankee City was akin to his friend Mayo's use of the Hawthorne experiments, extrapolating from a single case study to offer a generalized explanation of global developments. Warner's analysis of the consequences of the decline of craft under capitalism brought him close to some of Marx's views. However he was not a Marxist and he sought social equilibrium rather than revolution. Thus although many of his concerns were close to those of Braverman his conclusions were markedly different. Braverman was, of course, a self-proclaimed Marxist and deployed an analytical apparatus and vocabulary derived from the master. An examination of Braverman's Marxism forms the subject of the next section.

Braverman's Marxism

Marxism arrived in the United States during the mid-nineteenth century, carried there by migrant industrial workers from Europe. Many were German and among them was Joseph Weydemeyer, a friend of Marx, who founded the American Workers' League in New York. Described by McLellan as 'a cross between a party and a trade union, whose aim was to agitate for the immediate improvement of workers' conditions on a socialist basis', it was short lived (McLellan, 1979, p.313). German immigrants also featured prominently in the Socialist Labour Party (SLP) which was formed during the 1870s. Daniel De Leon joined the SLP in 1890 and, as editor of the party's English language paper *The People*, adopted an uncompromising Marxist position often to the alarm of more moderate members. In 1905 De Leon helped to found the International Workers of the World (IWW) a genuinely proletarian movement which soon embraced a syndicalist position, calling for direct action including sabotage. Divisions caused by De Leon's Marxism eventually produced a split in the SLP, the majority leaving to form the American Socialist Party. By the time De Leon died in 1914 the Socialist Party could number its members in tens of thousands and, in the presidential election of 1912, its candidate gained almost a million votes. The Socialist Party's ideology was, however, populist rather than Marxist and it was not until the First World War that Marxism re-emerged as a political force. The inspiration for this sprang from the victory of the Bolsheviks in the Russian Revolution of 1917. John Reed popularised the revolution in his book *Ten Days That Shook the World* and became a founder of the small Communist Labour Party. This party, together with the larger American Communist Party, were forced underground by wartime sedition laws. As McLellan has observed:

> by the time they re-emerged in 1921, Lenin's 'right turn' instructed them to engage in electoral activity and to work within the existing trade union movement (however)...they could make little headway in America where Taylorism and the production line were squeezing out craft industries and the mass production of consumer goods caused a decline in traditional ethnic radicalism.
>
> *(McLellan, 1979, p.317)*

The United States was to remain hostile territory for Marxism and indeed socialism and organized labour in general. The impact of Roosevelt's New Deal during the 1930s drew support away from the Socialist Party while 'the impact of the Second World War, the subsequent economic boom and the McCarthyite frenzy brought a period of stagnation and dissolution to Marxism which lasted from 1940 to 1960' (McLellan, 1979, p.317). Nevertheless, Marxism did enjoy some sort of revival in the early 1960s under the auspices of the New Left. Partly the revival of radicalism was stimulated by the United States involvement in Vietnam. Partly too it sprang from domestic considerations including civil rights issues and feminism. Certainly the New

Left was very different from what had gone before, combining elements of pop-culture and radical psychology with aspects of French existentialism and the products of the Frankfurt School. The Soviet Union, the motherland of the Old Left, was seen as being tainted by the ravages of Stalinism and the kind of imperialism pursued by the European nations in Africa and Asia and by the Americans in Vietnam. Many of the New Left's attitudes were summed up in Herbert Marcuse's *One-Dimensional Man: Studies in the Ideology of Advanced Industrial Society* which was frankly pessimistic about the possibility of a revolutionary transformation of society ever occurring in the industrialized West. The success of Western capitalism, Marcuse argued, had created a situation where the vast bulk of the population were materially satisfied. Thus, although the classic Marxist dichotomy between the bourgeoisie and the proletariat still existed it had been stripped of revolutionary potential. In Marcuse's view social unrest would in future come from those on the margins of society, the outsiders for whom Marx had allocated no historical role. However, although the populations of the industrial societies might be better off than ever before they were far from being fulfilled. On the contrary they were estranged from their work, each other and ultimately themselves – in a word they were 'alienated'. Further, according to Marcuse, they were trapped in a 'totalitarian' social system which eschewed naked political terror but deployed techniques of manipulation instead. As Marcuse described the situation:

> the distinguishing feature of advanced industrial society is its effective suffocation of those needs which demand liberation – liberation also from that which is tolerable and comfortable – while it sustains and absolves the destructive power and repressive function of the affluent society. Here the social controls exact the overwhelming need for the production and consumption of waste; the need for stupefying work where it is no longer a real necessity; the need for modes of relaxation which sooth and prolong this stupefaction; the need for maintaining such deceptive liberties as free competition at administered prices, a free press which censors itself, free choice between brands and gadgets.
>
> *(Marcuse, 1964/1991, p.7)*

Marcuse's philosophy was more at home on the university campus than the workshop floor. Certainly its mixture of alienation, pessimism and radical chic hardly offered a working ideology for the communist activist. Nevertheless it did help to create an intellectual climate which was sympathetic to Braverman's version of alienation through the degradation of work when it appeared in 1974.

Marcuse, and indeed the bulk of Western Marxists, drew their inspiration from the early works of Marx, particularly the *Economic and Philosophical Manuscripts*, sometimes referred to as the *Paris Manuscripts*. These had lain neglected after Marx's death until their translation and publication in 1932. In the words of McLellan the manuscripts 'gave the impression that a very different form of Marxism was available, one that could enter into fruitful dialogue with the increasingly popular philosophies of phenomenology, personalism and existentialism' (McLellan, 1979, p.281). Ironically Braverman was not influenced by the early Marx or by those later thinkers, such as Lukacs and Gramsci, whose theorizing had evolved along similar lines. Instead his starting point was Volume 1 of *Capital*, published in 1867, and particularly those parts of the book devoted to the labour process. Partly at least Braverman was prompted in this direction by the paucity of Marxist writing in the United States. The most original contributions had been made in the sphere of political economy with the publication of Paul Baran's *The Political Economy of Growth* in 1957 and Baran and Paul Sweezy's *Monopoly Capital* in 1965. Although Baran and Sweezy's insistence on the ever-increasing level of surplus value now seems somewhat dated, McLellan's description of *Monopoly Capital* as 'the most impressive overview of the United States economy' remains valid (McLellan, 1979, p.327). When Braverman came to write *Labor and Monopoly Capital* he placed it within a framework provided by Baran and Sweezy's political economy. Having said this, however, Braverman's Marxism ultimately derived from his own reading of, and reflection upon, the work of the mature Marx. As Braverman himself put it:

> neither the changes in productive processes throughout this century of capitalism and monopoly capitalism, nor the changes in the occupational and industrial structure of the working population have been subjected to any comprehensive Marxist analysis since Marx's death. It is for this reason that I cannot...attribute to any Marxists other than Marx himself a strong intellectual emphasis upon this study; there simply is no continuing body of work in the Marxist tradition dealing with the capitalist mode of production in the manner in which Marx treated it in the first volume of *Capital*.
>
> *(Braverman, 1974, p.9)*

Labour and monopoly capital

Braverman began his analysis of the apparent degradation of work under monopoly capital by briefly tracing the origins of wage labour. As he put it:

> while the purchase and sale of labor power has existed from antiquity, a substantial class of wage workers did not begin to form in Europe until the fourteenth century, and did not become numerically significant until the rise of industrial capitalism...in the eighteenth century. It has been the numerically dominant form for little more than a century, and this in only a few countries. In the United States, perhaps four-fifths of the population was self employed in the early part of the nineteenth century. By 1870 this had declined to one third and by 1940 to no more than one fifth; by 1970 only about one tenth of the population was self-employed. We are thus dealing with a social relation of extremely recent date. The rapidity with which it has won

supremacy…emphasizes the extra-ordinary power of the tendency of capitalist economies to convert all forms of labor into hired labor.

(Braverman, 1974, p.53)

In this situation, Braverman argued, workers were inevitably forced into paid employment because prevailing social conditions left them with no other way of making a livelihood. Meanwhile the employer, as the possessor of capital, pursued profits and in order to obtain them sought to dominate the labour process. In Braverman's words 'it becomes essential for the capitalist that control over the labor process pass from the hands of the worker into his own. This transition presents itself in history as the progressive alienation of the process of production from the worker; to the capitalist, it presents itself as the problem of management' (Braverman, 1974, p.58). On this basis industrial relations were bound to be antagonistic as capitalists and their hired managers struggled to gain and maintain control of their workers' activities. Whereas capitalists could readily evaluate the position of buildings, machinery, tools and materials in the labour process, they were unable to apply similar precision to the utilization of their workers. This was because capitalists did not purchase labourers as such but rather the labourers' time. As Braverman put it, 'what the worker sells, and the capitalist buys, is not an agreed amount of labor, but the power of labor over an agreed period of time' (Braverman, 1974, p.54). In order for the capitalists to gain profit from their activities it was obviously essential that the workers produced more than they consumed in wages. However, the amount produced was susceptible to variation depending upon the extent to which the workers applied themselves to their tasks. This subjective element was just as likely to lead to restriction as it was to maximization of output. Hence capitalists were constrained to seek means of minimizing workers' control over their work by developing techniques to increase certainty of performance. In the words of Pugh and Hickson:

managers, as representatives of owners, (are required) to design and re-design work in order to achieve competitive levels of profit. They need to have maximum control of workers and to be looking continually for ways of increasing that control. Typically, this has been achieved by increasing the division of labour into smaller and smaller, less and less demanding fragments of tasks. In this way increased output may be obtained from a workforce which is cheaper, since it is less skilled and less trained. Ford-type mass production epitomizes the results.

(Pugh and Hickson, 1989, pp. 94–95)

Braverman readily conceded that employers had always sought to control their workers. However, this search had reached its highest level with the development of Taylorism and the scientific management movement generally. As he put it:

it is impossible to over-estimate the importance of the scientific management movement in the shaping of the modern corporation and indeed all the institutions of capitalist society which carry on labor processes. The popular notion that Taylorism has been 'superseded' by later schools of industrial psychology or 'human relations', that it 'failed'...or that it is 'outmoded' because certain Taylorian specifics...have been discarded for more sophisticated methods: all these represent a woeful misreading of the actual dynamics of the development of management.

(Braverman, 1974, p.87)

Taylor, Braverman argued, had 'dealt with the fundamentals of the organization of the labor process and of control over it' whereas Elton Mayo, for example, had dealt 'primarily with the adjustment of the worker to the ongoing production process as...designed by the industrial engineer'. As far as the organization of work itself was concerned, it was arranged according to Taylorism. Personnel departments and their academic associates were merely engaged in those activities (such as selection, training, pacification and manipulation) which were necessary to adjust the workers to the demands of the work. Thus, according to Braverman, 'Taylorism dominates the world of production; the practitioners of 'human relations' and 'industrial psychology' are the maintenance crew for the human machinery. If Taylorism does not exist as a separate school today, that is because...it is no longer the property of a faction, since its fundamental teachings have become the bedrock of all work design' (Braverman, 1974, p.87). As far as Braverman was concerned the burgeoning clerical and service sectors of the economy were every bit as Taylorized as the workshop floor itself and, contrary to popular opinion, did not represent an upgrading of skills but a continuation of the de-skilling that characterized the development of work under capitalism. Similarly, automation only served to reduce the level of skill even further. As, for that matter, would any other technical development. Inevitably, technological innovation under capitalism would be 'used to increase the control of the labour process by capital in the interests of profit' (Pugh and Hickson, 1989, p.96).

Alongside the ever greater control over the labour process exercised by capital, Braverman claimed that a universal market had emerged. In the era of monopoly capitalism described by Baran and Sweezy, society was being transformed into a gigantic marketplace where everything became a commodity. When the bulk of the United States population had lived on farms or in small towns, Braverman argued, commodity production had been limited. Most material needs had been met through the direct work of the family. Further, even when work began to be transferred from the farm to the factory many of the former activities, such as carpentry, baking, preserving and the growing of crops, continued. However, this situation could not survive in the face of growing urbanization. As Braverman put it:

the tighter packing of urbanization destroys the conditions under which it is possible to carry on the old life. The urban rings close around the worker, and around the farmer driven from the land, and confine them within circumstances that preclude the former self-provisioning practices of the home...The pressure of social custom as exercised...by style, fashion, advertising, and the educational process (together with) the deterioration of skills (creates) the powerful urge in each family member towards an independent income...since the source of status is no longer the ability to make many things but simply to purchase them...The function of the family as a co-operative enterprise pursuing the joint production of a way of life is brought to an end.

(Braverman, 1974, pp.276–77)

The decline of family life, according to Braverman, was paralleled by the decline of community and the loosening of the former ties of the neighbourhood so as to exclude onerous tasks such as the care of the young, elderly and sick. Such tasks became increasingly institutionalized and operated as service industries for profit. The resultant atomized community generated problems of maladjustment and crime which created even greater institutional requirements, ranging from asylums to prisons. Meanwhile the working population became ever more dependent on commodities and, owing to specialization and division of labour, ever less competent to fulfil its many needs. As Braverman put it, in terms similar to those deployed by Marcuse:

the inhabitant of capitalist society is enmeshed in a web made up of commodity goods and commodity services from which there is little possibility of escape except through partial or total abstention from social life as it now exists. This is reinforced from the other side by a development which is analogous to that which proceeds in the workers' work: the atrophy of competence...We need not emphasize how badly this urban civilization works and how much misery it embraces. For the purposes of our discussion, it is the other side of the universal market, its dehumanizing aspects, its confinement of a large portion of the population to degraded labor, that is chiefly of interest.

(Braverman, 1974, p.281)

Thus the universal market and the degradation of labour are complementary phenomena, ensuring that the workers generate profit at the point of manufacture and consumption. Braverman does not offer an escape from the situation he describes through a revolutionary transformation of society. Neither does he anticipate an amelioration of the problems through the processes of trade union activity, political intervention and industrial democracy. Instead, he merely concedes what McLellan has termed 'capital's absolute domination over labour' (McLellan, 1979, p.329).

Critical summary

Braverman was not a management thinker. On the contrary he was anti-management, equating the managerial function with the erosion of skill and the degradation of work under capitalism. His attack on scientific management echoed that contained in the Hoxie Report of 1915 (see Chapter 2). Like Hoxie he took scientific management seriously and he provided a potent critique both of its claims and its impact. In a memorable phrase he described Taylorism as being not scientific management but 'a science of the management of other's work under capitalist conditions'. He also claimed that Taylor was not dealing with the general principles of management. Instead he was 'seeking...an answer to the specific problem of how best to control alienated labor – that is to say, labor power that is bought and sold' (Braverman, 1974, p.90). Braverman's pessimism concerning the decline of community, and the challenges to social harmony posed by industrialization and urbanization, brought him close to the concerns of Elton Mayo (see Chapter 11). However, his attitude to Mayo and indeed other 'human relations' thinkers was one of hostility and he depicted their role as being concerned 'primarily with the adjustment of the worker to the ongoing production process'. The extent to which Braverman was correct in seeing the evolution of work during the twentieth century as an ongoing process of degradation is, at least, problematical. Certainly some jobs have lost some or all of their skill content. Further, many jobs have disappeared entirely. Nevertheless much drudgery has been removed from working life and new skills have emerged. It is also difficult to support the argument that the many farmhands and unskilled labourers who flooded into the factories of, for example, Henry Ford, were actually being de-skilled. Nevertheless there are elements in Braverman's work which strike a chord among those who are concerned with the labour process. The appearance of *Labor and Monopoly Capital* coincided with a growing distaste in academic circles for the particular organization of work associated with mass production and, specifically, the assembly track. Thus Braverman had an influence beyond radical circles and contributed to the general climate of reformist management ideas that had been generated by such thinkers as Maslow, McGregor and Herzberg. Although, as has been seen, Braverman's critique is based on a Marxist analysis, the authenticity of his Marxism has been questioned, for example, by Rose who has characterized him as being a follower of the French thinker Proudhon rather than Marx. Further, it is possible to identify elements in Braverman's thought which bring him close to the concerns of the English craftsman and socialist William Morris. Nevertheless, these are quibbles and McLellan is surely correct when he says of Braverman that 'his forceful humanism, his direct style, and mastery of empirical studies make his treatment of the degradation of work in the twentieth century a worthy continuation of Marx' (McLellan, 1979, p.329).

Discussion questions

1. What did Braverman mean when he spoke of the degradation of work?
2. In what ways was Braverman's thinking influenced by Marxism?
3. How convincing is Braverman's argument that workers are forced into paid employment because prevailing social conditions leave them no other way to make a living?

Suggested reading

Braverman, H. (1974) *Labor and Monopoly Capital: the Degradation of Work in the Twentieth Century*, Monthly Review Press, New York.

McLellan, D. (1979) *Marxism After Marx: An Introduction*, Macmillan, London.

Marcuse, H. (1964/1991) *One-Dimensional Man: Studies in the Ideology of Advanced Industrial Society*, Routledge, London.

Pugh, D. and Hickson, D. (eds) (1989) *Writers on Organizations*, Penguin Books, Harmondsworth, ch.3.

Rose, M. (1988) *Industrial Behaviour: Research and Control*, Penguin Books, Harmondsworth, chs. 30 and 37.

Chapter 19

William Ouchi and Theory Z

In 1974 Richard Johnson and William Ouchi of the Graduate School of Business at Stanford University published an article under the title 'Made in America (under Japanese management)' in the *Harvard Business Review*. The authors began by highlighting the growing productivity gap between Japanese and American companies by citing a single example. In their own words:

> on the assembly line of a US company in Atlanta, Georgia, 35 American women put together transistor panels in a prescribed set of steps. In Tokyo, at another plant of this company, 35 Japanese assemblers used the same technology and the same procedure to manufacture the same part. The only real difference between the two lines is their productivity: the Japanese workers turn out 15 per cent more panels than do their American counterparts 7000 miles away.
>
> *(Johnson and Ouchi, 1974, p.61)*

For an American audience this was a shocking statement, confirming the worst fears of a decline in the USA's competitive edge over the rest of the world. Since the Second World War American manufacturers had grown accustomed to out-producing and out-performing every foreign competitor. The era of the Cold War had led the Americans to believe that the only danger to their general security sprang from communism and specifically the Soviet Union. The notion that their comprehensively vanquished enemies and strategic clients, the Japanese, might be poised to overhaul them technically and even economically was unpalatable, even unbelievable.[1] However, Johnson and Ouchi had more perplexing news to convey. As has been seen

---

1 Nevertheless it was true. By the 1990s Japan's *per capita* income was $23 570 compared to the United States' $21 653 (Oliver and Wilkinson, 1992, p.4).

throughout the bulk of this book the USA had led the world for much of the twentieth century in terms of management technique. From scientific management through mass production to applied industrial psychology the Americans had always been in the vanguard of development. The suggestion that Japanese management was out-performing the American competition, not just in Japan but in the USA itself, was almost outrageous. Nevertheless, according to Johnson and Ouchi, this was the case. As they put it:

> in Sony Corporation's plant at San Diego, California, some 200 Americans make 17-and 19-inch television sets on an assembly line that is identical with Sony's assembly line in Japan. In this case, however, the similarity does not end there: the American workers produce as much for Sony in San Diego as the Japanese assemblers do for Sony in Tokyo. What is more, our interviews with 20 other Japanese companies operating in the United States suggest that, in many instances, they are outperforming American companies in the same industries.
>
> *(Johnson and Ouchi, 1974, p.61)*

Given that Japanese management was gaining a tangible edge over the American competition what, asked Johnson and Ouchi, were the reasons for this and what could the Americans learn from the Japanese? The authors readily conceded that certain aspects of Japanese management technique were already common practice in the USA – indeed they had originated in America in the first place. F. W. Taylor's and other scientific management ideas, for example, had been known in Japan since before the First World War (see Chapter 2). As Wren has noted:

> the entrance into Japan of US ideas on management appears to have been inspired by the visit of Yukinori Hoshino, director of Japan's Kojima Bank, to the United States in 1911. Hoshino encountered Taylor's writings and obtained permission to translate Taylor's *Principles of Scientific Management*; Taylor's work appeared in Japanese in 1912 or 1913. Landing in fertile soil the seed of scientific management grew rapidly and led to a management revolution, replacing the entrepreneur-dominated age. A leading teacher, author, and consultant was Yoichi Ueno who authored a paper in 1912, *On the Efficiency*, which described the work of Taylor, Frank Gilbreth, and C. B. Thompson. The ideas of scientific management entered the journals, the educational system, and the practice of management in Japan. Carl Barth visited Japan in 1924, and a chapter of the Taylor Society was formed in 1925.
>
> *(Wren, 1994, p.205)*

Equally, argued Johnson and Ouchi, there were certain aspects of Japanese management which, as they put it, were 'inseparable from the Japanese culture itself' and could not therefore be used in America (Johnson and Ouchi, 1974, p.62). However, having made due allowance for similarities and distinctions, they nevertheless put forward five key areas of the Japanese approach to management which they felt were both different and exportable. These they summed up in the following five points:

> (1) emphasis on a flow of information and initiative from the bottom up; (2) making top management the facilitator of decision making rather than the issuer of edicts; (3) using middle management as the impetus for, and shaper of, solutions to problems; (4) stressing consensus as the way of making decisions; and (5) paying close attention to the personal well-being of employees.
>
> *(Johnson and Ouchi, 1974, p.62)*

The extent to which any of this was uniquely Japanese and did not already occur in the United States and other Western industrialized countries was arguable. Equally contentious was the extent to which any or all of these elements were responsible for the productivity improvements in Japanese companies operating within Japan and elsewhere. However, Ouchi's work soon developed beyond a narrow concern with the growing productivity gap between Japan and the USA to a consideration of the organization as the focus of identity and community.

In 1978 Ouchi co-authored with Alfred Jaeger, also of Stanford University, an article entitled 'Type Z Organization: Stability in the Midst of Mobility' which appeared in the *Academy of Management Review*. Drawing heavily on insights derived from, among others, Weber (see Chapter 6), Mayo (see Chapter 11), Homans (see Chapter 12) and Maslow (see Chapter 14) the authors explored the familiar ground of anomie as originally expounded by Durkheim. As they put it:

> society traditionally has relied upon kinship, neighbourhood, church, and family networks to provide the social support and normative anchors which made collective life possible. As Mayo pointed out, the advent of the factory system of production and the rapid rate of technological change produced high rates of urbanization, mobility and division of labour. These forces weakened the community, family, church and friendship ties of many Americans. Social observers point to this weakening of associational ties as the basic cause of increasing rates of alcoholism, divorce, crime, and other symptoms of mental illness at a societal level. While worrying over the disappearance of family, church, neighbourhood, and the friendship network, pre-dispositions can blind us to the most likely source of associational ties or cohesion; the work organization. The large work organization which brought about urbanization and its consequent ills can also provide relief from them.
>
> *(Ouchi and Jaeger, 1978, p.305–306)*

Of course, the centrality of the work organization as the focus of identity had already been extensively explored by industrial sociologists, most notably Elton Mayo and W. Lloyd Warner (see Chapter 18). Certainly by the time Ouchi and Jaeger were writing in the late 1970s it appeared that nothing new remained to be said on the subject. Indeed contemporary observers, including Schumacher (see Chapter 17) and Braverman (see Chapter 18) had successfully depicted the large work organization as being the source of alienation and loss of identity rather than 'the social umbrella under which people can live free, happy and productive lives' claimed by Ouchi and Jaeger.

Building on Ouchi's earlier research he and Jaeger now claimed that the success of Japanese companies sprang from:

> almost total inclusion of the employee into the work organizations so that the superior concerns himself or herself with the personal and family life of each subordinate; a collective, non-individual approach to work and responsibility; and extremely high identification of the individual with the company. These characteristics are largely the result of the lifetime employment system which characterizes large companies in Japan.
>
> *(Ouchi and Jaeger, 1978, p.306)*

Where Japanese companies were operating in the USA they were, according to Ouchi and Jaeger, attempting to establish the same sort of identity between company and worker that existed back home. Indeed, in spite of the American workers' reputed love of individual freedom and dislike of old-style paternalism, the evidence suggested that 'they favour a work organization which provided associational ties, stability, and job security' (Ouchi and Jaeger, 1978, p.307). The authors conceded that some American companies (including Kodak, IBM, Levi Strauss and Procte & Gamble) already displayed some of the elements of security and identity associated with their Japanese counterparts. This prompted Ouchi and Jaeger to claim that an emergent model of work organization could be discerned which possessed residual elements of the conventional American model and elements of the Japanese model. This hybrid they termed the 'Japanese-American mixed form' or 'ideal Type Z'. As they described it:

> the ideal Type Z combines a basic cultural commitment to individualistic values with a highly collective, non-individual pattern of interaction. It simultaneously satisfies old norms and present needs for affiliation. Employment is effectively (although not officially) for a lifetime, and turnover is low. Decision making is consensual, and there is often a highly self-conscious attempt to preserve the consensual mode.
>
> *(Ouchi and Jaeger, 1978, p.311)*

The authors conceded that the Type Z organization was not appropriate to all workers or every organization. However, where such organizations could be effectively established they would serve to fill the vacuum created by the relative decline of civil society. As the authors put it 'if American society is moving from high to low affiliation, people who are employed in a Type Z organization should be better able to deal with stress and should be happier than the population at large' (Ouchi and Jaeger, 1978, p.312).

From Type Z to Theory Z

In 1981 William Ouchi published what was to become the best selling book on Japanese management, *Theory Z: How American Business Can Meet the Japanese Challenge*. Ouchi, by now a professor at the Graduate School of Management, University of California, Los Angeles, turned to the work of Douglas McGregor and Chris Argyris (see Chapter 16) to provide the book's theoretical underpinning. In converting the Type Z organization of his earlier work into Theory Z Ouchi made a conscious allusion to McGregor's Theory X and Theory Y and the notion that managers' assumptions about workers would inevitably colour their management style. However, although McGregor's work provided a degree of influence it was the work of Argyris that proved the most influential. Referring specifically to Argyris's book *Integrating the Individual and the Organization* of 1964, Ouchi observed:

> Argyris argued that motivation in work will be maximal when each worker pursues individual goals and experiences psychological growth and independence. Close supervision diminishes motivation, retards psychological growth, and hampers personal independence and freedom. However, supervision can be supportive in Theory Y only when the supervisor trusts workers to use their discretion in a manner consistent with the goals of the organization. Thus the connection between an egalitarian style of management and mutual trust...Argyris challenged managers to integrate individuals into organizations, not to create alienating, hostile, and impersonally bureaucratic places of work. In a real sense, the type Z organization comes close to realizing that ideal. It is a consent culture, a community of equals who co-operate with one another to reach common goals. Rather than relying exclusively upon hierarchy and monitoring to direct behaviour, it relies also upon commitment and trust.
>
> *(Ouchi, 1981, pp.81 and 83)*

Type Z organizations, claimed Ouchi, worked better because they avoided the worst elements of hierarchy and bureaucracy and achieved a high state of consistency in their internal culture. As Ouchi put it, Type Z organizations were 'most aptly described as clans in that they are intimate associations of people engaged in economic activity but tied together through a variety of bonds' (Ouchi, 1981, p.83). Ouchi had borrowed, or rather adapted, the term 'clan' from Durkheim and used it to describe 'an intimate group of industrial workers who know one another well but who typically do not share blood relations' (Ouchi, 1981, p.274). Outstanding examples of the clan in action, claimed Ouchi, were the Quality Control Circles (Q-C Circles) which had been operating in Japan since the early 1950s. Ironically the quality control movement in Japan was largely inspired by American thinking, particularly the work of W. Edwards Deming and Joseph M. Juran.

In the immediate post-war years Japanese products had a reputation for poor workmanship and shoddy quality. The effort to improve the situation was spearheaded by American production engineers operating under the auspices of the Civilian Communications Section (CCS) of the Occupation Administration. Two of these engineers were Charles Protzman and Homer Sarasohn who, in the words of Tsurumi:

> wrote a complete course on industrial management, in which they covered the policy, organization, controls, and operations of what they considered to be a model American company. What they presented, however, frequently differed from what was being taught in the United States at that time, in as much as Protzman and Sarasohn were lecturing on what they felt American management ought to be practicing. In a fitting summation of their overall view, their manual's section on quality control quoted Andrew Carnegie: 'There lies still at the root of great business success the very much more important factor of quality'.
>
> *(Tsurimi, 1982, p.14)*

During the final months of 1949 and the early months of 1950 Protzman and Sarasohn conducted two eight week seminars in Tokyo and Osaka to which only top company managers were invited. Attendance at these seminars was obligatory for the participants and even when the Americans ceased holding them the Japanese took them over and continued for the next 25 years. Again in the words of Tsurumi, 'by 1974 about 5200 executives had attended these seminars. Those managers and Japanese scholars who actively disseminated what they had learned at the CCS seminars were the ones who invited Dr. Deming to Japan in 1950. It was primarily through their efforts that the Quality Control Circle movement took hold in Japan' (Tsurumi, 1982, p.14).

Interestingly, Protzman had been an engineer at the Hawthorne Works of Western Electric when the famous experiments had been conducted there during the late 1920s and early 1930s (see Chapter 11). He had been sceptical about the interpretation of the experiments put forward by Elton Mayo and his followers and saw the human relations approach to management as a prime example of what not to do. In the courses he prepared for his Japanese students he placed the emphasis on old style leadership on the model advocated by Fayol (see Chapter 5). He also stressed the value of discipline, teamwork and co-operation between managers and workers. As Tsurumi has commented 'Protzman's message struck a responsive chord in his Japanese students, who were bred in the Japanese tradition which said that true leaders were men of exemplary moral courage, self-sacrifice and benevolence' (Tsurumi, 1982, p.15).

Like Protzman (and indeed Joseph Juran) W. Edwards Deming was an employee at the Hawthorne Works of Western Electric. Deming trained as an electrical engineer at the University of Wyoming and gained a PhD in mathematical physics from Yale. During his period at the Hawthorne Works Deming became familiar with the work of Walter A. Shewhart, the founder of statistical quality control. In the early 1940s Deming established courses to teach Shewhart's methods to industrialists and engineers. It was these methods that he began teaching when he was invited to Japan in 1950. He met with phenomenal success there as the following comments by Horsley and Buckley show:

> W. E. Deming became a legend in Japan. He gave hundreds of lectures...to eager managers on the vital importance of statistical quality control...'Deming's Wheel', a diagram rationalizing the business of production management, was circulated widely...Among his pupils were many who were to become captains of Japanese industry in the 1960s and 1970s, heading firms like Nissan, Sharp and Nippon Electric Company (NEC). The annual Deming Prize for good management was highly coveted in the 1950s, and is still being awarded today. Deming was never so honoured in his own country.
>
> *(Horsley and Buckley, 1990, p.51)*

The interest which Deming stimulated in the subject of quality control prompted the Japanese to invite Joseph Juran to Tokyo in 1953. Juran had worked with Walter A. Shewhart and in 1951 had produced *The Quality Control Handbook* the first such manual of its kind. Together Deming and Juran inspired the Japanese quality control movement which was eventually emulated throughout the industrial world – not least in the USA itself. Although Ouchi acknowledged the contributions of Deming and Juran in the establishment of Q-C Circles, he placed far greater emphasis on what he described as 'the Japanese attention to the human side of organization'. Where Q-C Circles had been introduced by American companies in the USA, he claimed, they often neglected to combine the statistical techniques of modern quality control with the essential adjustments in human relations. As he put it:

> a successful implementation of the Q-C Circle in an American company can take place only if middle and upper levels of management truly understand the conditions necessary for the success of the program, and support them. This in turn means that the executive groups must offer the kinds of long-run and co-operative incentives without which co-operation at lower levels will not occur. Thus, the Q-C Circle cannot be understood in isolation, but only as one part of a larger and more complex organizational system – and such a system Theory Z offers.
>
> *(Ouchi, 1981, p.268)*

According to Ouchi a major factor underpinning Japan's post-war economic success was the system of lifetime employment operated by the country's biggest employers. Whilst readily conceding that it was limited to only some 35 per cent of Japan's workforce, he nevertheless felt justified in stating that, 'lifetime employment, more than being a single policy, is the rubric under which many facets of Japanese life and work are integrated' (Ouchi, 1981, p.17). The system whereby major companies and government employed a fresh intake of new workers from school or university every year, with the intention of retaining them until their retirement at the age of 55, served to enhance mutual dependency. As promotions in the individual organizations were made exclusively from within, a young (predominantly male) person joining a company could look forward to slow but sure career progression without threat from the external labour market. At the same time once embarked upon a career with a company the employee had little choice but to stay. As Pugh and Hickson have commented 'until retirement, an employee will not be dismissed for anything less than a major criminal offence, and dismissal is a harsh punishment since such a person has no possibility of finding work in a comparable major organization, and must turn to small low wage firms. So, the pressures to be aware of what the organization requires and to fit in with it are very strong' (Pugh and Hickson, 1989, p.108). Obviously such a system is at odds with the individualist assumptions of the West and is calculated to generate a far greater degree of collective consciousness than normally characterizes Western organizations. However, having said this, the differences between the two cultures can be exaggerated and until recently numerous organizations in the USA and Europe sustained staffing arrangements which, notwithstanding their operation in an open labour market, nevertheless provided the expectation of lifetime employment. Indeed, the expectation of employment far beyond the customary span in Japanese companies, extending very often to the age of 65. Of course, ultimately the capacity to sustain lifetime (or indeed any) employment depends upon economic considerations the bulk of which are beyond the control of the individual company, however large it might be. Technical change, competition, government policy and the recent development of globalization all serve to destabilize prevailing patterns of employment (see Chapter 20). Although various direct and indirect protectionist devices can be used (and the Japanese have deployed a number of these) organizations are nevertheless forced to adapt if they are to survive. Interestingly, at the time of writing, the Japanese system of lifetime employment is in a state of decay as Japan itself faces up to the challenge of international competition much of which comes from emerging Asian economies.

Beyond Theory Z, Anti-Theory Z and Japanization

Ouchi's work stimulated considerable debate in American academic circles. George W. England of the University of Oklahoma, for example, analysed Theory Z and summed it up in the following terms:

> the Theory Z approach to management quite simply suggests that involved workers are the key to increased productivity. Involved workers in large

Japanese organizations result from an internally consistent set of norms, practices, and behaviours which are grounded in trust and interpersonal intimacy. Japanese organizations foster lifetime employment, slow evaluation and promotion, non-specialized career paths, implicit control mechanisms, collective decision-making, collective responsibility, and wholistic concern in internally consistent ways which produce worker involvement and thus higher productivity.

(England, 1983, p.131)

England then went on to question the extent to which Theory Z was relevant to the bulk of organizations in the USA, given the self-evident differences in the cultures of America and Japan. As he put it, 'in Japan, Theory Z practices are consistent with the general social norms and are generally supported by the actions of labor organizations and governmental bodies. In a word, they form a highly consistent and integrated theoretical framework whose application works well in the Japanese setting' (England, 1983, p.140). However, he observed, in the USA 'over the past 20 years adversarial relations between government and business, and between labor organizations and business, have become sharper and less supportive of Theory Z applications' and he went on to conclude that 'Theory Z is not likely to become the norm in American companies to the extent it has in Japan' (England, 1983, p.140). Instead, therefore, of urging American business to conform to the alien practices of the Japanese it would be better for management thinkers to spend their time in attempting to discover 'what management philosophy and set of management processes would be sufficiently consistent internally, consistent with American societal norms and expections, and supported by major institutional actors such as government and labor unions' (England, 1983, p.141).

Although rejecting the general applicability of Theory Z to US circumstances, England nevertheless accepted Ouchi's work as a more or less accurate account of what happened in Japanese organizations. However, Jeremiah Sullivan of the University of Washington was unwilling to concede even this. In Sullivan's view Ouchi had willfully misrepresented the Japanese system of management. Sullivan saw the Japanese system as characterized by bureaucracy, hierarchy and a deference springing from Japanese social tradition. The elements which Ouchi had insisted on identifying as the keys to higher productivity were, on closer examination, amenable to an entirely different interpretation which Sullivan styled 'Anti-Theory Z'. In the case of consensus decision-making, for example, to which Ouchi gave considerable attention, Sullivan observed that:

consensus decision-making (if it exists as Ouchi describes it) and collective responsibility are a response to (rather than co-equal incentives with) non-specialization, lifetime employment, and promotion by age in Japanese Theory Z firms. Incompetent managers are protected by their subordinates in this way. The point is this: if a manager without special skills is automatically promoted into a job for which he has no competence, he will not make good decisions and cannot be given responsibility. He will have to rely on subordinates, and thus consensus decisions and collective responsibility will emerge. They will not be incentives to intimacy and trust so much as bi-products of Japanese practices of lifetime employment and non-specialized career paths. Their function will be to protect hierarchical relations so as to keep them useful to the organization's goal of production.

(Sullivan, 1983, p.138)

In Sullivan's view Ouchi had not provided an accurate account of what actually took place in Japanese organizations. Instead he had indulged in a piece of prescriptive writing largely concerned with what ought to be happening rather than what in fact took place. Further, he had extrapolated from this to create a theory that was insufficiently based on empirical research and as likely to damage American business as to bring about improvement. Finally, Sullivan doubted whether Theory Z was rooted in Japanese thinking. Instead it appeared to stem from Western thinking and specifically the work of Emile Durkheim. As Sullivan put it:

Theory Z does not really emerge out of Japanese conditions as Ouchi finds them. Japanese firms just exhibit bits and pieces of the theory. For example, trust clearly is of great importance in Japanese firms…, and co-operative social relationships are important parts of Japanese efforts to carry out tasks. However, Theory Z is really a modern variation in management theory of Durkheim's structuralist sociological work rather than a Japanese developed organization theory.

(Sullivan, 1983, p.139)

Although Ouchi's *Theory Z: How American Business Can Meet the Japanese Challenge* became the best-selling book on Japanese management, it was nevertheless only one text among a myriad books and articles on the subject that were published during the early 1980s. In 1984 J. Bernard Keys and Thomas R. Miller of Memphis State University published an article in the *Academy of Management Review* in which they attempted to 'classify and to clarify the state of knowledge of Japanese management'. They began their task by making the observation that those who had commented on Japanese management had often concentrated on a particular factor and neglected others. As they put it:

competing hypotheses abound…Some observers believe that excellence in Japanese management springs primarily from an emphasis on human resource development. Others maintain that the source of Japanese success is not found in social practices but rather in the profound understanding of the intricacies of the decision-making process. Several researchers laud the effective use of employee quality circles as the key element of Japanese success. Still others claim that Japanese expertise in technological development and in manufacturing management is the basis of their effectiveness. Yet another school of thought attributes Japanese achievement to their mastery of the use of statistical quality control applications. To those attempting to comprehend the Japanese phenomenon, it appears that a dense jungle of confusion has grown up consisting of conflicting 'theories' (using the term broadly), each of which offers hope of an explanation for the apparent superiority of the Japanese system of management.

(Keys and Miller, 1984, p.342)

Keys and Miller then went on to place the various conflicting theories into more or less self-explanatory categories (such as 'manufacturing management', 'quality circle', 'statistical quality control', 'long term, bottom line' and 'decision-making') depending on which of these received the greatest emphasis in any particular author's work. Further they also examined what they termed 'attempts at integrated models of Japanese management' where the authors had 'gone beyond the search for single-factor explanation in their efforts to develop more comprehensive theories'. Among the work they examined under this heading was that of Ouchi and his Theory Z. Whilst not rejecting his work out of hand, Key and Miller nevertheless made clear their support for the criticisms made by both England and Sullivan. They also saw fit to quote Gibney's verdict on Theory Z to the effect that 'Ouchi has given us a chrome-plated collection of hasty generalizations, slogan-type writing, and dimestore business sociology, based on what one might call a modified dart-board technique of research' (Gibney, 1981, p.17). Keys and Miller concluded that 'existing research efforts have failed to capture adequately the essence of Japanese effectiveness. Further, it seems unlikely that additional research seeking single-factor or dual-factor explanations of the Japanese success will be more successful; the panacea will continue to be elusive'. They went on to argue that 'a better understanding of the inter-relationships of the elements of the Japanese management system' was required in order that both commentators and practitioners might 'be better equipped to address the issues of emulation, adaptation, and implementation in American enterprises' (Keys and Miller, 1984, pp.351–352).

Of course, investment by Japanese companies in foreign countries was not limited to the USA alone. Investment also occurred in many other Western countries and particularly the UK where the Conservative Governments of the 1980s specifically set out to attract foreign investment. Further, by the 1980s attempts to emulate Japanese management practice had become almost commonplace within British organizations. In 1986 Peter Turnbull of the Cardiff Business School published an account of such a venture in the *Industrial Relations Journal*. The article dealt with the organizational changes being undertaken by the automobile components company Lucas Electrical which, Turnbull observed, were based on the production methods deployed in large Japanese firms and he coined the term 'Japanization' to describe the phenomenon. The term was subsequently taken up by two of Turnbull's colleagues, Nick Oliver and Barry Wilkinson, 'as an umbrella term to refer to the process by which some aspects of UK industry appeared to be converging towards a Japanese-style model of management practice'. And they observed that the 'process encompassed two strands – the emulation of Japanese manufacturing methods by Western manufacturers and also the increasing volume of Japanese direct manufacturing investment in Western economies' (Oliver and Wilkinson, 1992, p.1). When, in 1988, Oliver and Wilkinson published *The Japanization of British Industry* they suggested 'that British industry was undergoing a fundamental transformation, the nature of which was neatly captured by the term Japanization'. Their book rapidly became the foremost text on the development of Japanese-style management techniques in the UK and was followed, in 1992, by a second edition, *The Japanization of British Industry: New Developments in the 1990s*. Unlike Ouchi, Oliver and Wilkinson did not emphasize the significance of just one or two elements of the Japanese approach to management. On the contrary, they identified a bundle of elements which, taken together, characterized the Japanese 'system' and identified the significance of the social and political context in which it was set. As they put it:

> Japanization entails the successful management of the conditions generated by 'low waste' production systems…Japanization…is a complex but logically coherent process, with social and political as well as technical dimensions (and) to consider Japanization as simply involving the transferability (or otherwise) of Japanese management practices abroad is insufficient. This down-plays the equally important question of how well the various elements of a company's business strategy fit together…Our thesis is that at the heart of the success of the major Japanese corporations lies their ability to manage their internal and external dependencies in a more effective way than the vast majority of their Western counterparts have traditionally been able to do, and that they have been assisted in this by a supportive set of socio-economic conditions. If there is a 'secret' to Japan's success, we suggest that it lies in the synergy generated by a whole system, and not, as some have suggested, in specific parts of the system.
>
> *(Oliver and Wilkinson, 1992, p.88)*

Critical summary

Ouchi's work may be seen as part of an effort by Western management thinkers to account for the phenomenal success of Japanese industry. His view that higher productivity would be generated merely through greater worker involvement in the organization was contentious. Ironically the radical reconstruction of many industries as a result of Japanization often reduced workers' security rather than enhancing it. Further, Ouchi's ambitious scheme for deploying the business organization as a panacea for an increasingly atomized society was hardly plausible given the rapid job loss in many organizations during the 1980s. His insistence on emphasizing the human factors in Japanese management at the expense of the technical elements rendered his analysis simplistic. Also his determination to identify the organizational structures of Japanese business as always benign rather than sometimes hierarchical and bureaucratic and, often, authoritarian was self-evidently a distortion. However, Ouchi's work did provide a number of useful insights, not least the importance he gave to the concept of trust. As Peter Wickens aptly comments in his recent book *The Ascendant Organization*, 'time and again Ouchi returns to his central concept of trust. It manifests itself in his call for a redirection of attention to human relations…for an emphasis on a long-term relationship with customers and on value rather than efficiency'. However, as Wickens goes on to observe, 'the problem with Ouchi's analysis is not what he included, but what he left out. He virtually ignored the very strong "control" culture of the Japanese' (Wickens, 1995, pp.28–29).

Discussion questions

1. To what extent were Ouchi's ideas merely a re-working of Elton Mayo's?
2. What were the characteristics of a Type Z organization?
3. Why was Ouchi enthusiastic about Quality Control Circles?
4. What do you understand by the term Japanization?

Suggested reading

Aron, R. (1967/1990) Emile Durkheim. *Main Currents in Sociological Thought Volume 2*, Penguin Books, Harmondsworth.

England, G. (1983) Japanese and American Management: Theory Z and Beyond. *Journal of International Business Studies* **14** 131–142.

Johnson, R. and Ouchi, W. (1974) Made in America (under Japanese management). *Harvard Business Review* **52** (5) 61–69.

Keys, J. and Miller, T. (1984) The Japanese Management Theory Jungle. *Academy of Management Review* **9** 342–353.

Morita, A. (1987/1994) *Made in Japan: Akio Morita and Sony*, Harper Collins, London.

Oliver, N. and Wilkinson, B. (1992) *The Japanization of British Industry: New Developments in the 1990s*, Basil Blackwell, Oxford.

Ouchi, W. and Jaeger, A. (1978) Type Z Organization: Stability in the Midst of Mobility. *Academy of Management Review* **3** 305–314.

Ouchi, W. (1981) *Theory Z: How American Business Can Meet the Japanese Challenge*, Addison-Wesley, Reading, Mass.

Sullivan, J. (1983) A Critique of Theory Z. *Academy of Management Review* **8** 132–142.

Tsurumi, R. (1982) American Origins of Japanese Productivity: The Hawthorne Experiment Rejected. *Pacific Basin Quarterly* **7** 14–15.

Turnbull, P. (1986) The 'Japanization' of Production and Industrial Relations at Lucas Electrical. *Industrial Relations Journal* **17**(3) 193–206.

Chapter 20

Charles Handy and the future of work

Charles Handy was born in 1932 in Kildare in the Republic of Ireland where his father was a leading Anglican clergyman. After graduating from Oriel College, Oxford in 1956 Handy joined Shell International Petroleum, remaining with the company until 1965 when he left and spent a year working for Charter Consolidated in the City of London. In 1967 he went to the Sloan School of Management at the Massachusetts Institute of Technology (MIT), becoming International Faculty Fellow there. At MIT Handy came under the influence of the 'Sloan School gurus', including Warren Bennis and Chris Argyris who had in turn been strongly influenced by Douglas McGregor (see Chapter 16). Handy never resumed his business career. Instead, in 1968, he returned to Britain, joining the recently established London Business School (LBS) where he was responsible for organizing the Sloan Management Programme. In 1972 he was appointed professor at the LBS and remains a visiting professor in management there. Between 1977 and 1981 Handy was Warden of the private conference and study centre at St George's House in Windsor Castle. In 1976 he published his first book *Understanding Organizations* which became a standard text, going into its fourth edition in 1993. During the 1980s Handy continued to publish regularly, his themes developing beyond the narrower confines of organizational behaviour into the wider spheres of work, ethics and society. In 1984 he produced what is perhaps his most important book *The Future of Work* which is examined in the section which follows. Handy's recent work such as *The Age of Unreason* (1989) and *The Empty Raincoat* (1994) are written in popular rather than technical language and aimed at a wider readership than a merely 'professional' one. Through these later books, as well as through journal articles, lectures, radio and television broadcasts Charles Handy has established himself as Britain's leading management guru.

The context of *The Future of Work* and its sequels (*The Age of Unreason* and *The Empty Raincoat*) was provided by the emergence and persistence of historically high levels of unemployment, particularly in the UK. Briefly, during the post-war period the industrialized West had been more or less free of the threat of unemployment which had blighted the lives of many working people during the inter-war years (see Chapter 10). The long post-war economic boom produced a generation of workers who had little fear of losing their jobs. Optimistic assumptions concerning economic stability and progress were shared by economists, politicians and industrialists alike. Tight labour markets strengthened the trade unions and, generally speaking, managements were placed on the defensive. Management theorists shared the optimistic assumption that full employment could be sustained. In such a situation management techniques were calculated to persuade rather than coerce the worker. Maslow (see Chapter 14), Herzberg (see Chapter 15), together with McGregor and his associates (see Chapter 16) all advocated a soft managerial orientation which sought to gain commitment through providing opportunities for psychic growth. Even Braverman (see Chapter 18), who claimed to identify the process whereby work was being steadily degraded, did not prophesy the collapse of work itself. Having said all of this there were, at least in the British case, early indications that the post-war boom would not be sustainable. An example was the 'stop-go' economic policy pursued by the Conservative Governments of the 1950s. As Vickerstaff and Sheldrake have commented 'by the end of the decade many were arguing that stop-go and over reliance on financial policy to secure balance of payments equilibrium was resulting in low rates of investment, low productivity growth, low growth for the economy as a whole, a general decline in the international competitiveness of the British economy and steadily rising conflict' (Vickerstaff and Sheldrake, 1989, p.69).

Throughout the 1960s and 1970s successive British governments struggled to sustain the post-war policy consensus which placed the greatest emphasis on full employment. The prevailing economic orthodoxy of the period was derived from the work of Keynes and was concerned, at least at the level of political rhetoric, with sustaining economic demand as the means to avoid unemployment. Of course, the inflationary risks of this were well known but, broadly speaking, governments had been willing to accept them as the lesser of two evils. However, Britain's poor economic performance *vis-à-vis* her major competitors became an increasing cause for governmental concern. Between 1960 and 1976, for example, Britain's share of the world's exports of manufactured goods was halved. Meanwhile the phenomenon of 'stagflation', which saw low growth going hand in hand with rising inflation, raised the spectre of hyper-inflation and the dire social consequences associated with monetary collapse. An already difficult situation was gravely worsened by the hike in oil prices which followed the Arab-Israeli war of October 1973. The quadrupling of oil prices badly dislocated those economies, industrial and otherwise, which were dependent on imported oil. Although in the longer term Britain was able to exploit the substantial oil reserves of the North Sea, in the short term the country's fragile economy was seriously damaged. Unemployment rose from a little over 4 per cent in 1975 to reach in excess of 6 per cent in 1978. Meanwhile, inflation began to displace employment as the key issue for government. Peaking at over 24 per cent during 1975, inflation declined to around 8 per cent in 1978 only to climb back to 18 per cent by 1980. The Conservative Government which came to office in 1979 effectively abandoned the commitment to full employment, concentrating instead on reducing the level of inflation. Unemployment rose from a little over 5 per cent in 1979 to reach 13.5 per cent in 1985. Although the rate of unemployment did decline during the late 1980s, the days of full employment were apparently over. As Handy put it, 'the short answer to the question "will there be full employment again?" has to be "not in our lifetime"' (Handy, 1984/1994, p.37).

The future of work

Although this chapter has so far emphasized the unemployment difficulties experienced by Britain, problems were experienced by all the Western industrial nations, including the historically successful economies of West Germany and the USA. The impact of Japanese competition in manufacturing was noted in Chapter 19. During the 1970s a new global economy began to emerge in which rapid exchanges of goods, services and information transcended the constraints of national boundaries as never before. This phenomenon was facilitated by rapid technological innovation which, in turn, destroyed prevailing patterns of work. Soon the whole notion of what constituted work and the working life came under scrutiny as redundancy, plant closures and job loss became commonplace. Even though many new jobs were created they hardly replaced those that were lost. As Handy expressed the situation:

> it was during the 1970s…that the familiar scenery of our working lives began to show visible changes. The large employment organizations which had been day-time houses for so many people all their lives began to decline. Some famous names from our industrial past disappeared for ever. The names on the High Street shop fronts changed, and the way of life behind many of them changed too. The tradition of a man going out to work to support, by himself, a family at home became a statistical rarity; by the end of the decade only 14 per cent of households fitted this stereotype. 'Long term unemployment', 'youth unemployment' and 'redundancy' became familiar words, words which increasingly infected all social groups. Jobs began to be a scarce commodity, and 'work' started to mean other things besides the conventional full time job. Second and third careers, moonlighting and the (informal) economy became part of our language as did the chip and the video – all new words to herald new ways. The old patterns were breaking down; new patterns were forming.
>
> *(Handy, 1984, p.ix)*

If the conventional patterns of work that had developed since the nineteenth century were indeed breaking down what, other than terminal unemployment, was taking their place? According to Handy a whole range of developments could be discerned. First, the word work, in the sense of being only paid employment in an organization, was being challenged. Feminists had rightly claimed for some time that the activities of women in the home were work – albeit provided as a 'gift'. Second, the rise of part time employment, contractualization, temporary employment and 'odd jobs' was nudging people in the direction of having several jobs which, taken together, could provide a livelihood. Third, the expansion of voluntary work, particularly for those in the third age, offered the prospect of satisfying activity without the cash incentive. Handy summed all of this up as follows, 'there is more than one form of work. We can best describe the differences by thinking of three different forms of work:

1. job work, which is the paid job, including full time self-employment;
2. marginal work, which covers the work we do 'on the side' for extra earnings, which could be, but sometimes are not, declared (for tax purposes);
3. gift work, which includes all the work we do for free in the grey economy and in voluntary work.

(Handy, 1984/1994, p.52)

Briefly, Handy's thesis was that, in the future, it would no longer be viable to depend on the single, central life-time job to supply all, or even most, of an individual's economic, social and status needs. Instead people would be constrained 'to put together a portfolio of activities and relationships, each of which makes its own contribution to the package of things we want out of work and life' (Handy, 1984/1994, p.8). The 'portfolio' approach offered opportunities but also posed problems. The young, well educated individual, possessing transferrable skills and having limited responsibilities might readily adopt a portfolio lifestyle. Equally, the retired person with an adequate company pension, no mortgage and a grown up family might welcome the variety of the portfolio approach. But what of the poorly educated person with limited capacities and substantial outgoings and responsibilities? Would not the portfolio approach be merely a recipe for chronic insecurity? Handy recognized that there could well be difficulties. By illustration he turned to the phenomenon of 'Japanese drift' – the underside of Japanese industry not covered by life–time employment (see Chapter 19). As he put it:

there is a myth that everyone has a guarantee of lifetime employment in Japan. Not so…The truth is that large Japanese organizations float on a raft of small subcontractors…Japan is a country of small businesses which use low cost labour and do not offer lifetime employment…Japan also has a small army of the self-employed including a group of euphemistically called 'unpaid domestic workers', the unpaid members of the family who help in the one man business. Any reduction in hours worked by these self-employed, or by the workers in the sub-contracting firms, is hardly visible to the outside world. Of those working in these small businesses 8 per cent have no hours specified in their contracts. Underemployment is not the same as unemployment.

(Handy, 1984/1994, pp.91–2)

Given the increasing influence of Japanese practice on British management thinking, Handy envisaged a situation in which a UK version of what already occurred in Japan might well emerge. Large organizations were placing a whole range of their activities out to contractors, many of which were small businesses. Further, organizations were increasingly making use of temporary contracts and part time workers rather than employing workers in conventional full time jobs. One result of these phenomena was the emergence of the 'core and periphery', with the essential core workers of the company being relatively well paid, enjoying good service conditions and having job security and superannuation benefits. Meanwhile, the peripheral workers received poorer pay, had inferior service conditions, little or no job security and were not part of the superannuation scheme. Handy saw 'Japanese drift' as a threat to social cohesion as the development of a two tiered employment structure drove a wedge between those fortunate enough to be core workers and the rest.

Living with unreason and paradox

Many of the themes Handy had explored in *The Future of Work* were re-examined in *The Age of Unreason* (1989). He had ended the earlier text with a plea for radical re-thinking of the whole question of work and its social and economic ramifications. As he put it:

we are fixated, both as a nation and as individuals, by the employment organization. Work is defined as employment. Money is distributed through employment. Status and identity stem from employment. We therefore hang on to employment as long as we can; we measure our success in terms of it; we expect great things from it, for the country and for ourselves; and we cannot conceive of a future without it. And yet, ironically, we are very bad at it because there is an individualist streak in all of us which agrees with Marx that it is alienating to sell ourselves or our time to another.

(Handy, 1984/1994, p.188)

This final paradox had been ignored by the bulk of management thinkers although, as has been seen, some such as Maslow (see Chapter 14), Schumacher (see Chapter 17) and of course Braverman (see Chapter 18) had been aware that employment relationships were far from simple or satisfactory. Handy embraced the view that the organizations or corporations that had become the more or less dominant institutions of industrial societies, were beginning to wither away. The era when men such as Henry Ford could operate most effectively by concentrating an entire manufacturing capability on a single site, was fast giving way to one in which enterprises were becoming increasingly diffuse and amorphous. Worthwhile, well paid, secure jobs would no longer be guaranteed for even a minority of the labour force. Instead, the bulk of working lives would in future be characterized by jobs of short duration, involving the development of a portfolio approach and requiring the individual to be flexible, pragmatic and, hopefully, multi-skilled. The stark division between work and leisure that had developed with the onset of the industrial revolution would become ever more blurred.

A major consequence of this situation, argued Handy, would be necessary change in the nature of education and the education system. The British approach to education and training would no longer serve. The old assumptions that basic education and time served apprenticeship were adequate preparation for the forty-year working life were already redundant. Similarly, the notion that an individual completed her or his education and then spent the remainder of their active life in a job was equally passé. Instead the education system would have to develop in ways which facilitated more inclusive and more extensive educational opportunities for all. As Handy put it:

> if effective organizations need more and more intelligent people, if careers are shorter and more changeable, above all, if more people need to be more self-sufficient for more of their lives then education has to become the single most important investment that any person can make in their own destiny. It will not, however, be education as most of us have known it...the old British notion of education as something to be got rid of as soon as one decently could. Education needs to be reinvented.

(Handy, 1989/1990, p.168)

Of course, Handy readily conceded that this was easier said than done and that it would take a major shift in attitudes to achieve a situation in which everybody would embrace the notion of life-time learning. In fact it would require clear recognition by each individual, and by society at large, that the world of work was being irrevocably changed and that nothing could ever be quite the same again. Nevertheless, in spite of the self-evident dangers, problems and insecurities, Handy remained optimistic concerning the future. At least, he argued, the new world of work would generate the possibility of choice in a way that previous configurations of working life were more or less bound to deny. Perhaps discontinuous change would serve to liberate individuals from the confines of organizational life, thereby allowing 'more people to stop pretending earlier in their lives' (Handy, 1989/90, p.212).

The mood of *The Empty Raincoat* was far darker than that of Handy's earlier works. Indeed the book began with a statement by the author which read rather like an apology, or perhaps a confession. As he put it:

> four years ago, my earlier book, *The Age of Unreason*, was published. In that book I presented a view of the way work was being re-shaped and the effect

which the re-shaping might have on all our lives. It was, on the whole, an optimistic view. Since then, the world of work has changed very much along the lines which were described in the book. This should be comforting to an author, but I have not found it so. Too many people in institutions have been unsettled by the changes. Capitalism has not proved as flexible as it was supposed to be. Governments have not been all-wise or far-seeing. Life is a struggle for many and a puzzle for most.

(Handy, 1994, p.1)

Handy took the title for his book from a sculpture he had seen in an open air sculpture park in Minneapolis. The sculpture consisted of three shapes, the largest one being a bronze raincoat, standing erect and empty. Handy, somewhat confusingly perhaps, took the empty raincoat for what he called 'the symbol of our most pressing paradox'. As he observed, 'we were not destined to be empty raincoats, nameless numbers on a payroll, role occupants, the raw material of economics or sociology, statistics in some government report. If that is to be its price, then economic progress is an empty promise. There must be more to life than to be a cog in someone else's great machine, hurtling God knows where' (Handy, 1994, p.2).

In the remainder of the book Handy attempted to come to terms with some of the paradoxes which characterized life in the late twentieth century. For example, there was self-evidently an immense amount of work of all kinds to be done but there was apparently insufficient money available to pay the going rate for its accomplishment. Voluntary work had not taken up the slack because much of the labour required was not of the kind that a person would undertake except for money compensation. Further, those who had a regular paid occupation were under pressure to work ever harder. So hard in some cases that many had no time for anything other than work and eventually burnt out and were replaced by younger, hungrier people. Meanwhile, whole groups of people were increasingly marginalized from the world of paid work because they were too old, or lacked the necessary skills, or lived in the wrong place or whatever. Such people were effectively disenfranchised, not in terms of losing the right to vote in elections, but in terms of lacking the opportunity to obtain the necessary financial wherewithal essential in a society built on money. Of course, there was no shortage of money as such, it was merely that the distribution of wealth was so excessively unequal. As Handy commented:

over the period 1979–90, the bottom 10 per cent (in Britain) saw their income in real terms fall by 14 per cent, while the average income increased by 36 per cent. The wealth has been slightly less skewed in the other mature economies, but the trend has been the same. As ever, the rich got richer and the poor got, relatively, poorer the world over, and sometimes poorer in absolute terms. What held it all together was only the hope among the poor that, maybe, in a world of constant growth there would be room for some of them, too, amid the rich. It is beginning to seem a rather forlorn hope.

(Handy, 1994, p.12)

Self-evidently the developments in the nature of work which Handy had observed were eroding the notion that the work organization could provide either the focus of community or the basis of personal identity. Although some large production units still existed (in the automobile industry for example) they were becoming rarer and, in any case, working lives in such places were becoming shorter. Those individuals who had the necessary skills and motivation to become, in the jargon of the French existentialists, self-creating projects, might find greater freedom in the new, post-industrial future. However, many others (perhaps even the majority) would be condemned to a life of, at best, chronic insecurity or, at worst, dependence on the state or even crime. Such sombre reflections took Handy far from the comfortable assumptions of *Understanding Organizations*. In part he began to share some of the views concerning the future held by Schumacher (see Chapter 17) and outlined in his posthumously published *Good Work* of 1979. Schumacher had argued that the rising capital intensity of industry, together with the more extensive use of automation, would precipitate a crisis of unemployment and the industrial nations would be forced to examine their values and, possibly, 'return' to simpler methods of production. Handy also shared some of the views of the Marxist/existentialist thinker, Andre Gorz, contained in his book *Farewell to the Working Class* and published in an English translation in 1982. Gorz, like Handy, had identified the partial collapse of work in the Western industrial nations and sought to analyse its social ramifications. As he observed:

> the abolition of work is a process already underway and likely to accelerate. In each of the three leading industrialized nations of Western Europe, independent economic forecasts have estimated that automation will eliminate 4–5 million jobs in ten years...In the context of the current crisis and technological revolution it is absolutely impossible to restore full employment by quantitative economic growth...A society based on mass unemployment is coming into being before our eyes. It consists of a growing mass of the permanently unemployed on the one hand, an aristocracy of tenured workers on the other, and, between them, a proletariat of temporary workers carrying out the least skilled and most unpleasant types of work.

(Gorz, 1982, p.3)

Challenging the conventions of orthodox Marxism (see Chapter 18) Gorz argued that the industrial proletariat were no longer sufficiently numerous to be relevant to the process of industrial change. Instead, he identified what he called the 'non-class of non-producers' whom he claimed possessed the capacity to transform society. As he put it, 'only the non-class of non-producers...embodies what lies beyond productivism: the rejection of the accumulation ethic and the dissolution of all classes' (Gorz, 1982, p.74).

Like Gorz, Handy argued that changes in the nature and supply of work would bring about necessary personal and social transformation. However, although he shared some of Gorz's views he did not carry the same European intellectual baggage and the language he deployed was free of Hegelian rhetoric. For Handy the future was there to be seized by individuals and shaped to meet their desires. The new world of work could facilitate this by offering greater flexibility and the opportunity to build a working life free of the inhibiting constraints of the organization. There were of course many risks that the growing underclass would become ever larger, generating sharp polarities within society. Further, the loss of the big organization and the assumptions of the prolonged working life, might lead to a growing sense of personal isolation. There would, argued Handy, be the need to actively promote a sense of community and he pitched his hopes for the future at the micro –rather than the macro–level. As he concluded, in words worthy of Schumacher:

> nations are too big, the connections to the future not long enough. It is better to look smaller, to our now-smaller organizations, to local communities and cities, to families and clusters of friends, to small networks of portfolio people with time to give to something bigger than themselves. We have to fashion our own directions in our own places.
>
> *(Handy, 1995, p.267)*

Critical summary

Handy's later works reflected the growing perplexity generated by rapid social and technological change, globalization and persistently high levels of unemployment. During the 1980s and 1990s long standing, optimistic assumptions concerning economic goals and personal aspirations were placed under increasing challenge. The growing emergence of an underclass raised the spectre of a society divided against itself. The quality of working life seemed set to decline as the bulk of new jobs lacked intrinsic worth, security and the levels of pay necessary to sustain personal prosperity. In the sphere of management theory the notion that the employment organization could provide the focus of community and/or personal identity was more or less refuted. Handy attempted to analyse the opportunities, risks, and possible social developments besetting post-industrial society.

Discussion questions

1. Identify the factors which contributed to the persistence of relatively high levels of unemployment during the 1980s and 1990s.

2. What do the terms 'core' and 'periphery' mean in the employment context?
3. What did Handy mean by 'portfolio people'?
4. Why did Handy consider life–time employment to be a thing of the past?

Suggested reading

Clutterbuck, D. and Crainer, S. (1990) *Makers of Management: Men and Women Who Changed the Business World*, Macmillan, London, ch.2.

Gorz, A. (1982) *Farewell to the Working Class: An Essay in Post-industrial Socialism*, Pluto Press, London.

Handy, C. (1976) *Understanding Organizations*, Penguin Books, Harmondsworth.

Handy, C. (1984/1994) *The Future of Work: A Guide to a Changing Society*, Basil Blackwell, Oxford.

Handy, C. (1989/90) *The Age of Unreason*, Arrow Books, London.

Handy, C. (1994) *The Empty Raincoat: Making Sense of the Future*, Hutchinson, London.

Kennedy, C. (1991) *Guide to the Management Gurus*, Century, London, ch.11.

Schumacher, E. F. (1979) *Good Work*, Jonathan Cape, London.

Sheldrake, J. (1991) *Industrial Relations and Politics in Britain 1880–1989*, Pinter, London, chs. 5 and 6.

Chapter 21

Conclusion

This book has traced the evolution of management theory from the late nineteenth century to the present day – basically from Taylorism to Japanization. Until quite recently it was plausible to argue that this evolution was more or less coterminous with the development of a single nation, namely the United States. Scientific management developed in the crucible of American industrialization and subsequently spread throughout the industrial and industrializing world. The American system of manufacturing made possible the techniques of mass production deployed so effectively by US automobile manufacturers. Even the locus of the best publicized challenge to Taylorism, namely the Hawthorne Works of Western Electric, was operated on the basis of scientific management, mass production techniques and American welfare capitalism. The success of American industry based on technical edge, managerial expertise and sustained profitability continued until the 1980s. Since then, however, the industrial hegemony of the USA has been increasingly threatened by competition from the far East, most notably Japan. By the end of the century the focus of the world's manufacturing capacity will no longer be in the USA or even Europe but in Asia. This change, together with the globalization of industry and commerce, has challenged many assumptions – not least that of sustained high levels of employment. In such a situation managers face a formidable task– not just in managing their organization but in countering the scepticism and insecurity generated by unemployment. For example, it is hardly possible to do much in the direction of improving job satisfaction, let alone engendering self-actualization, when large scale redundancies are imminent. Nevertheless, although the optimistic belief that economic growth will provide a palliative for unemployment is certainly less secure than is was, it is futile to despair. Managers have to do their best in the circumstances in which they find themselves and these are not always easy as the examples of Fayol and Sloan, for example, clearly show. There is now a vast legacy of management theory available, including work inspired by Japanese industrial success. Hopefully, it will provide both guidance and inspiration in the difficult times ahead.

Bibliography

Aitken, H. (1960) *Taylorism at the Watertown Arsenal: Scientific Management in Action 1908-1915*, Harvard University Press, Cambridge, Mass.

Albrow, M. (1970) *Bureaucracy*, Pall Mall Press, London.

Argyle, M. (1972/1989) *The Social Psychology of Work*, Penguin Books, Harmondsworth.

Armytage, W. (1976) *A Social History of Engineering*, Faber, London.

Aron, R. (1967/1990) *Main Currents in Sociological Thought Volume 2*, Penguin Books, Harmondsworth.

Babbage, C. (1832/1971) *On the Economy of Machinery and Manufactures*, Augustus M. Kelley, New York.

Barnard, C. (1938/1968) *The Functions of the Executive*, Harvard University Press, Cambridge, Mass.

Barnard, C. (1948) *Organization and Management: Selected Papers*, Harvard University Press, Cambridge, Mass.

Belchem, J. (1991) *Industrialization and the Working Class: The English Experience 1750-1900*, Scolar Press, Aldershot.

Bendix, R. (1956/1974) *Work and Authority in Industry: Ideologies of Management in the Course of Industrialization*, University of California Press, Berkeley.

Booth, A. and Pack, M. (1985) *Employment, Capital and Economic Policy: Great Britain 1918-1939*, Basil Blackwell, Oxford.

Braverman, H. (1974) *Labor and Monopoly Capital: The Degradation of Work in the Twentieth Century*, Monthly Review Press, New York.

Briggs, A. (1961) *Social Thought and Social Action: A Study of the Work of Seebohm Rowntree*, Longman, London.

Briggs, A. (1979) *The Age of Improvement 1783-1867*, Longman, Harlow.

Chandler, A. (1980) The United States: Seedbed of Managerial Capitalism. Chandler, A. and Daems, H. (eds), *Managerial Hierarchies: Comparative Perspectives on the Rise of the Modern Industrial Enterprise*, Harvard University Press, Cambridge, Mass.

Chandler, A. (1962/1993) *Strategy and Structure: Chapters in the History of the American Industrial Enterprise*, MIT Press, Cambridge, Mass.

Child, J. (1969) *British Management Thought: A Critical Analysis*, Allen & Unwin, London.

Claeys, G. (1991) introduction to Owen, R. *A New View of Society and Other Writings*, Penguin Books, Harmondsworth.

Clark, W. (1922) *The Gantt Chart: A Working Tool of Management,* Ronald Press, New York.

Clutterbuck, D. and Crainer, S. (1990) *Makers of Management:Men and Women Who Changed the Business World*, Macmillan, London.

Cole, G. D. H. (1917/1972) *Self-Government in Industry*, Hutchinson, London.

Cole, G. D. H. (1923/1973) *Workshop Organization*, Hutchinson, London.

Coleman, T. (1965) *The Railway Navvies: A History of the Men who Made the Railways*, Hutchinson, London.

Copley, F. (1923) *Frederick W. Taylor: Father of Scientific Management*, Harper & Row, New York.

Daiute, R. (1964) *Scientific Management, Ideas, Topics, Readings*, Holt Rinehart & Winston, New York, 1964.

Daunten, P. (1962) *Current Issues and Emerging Concepts in Management*, Houghton, Boston.

Dintenfass, M. (1992) *The Decline of Industrial Britain 1870-1980*, Routledge, London.

Drucker, P. F. (1942/1995) *The Future of Industrial Man*, Transaction Publishers, New Brunswick.

England, G. (1983) Japanese and American Management: Theory Z and Beyond. *Journal of International Business Studies* **14** 131-142.

Fayol, H. (1949) *General and Administrative Management*, Pitman, London.

Follett, M. P. (1918) *The New State*, Longmans, Green, London.

Follett, M. P. (1924) *Creative Experience*, Longmans, Green, London.

Ford, H. (1923) *My Life and Work*, Heinemann, London.

Fox, A. (1985) *History and Heritage: The Social Origins of the British Industrial Relations System*, Allen & Unwin, London.

Gantt, H. (1910) *Work, Wages and Profit*, Engineering Magazine Co., New York.

Gantt, H. (1916) *Industrial Leadership*, Yale University Press, New Haven, Conn.

Gantt, H. (1919) *Organizing for Work*, Harcourt Brace Jovanovich, New York.

George, C. (1968) *The History of Management Thought*, Prentice Hall, Englewood Cliffs, N. J.

Gibney, F. (1981) Now It's Time To Imitate the Japanese. *Pacific Basin Quarterly* **6** 17–18.

Gilbreth, F. (1911) *Motion Study*, Van Nostrand Rheinhold, New York.

Gilbreth, F. (1912) *Primer of Scientific Management*, Van Nostrand Rheinhold, New York.

Gilbreth, F. and L. (1917) *Applied Motion Study*, Sturgis & Walton, New York.

Gilbreth, L. (1914) *The Psychology of Management*, Sturgis & Walton, New York.

Gilbreth, L. (1973) *The Quest for the One Best Way: A Sketch of the Life of Frank Bunker Gilbreth*, Hive, Eastern.

Gillespie, R. (1991) *Manufacturing Knowledge; A History of the Hawthorne Experiments*, Cambridge University Press, Cambridge.

Goodrich, C. (1920/75) *The Frontier of Control: A Study in British Workshop Politics*, Pluto Press, London.

Gorz, A. (1982) *Farewell to the Working Class: An Essay in Post-Industrial Socialism*, Pluto Press, London.

Graham, P. (1987) *Dynamic Managing: The Follett Way*, British Institute of Management, London.

Graham, P. (1995) *Mary Parker Follett – Prophet of Management*, Harvard Business School Press, Boston, Mass.

Greenwood, R. G., Bolton, A. and Greenwood, R. A. (1983) Hawthorne a Half Century Later: Relay Assembly Participants Remember. *Journal of Management* **9**(2) 217–231.

Gulick, L. and Urwick, L. (eds) (1937), *Papers on the Science of Administration*, Institute of Public Administration, Columbia University, New York.

Habakkuk, H. (1962) *American and British Technology in the Nineteenth Century: the Search for Labour-Saving Inventions*, Cambridge University Press, Cambridge.

Handy, C. (1976) *Understanding Organizations*, Penguin Books, Harmondsworth.

Handy, C. (1984/1994) *The Future of Work: A Guide to a Changing Society*, Basil Blackwell, Oxford.

Handy, C. (1989/1990) *The Age of Unreason*, Arrow Books, London.

Handy, C. (1994) *The Empty Raincoat: Making Sense of the Future*, Hutchinson, London.

Hannah, L. (1976) *The Rise of the Corporate Economy*, Methuen, London.

Harris, J. (1994) *Private Lives, Public Spirit: Britain 1870–1914*, Penguin Books, Harmondsworth.

Herzberg, F. (1966/1974) *Work and the Nature of Man*, Crosby Lockwood Staples, London.

Herzberg, F., Mausner, B. and Snyderman, B. (1959/1993) *The Motivation to Work*, Transaction Publishers, New Brunswick, New Jersey.

Heskett, J. (1987) *Industrial Design*, Thames & Hudson, London.

Heyl, B. (1968) The Harvard 'Pareto Circle'. *Journal for the History of the Behavioural Sciences* **4** 316–333.

Homans, G. (1962) *Sentiments and Activities: Essays in Social Science*, Routledge & Kegan Paul, London

Horsley, W. and Buckley, R. (1990) *Nippon New Superpower: Japan Since 1945*, BBC Books, London.

Hoxie, R. (1915) *Scientific Management and Labor*, Appleton, New York.

Johnson, R. and Ouchi, W. (1974) Made in America (Under Japanese Management). *Harvard Business Review*, **52**(5) 61–69.

Joyce, P. (1982) *Work, Society and Politics: The Culture of the Factory in Later Victorian England*, Methuen, London.

Kakabadse, A, Ludlow, R and Vinnicombe, S (1988) *Working in Organizations*, Penguin Books, Harmondsworth.

Kasler, D. (1988) *Max Weber: An Introduction to His Life and Work*, Polity Press, Cambridge.

Kennedy, C. (1991) *Guide to the Management Gurus*, Century, London.

Keys, J. and Miller, T. (1984) The Japanese Management Theory Jungle. *Academy of Management Review* **9** 342–353.

Landes, D. (1969) *The Unbound Prometheus: Technological Change and Industrial Development in Western Europe from 1750 to the Present*, Cambridge University Press, Cambridge.

Landsberger, H. (1958) *Hawthorne Revisited: 'Management and the Worker', its Critics, and Developments in Human Relations in Industry*, Cornell University, Ithaca, New York.

Lane, C. (1989) *Management and Labour in Europe*, Edward Elgar, Aldershot.

Levine, A. (1967) *Industrial Retardation in Britain 1880–1914*, Weidenfeld & Nicolson, London.

MacRae, D. (1974) *Weber*, Woburn Press, London.

McGregor, D. (1960/1987) *The Human Side of Enterprise*, Penguin Books, Harmondsworth.

McGregor, D. with McGregor, C. and Bennis, W. (eds) (1967) *The Professional Manager*, McGraw–Hill, New York.

McLellan, D. (1979) *Marxism After Marx: An Introduction*, Macmillan, London.

Marcuse, H. (1964/1991) *One-Dimensional Man; Studies in the Ideology of Advanced Industrial Society*, Routledge, London.

Maslow, A. (1943) A Theory of Human Motivation. *Psychological Review* **50** 370–396.

Maslow, A. (1954) *Motivation and Personality*, Harper & Row, New York.

Maslow, A. (1965) *Eupsychian Management*, Richard Irwin, Homewood, Illinois.

Maslow, A. (1971) *The Farther Reaches of Human Nature*, Viking Press, New York.

Mayo, E. (1919) *Democracy and Freedom: An Essay in Social Logic*, Macmillan, Melbourne.

Mayo, E. (1933/1960) *The Human Problems of an Industrial Civilization*, Viking Press, New York.

Mayo, E. (1949) *The Social Problems of an Industrial Civilization*, Routledge & Kegan Paul, London.

Merkle, J. (1980) *Management and Ideology: The Legacy of the International Scientific Management Movement*, University of California Press, California.

Merrill, H. (ed) (1960) *Classics in Management*, American Management Association, New York.

Metcalf, H. and Urwick, L. (eds) (1941) *Dynamic Administration: The Collected Papers of Mary Parker Follett*, Management Publications Trust, Bath.

Meyer, S. (1981) *The Five Dollar Day: Labor Management and Social Control in the Ford Motor Company 1908–1921*, State University of New York Press, Albany.

Mingay, G. (1976) *Rural Life in Victorian England*, Heinemann, London.

Mintzberg, H. (1983) *Structure in Fives: Designing Effective Organizations*, Prentice Hall, Englewood Cliffs, N. J.

Morita, A. (1987/1994) *Made in Japan: Akio Morita and Sony*, Harper Collins, London.

Nadworny, M. (1953) The Society for the Promotion of the Science of Management. *Explorations in Entrepreneurial History* **5** 244–247.

Nadworny, M. (1957) Frederick Taylor and Frank Gilbreth: Competition in Scientific Management. *Business History Review* **31**(1) 23–34.

Nelson, D. (1975) *Managers and Workers: Origins of the New Factory System in the United States*, University of Wisconsin Press, Maddison.

Nevins, A. (1954) *Ford: the Times, the Man, the Company*, Charles Scribner's, New York.

Oliver, N. and Wilkinson, B. (1992) *The Japanization of British Industry: New Developments in the 1990s*, Basil Blackwell, Oxford.

Ouchi, W. and Jaeger, A. (1978) Type Z Organization: Stability in the Midst of Mobility. *Academy of Management Review*, **3** 305–314.

Ouchi, W. (1981) *Theory Z: How American Business Can Meet the Japanese Challenge*, Addison–Wesley, Reading, Mass.

Perrow, C. (1986) *Complex Organizations: A Critical Essay*, Random House, New York.

Pimlott, B. (1986) *Labour and the Left in the 1930s*, Allen & Unwin, London.

Pollard, H. (1974) *Developments in Management Thought*, Heinemann, London.

Pollard, S. (1965) *The Genesis of Modern Management: A Study of the Industrial Revolution in Great Britain*, Edward Arnold, London.

Porritt, J. (1993) introduction to Schumacher, E. F. *Small is Beautiful: A Study of Economics as if People Mattered*, Vintage Books, London.

Price, R. (1986) *Labour in British Society: An Interpretative History*, Croom Helm, Beckenham.

Pugh, D. and Hickson, D. (eds) (1989) *Writers on Organizations*, Penguin Books, Harmondsworth.

Pugh, D. (ed) (1990) *Organization Theory: Selected Readings*, Penguin Books, Harmondsworth.

Rae, J. (1959) *American Automobile Manufactureres: The First Forty Years*, Chilton, Philadelphia.

Rathe, A. (ed) (1960) *Gantt on Management: Guidelines for Today's Executive*, American Management Association and The American Society of Mechanical Engineers, New York.

Roethlisberger, F. and Dickson, W. (1939/1964) *Management and the Worker: An Account of a Research Program Conducted by the Western Electric Company, Hawthorne Works, Chicago*, Wiley & Sons, New York.

Rose, M. (1988) *Industrial Behaviour: Research and Control*, Penguin Books, Harmondsworth.

Rosenfeld, J. and Smith, M. (1966) Mary Parker Follett: The Transition to Modern Management Thought. *Advanced Management Journal* **31**(4) 33–37.

Schumacher, E. F. (1973/1993) *Small is Beautiful: A Study of Economics as if People Mattered*, Vintage Books, London.

Schumacher, E. F. (1979) *Good Work*, Jonathan Cape, London.

Sheldrake, J. (1988) *The Origins of Public Sector Industrial Relations*, Avebury, Aldershot.

Sheldrake, J. (1991) *Industrial Relations and Politics in Britain 1880-1989*, Pinter, London.

Sloan, A. (1963) *My Years With General Motors*, Sidgwick & Jackson, London.

Smith, A. (1776/1986) *The Wealth of Nations*, Penguin Books, Harmondsworth.

Spriegel, W. and Myers, C. (eds) (1953) *The Writings of the Gilbreths*, Richard Irwin, Holmwood, Illinois.

Stevenson, J. (1992) *Popular Disturbances in England 1700-1832*, Longman, Harlow.

Sullivan, J. (1983) A Critique of Theory Z. *Academy of Management Review* **8** 132-142.

Taylor, F. W. (1903) *Shop Management*, Harper & Row, New York.

Taylor, F. W. (1911) *The Principles of Scientific Management*, Harper & Row, New York.

Taylor, F. W. (1972 edition) *Scientific Management*, Greenwood Press, Westport, Conn.

Trahair, R. (1984) *The Humanist Temper: the Life and Work of Elton Mayo*, Transaction Books, New Brunswick, New Jersey.

Tsurumi, R. (1982) American Origins of Japanese Productivity: The Hawthorne Experiment Rejected. *Pacific Basin Quarterly*, 7 14-15.

Turnbull, P. (1986) The 'Japanization' of Production and Industrial Relations at Lucas Electrical. *Industrial Relations Journal*, **17**(3) 193-206.

Ure, A. (1835/1967) *The Philosophy of Manufactures or An Exposition of the Scientific, Moral and Commercial Economy of the Factory System of Great Britain*, Frank Cass, London.

Urwick, L. (1929) *The Meaning of Rationalisation*, Nisbet, London.

Urwick, L. (1938) Rationalisation *British Management Review*, **3** 13-30.

Urwick, L. (ed) (1956) *The Golden Book of Management*, Newman Neame, London.

Urwick, L. (1970) Theory Z. *SAM Advanced Management Journal* **35** 14-21.

Urwick, L. and Brech, E. (1945) *The Making of Scientific Management Volume 1: Thirteen Pioneers*, Management Publications Trust, London.

Vickerstaff, S. and Sheldrake, J. (1989) *The Limits of Corporatism: British Experience in the Twentieth Century*, Avebury, Aldershot.

Vroom, V. (1964) *Work and Motivation*, Wiley & Sons, New York.

Warner, W. L. and Low, J. (1947) *The Social System of the Modern Factory*, Yale University Press, New Haven.

Weber, M. (1947) *The Theory of Social and Economic Organization*, The Free Press, Illinois.

Whitehead, T. N. (1938) *The Industrial Worker: A Statistical Study of Human Relations in a Group of Manual Workers*, Harvard University Press, Cambridge, Mass.

Whyte, W. F. (1987), From Human Relations to Organizational Behavior: Reflections on the Changing Scene. *Industrial and Labor Relations Review*, **40**(4) 487–499.

Wickens, P. (1995) *The Ascendant Organization: Combining Commitment and Control for Long Term, Sustainable Business Success*, Macmillan, London.

Wiener, M. (1981/1985) *English Culture and the Decline of the Industrial Spirit 1850–1980*, Penguin Books, Harmondsworth.

Wolf, W. (1974) *The Basic Barnard: An Introduction to Chester I. Barnard and His Theories of Organization and Management*, Cornell University, Ithaca, New York.

Wrege, C. (1976) Solving Mayo's Mystery: The First Complete Account of the Origin of the Hawthorne Studies – The Forgotten Contributions of C. E. Snow and H. Hibarger. *Academy of Management Proceedings* 12–16.

Wrege, C. and Greenwood, R. (1991) *Frederick W. Taylor, Father of Scientific Management: Myth and Reality*, Business One Irwin, Homewood, Illinois.

Wren, D. (1979) *The Evolution of Management Thought*, Wiley & Sons, New York.

Wren, D. (1994) *The Evolution of Management Thought*, Wiley & Sons, Chichester.

Index